NEW STUDIES IN BIBLI

BIBLICAL THEOLOGY
ACCORDING TO THE
APOSTLES

NEW STUDIES IN BIBLICAL THEOLOGY 52

Series editor: D. A. Carson

BIBLICAL THEOLOGY ACCORDING TO THE APOSTLES

How the earliest Christians told
the story of Israel

Chris Bruno, Jared Compton and
Kevin McFadden

APOLLOS

Academic
An imprint of InterVarsity Press
Downers Grove, Illinois

APOLLOS (an imprint of Inter-Varsity Press, England)
36 Causton Street, London SW1P 4ST, England
Website: www.ivpbooks.com
Email: ivp@ivpbooks.com

InterVarsity Press, USA
P.O. Box 1400, Downers Grove, IL 60515, USA
Website: www.ivpress.com
Email: email@ivpress.com

Inter-Varsity Press, England, publishes Christian books that are true to the Bible
and that communicate the gospel, develop discipleship and strengthen the church for its
mission in the world.

IVP originated within the Inter-Varsity Fellowship, now the Universities and Colleges
Christian Fellowship, a student movement connecting Christian Unions in universities and
colleges throughout Great Britain, and a member movement of the International Fellowship
of Evangelical Students. That historic association is maintained, and all senior IVP staff and
committee members subscribe to the UCCF Basis of Faith. Website: www.uccf.org.uk.

InterVarsity Press®, USA, is the book-publishing division of InterVarsity Christian Fellowship/
USA® and a member movement of the International Fellowship of Evangelical Students.
Website: www.intervarsity.org.

First published 2020

Set in 10/13.25pt Minion Pro and Gill Sans Nova
Typeset in Great Britain by CRB Associates, Potterhanworth, Lincolnshire
Printed and bound in Great Britain by Ashford Colour Press Ltd, Gosport, Hampshire

UK ISBN: 978-1-78359-956-1 (print)
UK ISBN: 978-1-78359-957-8 (digital)

US ISBN: 978-0-8308-2020-7 (print)
US ISBN: 978-0-8308-7115-5 (digital)

British Library Cataloguing-in-Publication Data
A catalogue record for this book is available from the British Library.

Library of Congress Cataloging-in-Publication Data
A catalog record for this book is available from the Library of Congress.

To Patrick Griffiths

Contents

Series preface

New Studies in Biblical Theology is a series of monographs that address key issues in the discipline of biblical theology. Contributions to the series focus on one or more of three areas: (1) the nature and status of biblical theology, including its relations with other disciplines (e.g. historical theology, exegesis, systematic theology, historical criticism, narrative theology); (2) the articulation and exposition of the structure of thought of a particular biblical writer or corpus; and (3) the delineation of a biblical theme across all or part of the biblical corpora.

Above all, these monographs are creative attempts to help thinking Christians understand their Bibles better. The series aims simultaneously to instruct and to edify, to interact with the current literature and to point the way ahead. In God's universe mind and heart should not be divorced: in this series we will try not to separate what God has joined together. While the notes interact with the best of scholarly literature, the text is uncluttered with untransliterated Greek and Hebrew, and tries to avoid too much technical jargon. The volumes are written within the framework of confessional evangelicalism, but there is always an attempt at thoughtful engagement with the sweep of the relevant literature.

This book is a fresh entry into the crowded field of biblical theology. One form of biblical theology seeks to unpack the distinctive theological voice of each biblical book and corpus; another very common form of biblical theology traces themes across the canon, watching them develop and sometimes even take on a typological life of their own. The approach adopted by the three authors of this volume follows neither pattern. Instead, they set themselves the task of studying how the story of Israel is picked up in various ways in the NT, whether directly or allusively. What does Matthew's handling of Jesus' genealogy disclose about the evangelist's understanding of Israel's history? What about the treatment of Israel by Stephen in Acts 7, by Paul in Romans 9 – 11, by the author of Hebrews in Hebrews 11? The journey through these and other texts is surprisingly interesting, and contributes mightily to a fresh understanding of some of the ways in which the biblical documents intertwine so as to flesh out the good news of Jesus the Messiah.

D. A. Carson
Trinity Evangelical Divinity School

Authors' preface

Biblical theology is often oriented towards understanding the overarching narrative, or story, of the Bible. Within that larger story, Israel's story in the OT plays a crucial role. Several years ago Jared Compton initiated this project by pointing out to Chris Bruno and Kevin McFadden that the NT summarizes the story of Israel in a number of different ways with unique emphases that often go unnoticed. Our goal in this study is to consider these infrequently noticed summaries to glean a better understanding of the biblical theology of the apostles themselves. We will suggest that the NT offers a biblical-theological rule of faith that can guide our own biblical theology, providing a framework within which we can both do faithful biblical theology and OT interpretation with the grain of the earliest Christians. While our hope is that many interpreters of Scripture will benefit from this book, we cannot apologize for our view of both the OT and NT as Christian Scripture, revelation from God for which we are ultimately accountable before him.

This book is the fruit of a number of years of research and conversation among us three authors. The ideas in several of the chapters have been tested in different conference and classroom settings, and we are thankful for the input we have received along the way. We are especially grateful to the students from Chris's biblical theology and use of the OT in the NT courses at Bethlehem College and Seminary. The conclusions of the book were hammered out over a few long, gruelling (but enjoyable) days together in Kenosha, Wisconsin, where we were able to work through the whole manuscript and get onto the same page (well, mostly the same page). We are grateful to the Lord for giving us unity in this project and for strengthening us to finish it.

Thanks are due to many others who have contributed to this book along the way. Don Carson, the editor of this series, provided valuable guidance and input at various stages of the project. Philip Duce at Inter-Varsity Press has been a generous and gracious help (as he endured a number of delays in the submission of the manuscript). Much the same, in fact, could be said for our skilful and diligent copy editor, Eldo Barkhuizen.

John Biegel, Bruce Compton, Joel Compton, Justin Denney, Joe McCulley, Tyler Rodkey, Patrick Schreiner, Tom Schreiner and Mike Stanislawski read portions of the manuscript and provided valuable input. Jenny Andrus, Cody Irwin, Joe McCulley and Katrina Selby were great helps in formatting and editing portions of the manuscript. Cody Irwin went above and beyond the call of duty in helping to prepare the indices. Jared Compton wishes to express his thanks to the staff at University of St Mary of the Lake for their kind hospitality, Chris Bruno thanks Barbara Winters and the staff at Bethlehem College and Seminary's library for their research help, and Kevin McFadden is grateful to Stephanie Kaceli and the staff at Cairn University's Masland Library for their support, as well as the staff at the Princeton Theological Seminary Library for their exceptional hospitality.

We are especially grateful for the institutional support we have received to finish this project. The leadership team at CrossWay Community Church generously gave Jared Compton time to work on this project, and the administrative and academic leadership at Bethlehem College and Seminary have been very supportive of Chris Bruno. Kevin McFadden wishes to thank his former provost Brian Toews and dean Jonathan Master for carving out time in his schedule for this project as well as his colleagues in the school of divinity at Cairn University for helping to teach some of his classes and for encouraging him along the way.

Our families have been nothing but gracious and encouraging as we have written this book. Thanks to our wives, Katie Bruno, Charisse Compton and Colleen McFadden, for praying for, helping to edit and supporting this project in so many ways. Luke, Simon, Elliot and Noah Bruno and Asher, Jude and Haven Compton: thank you for all the ways you have helped, encouraged and prayed for your dads as they wrote this book.

Finally, this book is unique in the NSBT series, for we are rather confident that it is the only volume written by three authors who went to elementary, junior high and high school together. In the spring of 1998 we all graduated from Inter-City Baptist High School together. We have stayed close through the years, so it has been especially gratifying to work together on this project. However, it is no accident that we all have continued to pursue serious study of the Bible. Our Bible teacher during our high school years, Patrick Griffiths, encouraged us to follow the example of the Bereans, who 'examined the Scriptures every day to see if what Paul said was true' (Acts 17:11). We happily dedicate this book to Pat, with the hope that many others will follow in the path that he forged for us decades ago.

Chris Bruno
Jared Compton
Kevin McFadden

Abbreviations

Abbreviations

CJT	*Canadian Journal of Theology*
CTR	*Criswell Theological Review*
CurBR	*Currents in Biblical Research*
DSD	*Dead Sea Discoveries*
EBC	Expositor's Bible Commentary
EDEJ	*The Eerdmans Dictionary of Early Judaism*, ed. J. J. Collins and D. C. Harlow, Grand Rapids: Eerdmans, 2010
ESV	English Standard Version
ETL	*Ephemerides theologicae lovanienses*
ExAud	*Ex Auditu*
Exch	*Exchange*
HvTSt	*Hervormde Teologiese Studies*
ICC	International Critical Commentary
JBL	*Journal of Biblical Literature*
JETS	*Journal of the Evangelical Theological Society*
JPTS	Journal of Pentecostal Theology Supplement Series
JSNT	*Journal for the Study of the New Testament*
JSNTSup	Journal for the Study of the New Testament Supplement Series
JSPL	*Journal for the Study of Paul and His Letters*
JSPSup	Journal for the Study of the Pseudepigrapha Supplement Series
JSS	*Journal of Semitic Studies*
JTI	*Journal for Theological Interpretation*
Jub.	*Jubilees*
L.A.B.	*Liber antiquitatum biblicarum*
LNTS	The Library of New Testament Studies
LW	*Luther's Works*, ed. J. Pelikan, St. Louis: Concordia, 1963
LXX	Septuagint
MT	Masoretic Text
Mart. Ascen. Isa.	*Martyrdom and Ascension of Isaiah*
N/A	not applicable
NAC	New American Commentary
NB	nota bene (note well; observe carefully)
Neot	*Neotestamentica*

Abbreviations

NETS	New English Translation of the Septuagint
NICNT	New International Commentary on the New Testament
NIGTC	New International Greek Testament Commentary
NIVUK	New International Version (anglicized edition)
NovT	*Novum Testamentum*
NovTSup	Supplements to Novum Testamentum
NRSVA	New Revised Standard Version, Anglicized
NSBT	New Studies in Biblical Theology
NT	New Testament
NTS	*New Testament Studies*
OT	Old Testament
PCNT	Paideia Commentaries on the New Testament
PNTC	Pillar New Testament Commentary
PRSt	*Perspectives in Religious Studies*
Pss Sol.	*Psalms of Solomon*
RB	rewritten Bible
RTR	*The Reformed Theological Review*
SBJT	*Southern Baptist Journal of Theology*
SBLDS	Society of Biblical Literature Dissertation Series
SIS	summary/summaries of Israel's story
SJT	*Scottish Journal of Theology*
SNTSMS	Society for New Testament Studies Monograph Series
s.v.	sub verbo (under the word)
TDNT	*Theological Dictionary of the New Testament*, ed. G. Kittel and G. Friedrich; tr. G. W. Bromiley, 10 vols, Grand Rapids: Eerdmans, 1964–76
Tg. Jon.	*Targum Jonathan*
TJ	*Trinity Journal*
TOTC	Tyndale Old Testament Commentary
tr.	translated, translation
TynBul	*Tyndale Bulletin*
WBC	Word Biblical Commentary
WTJ	*Westminster Theological Journal*
WUNT	Wissenschaftliche Untersuchungen zum Neuen Testament

ZECNT	Zondervan Exegetical Commentary on the New Testament
ZNW	*Zeitschrift für die neutestamentliche Wissenschaft und die Kunde der älteren Kirche*

1

Introduction

How did the apostles do biblical theology, and what can we learn from them? The goal of this book is to address these questions.

There has been a growing interest in the practice of biblical theology among evangelical Christians in the West, an interest seen in the very existence of this series of books. And even many laypeople are now familiar with the idea that the Bible is not only a collection of individual stories but also contains a larger story that stretches from the garden to the new creation.

From one perspective this is a new phenomenon in the church. The discipline of biblical theology was originally given a home in the academy through the work of post-Enlightenment historical critics who made a distinction between the theology of the Bible (biblical theology) and the theology of the church (dogmatic theology).[1] This modern, dogged interest in the historical development of the theology of the Bible was then baptized by orthodox theologians who used the new method to analyse the history of redemptive revelation.[2]

From another perspective, however, recounting the theological teaching of the Bible as a story with historical development was certainly a part of pre-Enlightenment theologizing as well. Perhaps the second-century

---

[1] Many trace the origin of the discipline of biblical theology to the 1787 address by J. P. Gabler. Gabler saw the distinction between biblical theology and dogmatic theology as a way to get beyond the many differences in systematic theology and back to the unchanging, divine religion of the Bible (for a translation and commentary on his address see Sandys-Wunsch and Eldredge 1980).

[2] Most notably by Geerhardus Vos, professor of biblical theology at Princeton Seminary in the late nineteenth and early twentieth centuries. Although a century and a half before Vos, and even before Gabler, the great American theologian Jonathan Edwards anticipated the historical turn in theology and purposed to write 'a body of divinity in an entire new method', which would be a history of the work of redemption (Marsden 2003: 473). Unfortunately, his untimely death prevented him from accomplishing this endeavour (see ibid. 472–489).

Christian bishop Irenaeus is most famous for taking this approach.[3] And yet long before Irenaeus Jewish interpreters of the Bible summarized their understanding of holy writ in narrative historical form. Such summaries are found both within the OT (e.g. Neh. 9; Pss 105; 106; etc.) and outside it (e.g. Sir. 44–50). Our interest in this book, however, is not in these pre-Christian summaries, but rather in the summaries of Israel's story composed after the coming of Jesus Christ in the apostolic witness of the NT.

Our idea: exploring the exposed iceberg

In the last century of biblical scholarship and especially in the last few decades the use of the OT in the NT has been explored at great length. For a time there was an intense interest in parallels between NT exegesis and the uses of the OT found at Qumran (pesher) or those found in the later rabbis (midrash).[4] More recently there has been an interest in literary studies that consider factors behind the text such as the subtler echoes of the OT in the NT, ways that the OT story shapes the Gospels, or OT narratives that may lie underneath Paul's arguments.[5]

If we use the metaphor of an iceberg, many of these studies have been deep-sea explorations attempting to shine a spotlight on things that are submersed in dark and frigid places, such as Paul's Pharisaic training (midrash) or the philosophical echo chamber in which ancient texts find new resonations (intertextuality). We have all benefited from these studies but our project takes a more direct approach. Our goal is to explore those parts of the iceberg that are standing in plain sight under the light of the sun. Sometimes the most difficult thing to observe carefully is the thing that you see all the time, such as the famous 'hall of faith' in Hebrews 11. And yet Hebrews 11 is not only one of the most important examples of the use of the OT in the NT, but is also an inspired example of how to put the story of the Bible together.

The iceberg metaphor can also be usefully applied to our goal of understanding the *biblical theology* of the apostles by means of these passages. One difficulty in this discipline is that no one agrees about what exactly 'biblical theology' is. A recent volume entitled *Understanding Biblical*

---

[3] 'For Irenaeus the Bible was a single narrative whose chief actor was God' (Wilken 2003: 63).
[4] E.g. Longenecker 1999 (1st edn 1975).
[5] One thinks especially of Richard Hays's work on Paul (1989) and now the Gospels (2016).

Theology finds no fewer than five different approaches represented by modern scholars (Klink and Lockett 2012). These approaches range from those who view the discipline as merely a descriptive, historical discipline, unearthing the religion of the human authors of the Bible,[6] to those who argue that it should fully embrace the same categories and methods as systematic theology.[7] This is why on a practical level the term 'biblical theology' may describe the exploration of one biblical author such as Paul (Schreiner 2001), of a larger corpus such as the OT (Dempster 2003), of the development of the OT in the NT (Beale 2011), of the central theme of the entire Bible (Hamilton 2010)[8] or even of a view of God that accords with the Bible.[9]

Thus, an exploration of the 'biblical theology' of the apostles could in one sense be a study of everything the NT authors say and especially what they say about their Bible, the OT. Our goal in this project is not to explore the *entire* biblical theology of the apostles but to explore the exposed tip of the iceberg, their explicit summaries of Israel's history. While there are many different approaches to the discipline of biblical theology, one characteristic of most of them is the attempt to come to terms with the post-Enlightenment focus on the Bible as a historical book. The passages in the NT that have the most bearing on this kind of study are those that narrate the history recounted in the OT from Abraham to the exile and beyond. These summaries are not everything the NT authors have to say about biblical theology, but are the clearest examples of apostolic reflection on the history or story of the Bible. Moreover, studying the exposed part of the iceberg will help us better understand what lies below the surface.

Our criteria: New Testament summaries of Israel's story

Movement in this direction has already begun in the recent article of Hood and Emerson, who attempt to isolate 'summaries of Israel's story' (SIS) as a compositional category. This article reviews modern research in

---

[6] E.g. James Barr (see Klink and Lockett 2012: 29–56).

[7] E.g. Francis Watson (see Klink and Lockett 2012: 157–182).

[8] Note Graeme Goldsworthy's definition of biblical theology: 'the study of how every text in the Bible relates to Jesus and his gospel' (2008: 7).

[9] This is the way Mark Dever speaks about the mark of 'biblical theology' in his *Nine Marks of a Healthy Church* (2004: 57–75).

this 'genre-transcending literary category',[10] presents criteria to identify the category SIS and then gives a provisional list of about seventy to eighty such summaries in Jewish and Christian literature found both inside and outside the Bible.

Hood and Emerson trace the beginning of their history of research to the publication of Ethelbert Stauffer's *New Testament Theology* in the mid-twentieth century that contained in an appendix 'an apparently unprecedented list' of 121 'theological summaries of history'.[11] Stauffer perceived in these summaries support for his own view of biblical theology, which is rooted in the sacred history:

> The theology of the early church was a process of ordering. What went on was not the making of metaphysical concepts, nor yet the construction of a system, but an ordering of thought, that sought to discover the actual relationships between the different elements of the world of human experience. The answer that was found as a result of the search was like this: God ordered all reality in history . . . In this sense the theology of history is the primary and canonical form of Christian thinking . . .[12]

Hood and Emerson next survey several other scholars after Stauffer who have studied these summaries. They observe however that

> none of these scholars address these summaries as a distinct compositional category as Stauffer did . . . Scholars usually focus on one or a handful of closely related forms [e.g. those that follow the 'deuteronomic' sin–exile–return view of history] rather than giving attention to summaries as a form-transcendent phenomenon.[13]

They also survey scholars associated with the 'narrative turn' in biblical scholarship (e.g. N. T. Wright) who have brought attention back to Israel's story but do not cite Stauffer and his list of summaries.[14]

---

[10] Hood and Emerson 2013: 330.
[11] Hood and Emerson 2013: 329. Stauffer is apparently the first to label these 'summaries' (according to Hood and Emerson 2013: 330).
[12] Stauffer 1955: 173–174.
[13] Hood and Emerson 2013: 332.
[14] Ibid. 332–334.

Joachim Jeska, influenced by Stauffer, has given 'the fullest review and the sole attempt in the extant literature to establish a technical term for this phenomenon, *Summarien der Geschichte Israels*'.[15] He views these summaries not merely as 'historical reporting, but attempts to *actualize* Israel's history, bringing it to bear for present or future purposes, sometimes implicitly by the creation of patterns, sometimes by explicit comment'.[16] He comes up with a much shorter list than Stauffer (twenty-seven examples), partly because he does not use the shorter texts and partly because he restricts his investigation to ancient Jewish summaries that tell the story from Genesis to 2 Kings.[17] Hood and Emerson observe that, although Jeska arranges his lists according to genre, he 'follows Stauffer in accumulating examples from a variety of forms and genres',[18] treating these summaries as a compositional category that transcends genre and can be examined in their own right.

In the final section of their article Hood and Emerson suggest various criteria by which they delineate the compositional category of SIS. It should be observed that they purposely use the English word 'story' rather than 'history', not to deny the *realis* nature of Israel's narrative, but to describe a narrative that moves beyond the past into the present and even the future.[19] They first identify SIS as a 'shorter version of the phenomenon known as rewritten Bible' (RB), for example, the retelling of Genesis and Exodus in *Jubilees* or Josephus's longer history of the Jewish people (*Jewish Antiquities*).[20] The difference between this genre of literature and the compositional category of SIS is that an SIS is 'highly condensed' rather than being a lengthy summary and is always found '*within* a work' rather than standing on its own.[21]

Next they suggest several criteria, which can be summarized with the following: an SIS recounts the 'characters, events, and institutions' of Israel's history in 'chronological order' and at 'substantial length'.[22] By 'substantial length' they are attempting to eliminate briefer references to Israel's history such as Jesus' statement that 'many will come from the

---

[15] Ibid. 334.
[16] Ibid.; emphasis original.
[17] Ibid. 335.
[18] Ibid. 336.
[19] Ibid.
[20] Ibid. 337.
[21] Ibid.; emphasis original.
[22] Ibid. 339.

east and the west, and will take their places at the feast with Abraham, Isaac and Jacob in the kingdom of heaven' (Matt. 8:11). By 'chronological order', Hood and Emerson refer to a passage that 'moves in proper "historical" direction', allowing for 'minor chronological digression' such as in Hebrews 11.[23]

With these criteria in place, Hood and Emerson write out their list of Jewish and Christian SIS. Since our concern is with the apostolic witness to Israel's story, we will list only the seven summaries they find in the NT: Matthew 1:1–17; Mark 12:1–23//Matthew 21:33–46//Luke 20:9–18; Acts 7; Acts 13:16–41; Romans 9 – 11; Hebrews 11:1 – 12:2; and Revelation 12:1–12.

Our study of apostolic biblical theology follows Hood and Emerson's criteria exactly, although our list of summaries is slightly different. We have selected the passages in the NT that recount the characters, events and institutions of Israel's story in chronological order and at substantial length. Following these criteria we have excluded many texts that recount elements of Israel's story but not in chronological order or at substantial length.[24] One thinks of the brief recounting of certain episodes in the Gospels such as Jonah and the huge fish or Solomon and the Queen of the South (Matt. 12:39–42), Peter's sermons in the early chapters in Acts (Acts 2:14–36; 3:12–26), or even the more substantial reflections of Paul on Abraham (Rom. 4) and Adam (Rom. 5:12–21; 1 Cor. 15) that do not show chronological or historical movement. In other words, while these recountings appeal to characters or events from the story of Israel, they do not really tell that story.

The application of Hood and Emerson's criteria, of course, involves a measure of subjectivity. In fact, upon reflection we decided to exclude one of their NT examples of SIS (Rev. 12:1–12) and include another that they do not (Gal. 3 – 4). In the former case we were convinced that Revelation 12:1–12 is really about only a part of the biblical story – the defeat of the devil and his persecution of the church – rather than a recounting of the entire story of Israel.[25] And in the latter case we saw all the earmarks of an SIS: Israel's characters, events and institutions in chronological order, at substantial length and in summary form. Galatians 3 – 4 names

---

[23] Ibid.

[24] 'In order to be labeled SIS or RB, a text should cover multiple periods in Israel's history' (Hood and Emerson 2013: 338).

[25] This is true whether one sees the defeat of the devil as a reference to primeval history, to the incarnation or to his future defeat (on these views, see Koester 2014: 550–551).

Abraham, Hagar, Sarah, Ishmael, Isaac, Moses and Jesus Christ, recounts events in the life of Abraham, the giving of the law and God's sending of his Son and Spirit, and elucidates the significance of one Jewish institution at length – the law – along with some tantalizingly brief comments about the city of Jerusalem.

Some readers may question our inclusion of certain passages. For example, Snodgrass argues that the parable of the tenants is not exactly a story of Israel. 'It is not precise to describe the parable as a graphic presentation of the course of salvation-history since this would require a much fuller treatment similar to that in Acts 7.'[26] While we concede that this retelling of Israel's story is more allusive and poetic than Stephen's speech in Acts 7 or even Matthew's genealogy, it nonetheless can be seen as a story of Israel's history. If indeed the vineyard in some way represents Israel, then we have a story of Israel's founding and their failure. On the other hand, some readers may be disappointed that we excluded other passages. For example, we could see someone making a good argument for Romans 5:12–21, which begins with Adam, refers to Moses and the coming of the law and ends with the reign of grace through Christ. However, in our view this passage is fundamentally a typological comparison between Adam and Christ and does not attempt to show the historical progression of Israel's story.

At the end of the day, however, we had to draw the line somewhere. Our goal once again was not to analyse every passage pertaining to the apostles' biblical theology but to explore the exposed parts of the iceberg; that is, the NT SIS. While not all may agree about which parts of the iceberg are exposed, we believe our selections provide a representative picture of the biblical theology of the earliest Christians. Even if we have missed some of that territory, we hope to expose our readers to enough of it to be able to follow the major plot points of Israel's story and see a glimpse into how the apostles put their Bible together.

Our method: context, content and contribution

Guided by Hood and Emerson's criteria, we have identified seven SIS in the NT: (1) the genealogy in Matthew (Matt. 1:1–17); (2) Jesus' parable of

---

[26] Snodgrass 2011: 106.

the tenants (Matt. 21:33–46; etc.); (3) Stephen's speech (Acts 7); (4) Paul's sermon in Pisidian Antioch (Acts 13:16–41); (5) Paul's argument from salvation history in Galatians (Gal. 3 – 4); (6) his defence of God's faithfulness to Israel in Romans (Rom. 9 – 11); and (7) the author of Hebrews's exhortation to his readers about persevering faith (Heb. 11). A chapter will be given to each NT book that includes these summaries. For Matthew and Acts we will address the two summaries in each of these books together to some degree. While we recognize them as distinct SIS, we must also recognize Matthew's and Luke's respective agendas in including two stories in their composition and so treat them accordingly.

Our method of analysis in each chapter will follow a similar pattern, even though there will be some differences due to the genre in which the SIS is placed and the unique content of each summary. Each chapter will first examine the *context* of the story. Our goal here is to place each SIS in the context of its individual book and to understand *why* this author has told Israel's story. The SIS in the NT and beyond are not merely recounting Israel's story for historical interest but telling the story for specific reasons. If we can identify these reasons (i.e. the function the author intends the summary to serve), then it will help us to see how he understands the story and what he expects readers to take away. We do not mean to suggest here that SIS are merely a function of the author's rhetorical goals – that he skews the story to fit these goals – but rather to see the main thing the author notices in the OT story of Israel and chooses to highlight for a specific situation.[27]

Second, we will examine the *content* of each story. *How* does the author tell the story in order to accomplish his rhetorical goals? SIS are by their nature highly condensed and therefore truncated accounts of Israel's history. Which parts of the story does the author highlight and what exactly does he say about these parts? This section will give a careful exegetical analysis of each summary and thus will be the longest and most important part of each chapter.

Finally, we will reflect on the *contribution* that each story makes to biblical theology. Once we have done the preliminary groundwork of analysing *why* the author recounts Israel's story and *how* he recounts that story, we will be in a position to understand *what* the author's exact

---

[27] As noted above, Jeska observes that SIS are told to *actualize* the story for a present or future situation (Hood and Emerson 2013: 334).

contribution to biblical theology is. This section will attempt to skim off the top what we have learned from our analysis of each NT SIS.

In the next chapter, 'Matthew and Israel's continuing story', we will explore how Matthew relates the story of Jesus to the story of Israel in the evangelist's opening genealogy and in the parable of the tenants. Chapter 3, 'Luke, Acts and the climax of Israel's story', will examine the covenantal structure of Israel's story as recorded in Stephen's speech and Paul's sermon in Pisidian Antioch. Chapter 4, 'Galatians and Israel's law', will examine how the story of Israel proves that the inheritance does not come by the law but by the Abrahamic promise. Chapter 5, 'Romans and Israel's identity', will highlight Paul's nuanced definition of Israel's identity in his defence of God's faithfulness. Chapter 6, 'Hebrews and Israel's inheritance', will explore how the author of Hebrews uses the nature of Israel's inheritance to sustain his audience's faith. Finally, in chapter 7, we will summarize our observations and draw out implications. In the main body of the book our reflection on the contributions of each summary will only be descriptive. Then, in chapter 7, we will offer some prescriptive points about how apostolic biblical theology should guide our own practice of biblical theology. This after all is our ultimate goal – not only to understand how the apostles did biblical theology, but to understand what we can (and should) learn from them.

2

Matthew and Israel's continuing story

The NT begins with a story of Israel. The genealogy that begins the Gospel of Matthew, the first book in every known order of the NT, is not simply a way to demonstrate that Jesus is a descendant of Abraham and David, but is also a carefully constructed presentation of Israel's story. As he invokes Israel's story, Matthew reveals his understanding of the overall shape of Israel's history and invites the reader into an already unfolding story.[1] The genealogy introduces the links between the story of Israel and the story of Jesus the Messiah, links that will be further explained as the Gospel progresses. Throughout his Gospel Matthew points back to the story of Israel and reminds his readers that they are continuing Israel's story. Near the end of the Gospel Matthew tells the story of Israel again as Jesus recounts the parable of the tenants; this story points to the surprising climax and continuation of Israel's story.

In this chapter we will consider how Matthew invites us into this story through the SIS found in the genealogy in Matthew 1 and the parable of the tenants in chapter 21. As noted in the first chapter, while our discussion of each story of Israel will be unique, each chapter will follow the same general pattern. We will move from the context in which the summary is found to the content of the story, and then conclude with the contributions of each story to the author's biblical theology. From this we will better understand why the author tells the story of Israel in the way that he does and how his understanding of this story supports his larger agenda in the

---

[1] A number of scholars have recognized that the genealogy is a story of Israel. For an overview, see Hood 2011: 20–27. While following Hood's work in his overall approach, our investigation of the genealogy will differ from his in several key points; nonetheless, his investigation serves as a helpful catalyst for our project in both this text and the others that follow.

book. Because this chapter examines two summaries, we will summarize the content of each story and make some concluding observations about each individually; however, we will reserve our reflections on the contributions of these two stories until the end of the chapter, where we will be able to treat them together.

In what follows we will observe that in Matthew the story of Israel, though appearing to be a tragedy, takes a hopeful turn as it continues the coming of the Messiah, Jesus. Both the genealogy and the parable of the tenants emphasize the failure of Israel, particularly its leaders. In different ways they recount God's covenant blessings to Israel, and the genealogy in particular emphasizes the way the covenants form the structure of Israel's history. Along with these covenant blessings, however, Matthew also recounts Israel's heartbreaking failure to remain faithful to the covenant God. The genealogy and the parable of the tenants also indicate that Israel's story continues as Jesus reconstitutes Israel in the new-covenant era. The Gospel then concludes with Jesus' commissioning his apostles to continue the story of Israel as his kingdom extends to the nations.

The context of Matthew's genealogy

As we begin our investigation of the two summaries in Matthew's Gospel, we might note that the Gospel of Matthew as a whole is in some way retelling all or part of Israel's story. While we recognize that not all scholars agree on the outline of Matthew, it is likely that the main structure of the book follows five 'narrative-discourse' sections.[2] In the early twentieth century Benjamin Bacon suggested that the five discourse sections of the book correspond to the five books of the Torah.[3] Others have modified Bacon's proposal, including the recent suggestion of Peter Leithart, who proposes that the five sections roughly parallel the eras of Moses (3:1 – 7:28), Joshua (8:1 – 11:1), Solomon (11:2 – 13:53), Elijah

---

[2] The end of each discourse is clearly marked with some variation of the phrase *kai egeneto hote etelesen ho Iēsous* ('and it came to pass when Jesus had finished'; see 7:28; 11:1; 13:53; 19:1; 26:1). For major options on the structure of Matthew, see Osborne 2010: 40–47.

[3] Benjamin Bacon was largely responsible for the modern popularization of this theory (1930). However, Bacon traces his theory to very early interpreters of Matthew, including Papias, who commented on the 'ordered arrangement' of the Gospel (see Eusebius, *Ecclesiastical History* 3.39.14–16).

(13:54 – 19:1a) and the prophets just before the exile (19:1b – 26:1).[4] The genealogy would then serve as an introduction to this recapitulation of Israel's history. Regardless of how they understand the structure, most interpreters of Matthew agree with N. T. Wright's assessment: 'Matthew's plot and structure presuppose the entire Jewish story-line to date.'[5]

While it is likely that the Gospel of Matthew in some way recapitulates the story of Israel on a number of horizons, it is insufficient to say that the whole of the book retells Israel's story without also seeing that within its constituent parts Matthew is telling the story of Israel as well. In brief, the Gospel opens with a story of Israel in the genealogy, frames the life of Jesus as a recapitulation of Israel's history and, near the end of his ministry, Jesus vividly tells this same history in the parable of the tenants. These retellings function individually as stories of Israel to themselves while also providing us with a guidepost for reading the rest of the Gospel as a macro-story of Israel.

In order to understand how the Gospel of Matthew summarizes the story of Israel, therefore, we will begin in the genealogy and let this retelling of the story frame our discussion moving forward. Because of its prominence in the NT canon and its focus on Jesus the Messiah as the culmination of Israel's history, the genealogy in Matthew's Gospel sets the stage for both the rest of the Gospel and the rest of our observations in this volume.

The content of Matthew's genealogy (Matt. 1:1–17)

Our task is not so much to consider why Matthew included the particular men and women that he did in the genealogy, as if a brief summary of the life of each ancestor of Jesus would clarify Matthew's aims. As we will observe below, the individual players are certainly relevant to the story. However, our first task is to consider the structure of his genealogy as a whole. As we trace the broad structure of Matthew's genealogy, we must also ask how the genealogy serves as an introduction to the whole book. Doing so will help us better understand the way the story of Israel functions throughout Matthew. After we determine the function of the

---

4 See Leithart 2018: 21, 26–40.
5 Wright 1992: 385–386.

genealogy in the whole book, we will give closer attention to the individuals and events that Matthew includes in it.

Unlike Luke, who begins his genealogy with Adam, Matthew's genealogy starts with Abraham, the founding patriarch of Israel.[6] From there he signals David's reign and the Babylonian captivity as the other key points in Israel's history. In other words, the Gospel begins with an emphasis on the Messiah from Israel and for Israel.[7] For any of Matthew's readers with some knowledge of the OT, this is unsurprising. The Abraham–David–exile–Jesus sequence may strike modern ears as a boilerplate SIS. However, as we examine this genealogy in more detail in the light of Matthew's unfolding narrative, we may discover that this telling of Israel's story reveals more than modern readers often realize.[8]

Richard Hays observes that the structure of Matthew's genealogy 'outlines the *plot* of Israel's story'.[9] In our study of the genealogy we will consider the structure and significance of this version of the plot.[10] Matthew tells the story of Israel in three acts. First, from Abraham until the reign of King David. Next, from David's reign until the exile. Finally, from the exile until the arrival of the Messiah, Jesus. The first group of names, from Abraham to David, matches the sequence of the genealogies found in the OT, particularly the list in 1 Chronicles 1 – 2 and Ruth 4. However, the second group, from David to the exile, omits three of David's descendants from the list in 1 Chronicles 3:1–16 (LXX).[11] Moreover, the fulfilment of God's covenants with Israel serves as the necessary background for each of these acts.

---

[6] For observations on the differences between the Lukan and Matthean genealogies, see LéGasse 1998: 443–454. However, LéGasse concludes that Luke's version is likely more historically accurate because it includes more obscure figures and is therefore less stylized than Matthew's (ibid. 454).

[7] This Israel-centric focus in the genealogy need not exclude the inclusion of the Gentiles, for, as we will see below, Matthew ends his Gospel with a focus on the nations.

[8] Much of the recent study of Matthew's genealogy is indebted to Nolland 1996: 115–122. Nolland classifies Matthew's work as an 'annotated genealogy'. Hood provides a useful overview of the development of this label (2011: 27–33).

[9] Hays 2016: 110; emphasis original.

[10] Hakh argues, 'Matthew did not aim to present a history of Israel, but instead to develop a theology about who Jesus is for his community' (2014: 114). However, this creates a false dichotomy. It is better to say that Matthew is presenting a history of Israel *in order to* develop a theology about who Jesus is.

[11] See discussion in Waetjen 1976: 207–211. While some scholars suggest that Matthew was operating from a text that omitted these names, it is impossible to determine whether this is the case. Regardless, Matthew himself highlights the three sets of fourteen generations in Israel's history.

Exile

Nicholas Piotrowski has helpfully classified the genealogy as an 'interrupted chiasm'.[12] That is, the neat 'Messiah – David – Abraham// Abraham – David – Messiah' symmetry is broken by the exile (Matt. 1:17). This literary device reflects the historical circumstances well. The history of Israel was indeed 'interrupted' by the exile. Therefore, our reading of Matthew's retelling of Israel's story in Matthew – and of the entire Gospel – should be informed by this interruption.

Piotrowski comments, 'If Matthew were a play, the first four chapters would be like arriving at the theatre to watch the crew set up the stage.'[13] As we observed above, it is better to think of the genealogy as a three-act play. Or, if we could adjust the metaphor, we might also say that if Israel's story were a television programme, the genealogy would be a recap of the previous series. Series one runs from Abraham to the reign of David, series two from David until the exile, and series three from the exile until the birth of the Messiah. Thus, Matthew 1:18 picks up the story at the beginning of the fourth series – or more accurately, at the very end of the third.[14] When this background is understood, it not only helps us understand Matthew's interrupted chiasm but also helps us make sense of Matthew's reading of Israel's story as a whole.

In addition to his valuable observations about the structure of Matthew's genealogy, Piotrowski has also provided a helpful summary of the function of the noun *metoikesia* in this context. In short, the word refers to 'the initial deportation to Babylon *but not the full experience of captivity*'.[15] That is to say, it refers to the beginning, but not the end, of the exile.

Matthew does not mention the return to Judea nor any of the events surrounding this return. In fact, he includes Jeconiah and Shealtiel in the section after the deportation to Babylon, and neither of them is associated with the return from exile. Moreover, in the following chapter Herod, an Idumean king and Roman vassal, rules over the Jews, and the Davidic

---

[12] Piotrowski 2015: 193.

[13] Ibid. 190.

[14] Davies and Allison conclude that 'Matthew set out to compose in some sense a counterpart to Genesis', thus beginning a new cycle of Israel's history (1988: 187).

[15] Piotrowski 2015: 197; emphasis original. For the full argument, see Piotrowski 2015: 194–196.

throne remains vacant. Given the close connection between the restoration of the Davidic monarchy and the end of exile, Matthew's implication is that the exile continues until the coming of the Messiah.[16] Therefore, the phrase 'after the exile to Babylon' (*meta de tēn metoikesian Babylōnos*) in Matthew 1:12 does not refer to the conclusion of the exile or the whole period of exile, as the NIVUK translation may imply, but rather to the period following the beginning of the exile. '*Thus*', Piotrowski concludes, '*in the genealogy exile is marked, at least in part, by the lack of the Davidic king, which doubles as unfulfilled promises to Abraham.*'[17]

Abraham to David

Matthew begins with a reference to Abraham, but this reference also assumes the background to the Abraham narrative in Genesis 1 – 11. Israel's God, the creator of the world, was committed to redeeming the world through the family of Abraham. We are stepping into a narrative world that is pregnant with these presuppositions. To continue with cinematic analogies, Matthew's genealogy is somewhat like watching the original *Star Wars* trilogy in preparation for watching the new episodes.[18]

We need not examine the unfolding story of Abraham, Isaac, Jacob and their descendants in any detail. Rather, our task will be to consider the significance of the characters who appear in the genealogy (see Table 2.1). We will give particular attention to the places where Matthew's genealogy appears to deviate from the order or emphasis of the OT genealogies and/ or when he includes additional annotations – especially female ancestors of Jesus, for, as Bauckham notes, 'Jewish genealogies of this kind (tracing someone's descent through the male line) included women, as wives and mothers, only for definite reasons.'[19]

---

[16] See Ezek. 34:23–24; 37:24.

[17] Piotrowski 2015: 197; emphasis original.

[18] Of course, one could say the prequel trilogy provides even more background and helps us understand how the empire came to power and the need for deliverance that is more or less assumed in the original trilogy. We could even argue that Matthew's genealogy more or less assumes a knowledge of Gen. 1 – 11 that leads us to the beginning of Israel's story with Abraham in Gen. 12. In the same way one might assume a knowledge of episodes 1, 2 and 3 when watching the original *Star Wars* films. Of course, one could also assume that this analogy is merely a deluded attempt to wed *Star Wars* and biblical theology.

[19] Bauckham 1995: 313. While Nowell is right to consider the role of all of the women in the family line of Jesus in the OT, to impute that intention to Matthew likely moves beyond his purposes for including these particular women in the line (2008: 1–15).

Table 2.1 Abraham to David

Character	Description
Abraham	Father of Isaac
Isaac	Father of Jacob
Jacob	Father of Judah *and his brothers*
Judah	Father of Perez and Zerah, *whose mother was Tamar*
Perez	Father of Hezron
Hezron	Father of Ram
Ram	Father of Amminadab
Amminadab	Father of Nashon
Nashon	Father of Salmon
Salmon	Father of Boaz, *whose mother was Rahab*
Boaz	Father of Obed, *whose mother was Ruth*
Obed	Father of Jesse
Jesse	Father of King David[20]

Because Matthew does not deviate from the genealogical lists in 1 Chronicles 1 – 2, both ancient and modern readers might assume that the fourteen generations listed in this first section are little more than a prosaic genealogical record. However, a closer look reveals a subtle emphasis on events in the history of Israel when the line of promise encountered a particular danger or threat. The first of these events is focused on Judah and his sons Perez and Zerah, born to his daughter-in-law Tamar. It is likely that Tamar is mentioned not only because she was a woman or a Gentile, but also because of her unique role in preserving the line of promise in spite of the sin of Judah. While the significance of these events is not always spelled out in other early Jewish texts, Bauckham rightly notes Tamar's action was universally praised.[21]

The same might be said of Ruth and Rahab in verse 9. As we will observe, the significance of the women in Matthew's genealogy does not lie with sexual improprieties or other irregularities that surround them. Rather, as Hays rightly concludes, 'They are characterized in the stories

---

[20] David both concludes the first section and begins the second section; however, his description as 'the father of Solomon, whose mother had been Uriah's wife' properly belongs to the second section.

[21] Bauckham 1995: 319.

not by their doubtful reputations but by their tenacious fidelity.'[22] And in all three cases this fidelity was a means by which God preserved the Abrahamic line of promise.

Gentile women as saviour figures

Although Matthew does not give particular emphasis to the events in Abraham's life, he highlights those figures and events that serve to demonstrate God's commitment to keeping his promises to Abraham. The promises to Abraham are most prominent in Genesis 12:1–3; 15:17–20; and 22:15–18.[23] Scholars have devised many different schemata for organizing the promises, but the consistent thread that runs through these three texts is God's gift of the land to Abraham (Gen. 12:1; 15:18–21; 22:17), where his numerous offspring would live (Gen. 12:2; 15:18; 22:17). Beyond that, two of these texts assert that the covenant promises were to be a means of blessing to the nations (Gen. 12:3; 22:18; 35:11).

While the Abraham, Isaac and Jacob narratives are obviously important to Israel's history, Matthew passes them by without additional comment. It is likely that he mentions the brothers of Judah in verse 2 to distinguish the messianic line as pre-eminent over the rest of the tribes of Israel.[24] However, in verse 3 Matthew mentions the first character in the genealogy who is not a direct descendent of Abraham, Tamar. Though the reason for Tamar's inclusion is not immediately obvious, it is noteworthy that the incident with Judah and Tamar was the first threat to the line of Judah (Gen. 38:1–30).

After the deaths of his two oldest sons, Judah refused to allow his third son, Shelah, to marry Tamar. Whether through fear or cunning, Judah had directly threatened the continuation of his own line. However, through an uncomfortable series of events, Tamar essentially tricked Judah into fathering his own twin grandsons. Through the second-born son/grandson, Perez, the line of Judah continued.[25] Therefore, in a very real sense, a Canaanite woman rescued the line of promise.[26] Matthew is

---

[22] Hays 2016: 112.

[23] These promises are reiterated for Isaac and Jacob in Gen. 26:2–24; 28:3–14; and 46:3.

[24] So Hood 2011: 65–75.

[25] In 1 Chr. 2:3–4 Judah is listed as having five sons in total; therefore, if Shelah had no legitimate sons, the births of Terah and Perez were the only means for the line to continue.

[26] Some early Jewish texts imply that Tamar was not a Gentile (i.e. *Jub.* 41.1; *L.A.B.* 9.5). However, Bauckham argues that Philo understood her to be a Canaanite woman (see *On the Virtues* 220–222). More significantly for our purposes, the text of the OT itself describes Rahab and her family as residents of Jericho/Canaan (see Josh. 2:1–2, 13; Bauckham 1995: 320).

not simply highlighting the inclusion of the Gentiles or women in the genealogy of Jesus, but is rather insisting that the Gentile women play a significant role in the preservation of the line of promise and in the story of Israel itself.[27]

In the next five generations the genealogy continues without interruption. However, the last five generations of this section include two more Gentile women who were also instrumental in the preservation of the line of promise. The first of these, Rahab, is somewhat difficult to identify.[28] While the most likely candidate is Rahab the prostitute in Joshua 2, who aided the spies entering the Promised Land, this immediately raises the question of whether Rahab and the generation of the conquest could have lived in such close proximity to King David.

Many have rightly noted that this objection demands a level of precision in the generations that neither the OT genealogies nor Matthew's Gospel intend to provide.[29] Rather, as D. A. Carson points out:

> Approximately four hundred years (Ge 15:13; Ex 12:40) are covered by the four generations from Perez to Amminadab. Doubtless several names have been omitted ... Similarly, the line between Amminadab and David is short. More names may have been omitted. Whether such names properly fit before Boaz, so that Rahab was not the immediate mother of Boaz (just as Eve was not immediately 'the mother of all the living,' Ge 3:20), or after Boaz, or both, one cannot be sure.[30]

Assuming that the Rahab in Matthew's genealogy is the prostitute of Jericho, what, then, might be the significance of including her in the genealogy? When seen in the light of the sexual improprieties that surrounded the incident with Judah and Tamar, some have argued that Matthew sees Tamar as a hint at the 'holy irregularity' of the virgin birth

---

[27] For a fuller overview of the debate, see Hood 2011: 88–118. Hood concludes that the named women plus Uriah are 'four praiseworthy non-Jews'. It is likely that Matthew intends to highlight the named women, and perhaps even Uriah, as a contrast to the unrighteousness of the king, as exemplars of righteousness. However, Hood does not see the decisive actions of the Gentile women as foreshadows of the Messiah in the way that we argue here.

[28] See Bauckham 1995: 320–329.

[29] As noted above, the first section of Matthew's genealogy includes the generations from Abraham to David listed in the OT such as the one found in 1 Chr. 2.

[30] Carson 2010: 91.

later in Matthew 1.[31] While these incidents are certainly part of the larger 'holy irregularity' that is the history of Israel writ large, Matthew's purpose is likely not tracing a line of scandalous events that eventually led to the Messiah, as Stendahl argues.[32] Rather, like Tamar, Rahab, a Gentile woman, encountered the line of promise at a moment of threat and danger. As we will note below, this is also the case with the birth of the Messiah, Jesus.

In Rahab's case the direct threat was against the spies Joshua and Caleb (Josh. 2:1–21). It was commonly recognized that Rahab played a decisive role in protecting the spies. Josephus portrays Rahab as speaking of her 'preservation' of the spies (*Jewish Antiquities* 5.11). Additionally, one might even say that just as these men were representatives of the nation as a whole, by extension they were representatives of Israel's God. Thus, Rahab's preservation of the spies was indeed protection of the line of promise when under threat. Significantly, the incident with Rahab came just as the Hebrews were about to enter the land promised to Abraham. The intervention of Rahab the Gentile prostitute became the means that God used to preserve the line of promise and grant the Hebrews access to the land. Moreover, through her preservation of Israel, she also saved herself, which surprisingly became a means of preserving the messianic line.[33]

In the third generation before David was born we find the same basic pattern as we have observed with Tamar and Rahab. Though the circumstances are again different for the birth of Obed to Boaz and Ruth, this episode is similar to the previous events in one important respect. The line of promise was again in danger on several fronts and the strategic action of a Gentile woman became the means that God used to preserve the line of promise.

At the beginning of the book of Ruth the author informs us that a famine in Judah had threatened God's covenant people (Ruth 1:1). Because of this, Elimelech, a descendant of Judah, his wife Naomi and their sons travelled to Moab to escape the famine. While there, another threat emerged when Elimelech and his sons died without heirs. The line of promise, or at least this branch of it, had ended. However, the rest

---

[31] See e.g. Stendahl 1960: 94–105; repr. in Stanton 1995: 69–80.
[32] Stendahl 1960: 73–74.
[33] It is possible that Matthew is rooting the marriage of Rahab and Salma/Salmon in the genealogical lists in 1 Chr. 2. See Bauckham 1995: 325.

of the book of Ruth tells the story of the surprising preservation of that line through the marriage of Boaz, the relative of Naomi and Elimelech, to Ruth, their Moabite daughter-in-law. From this union the remaining three generations in this first division of Matthew's genealogy would be born. The actions of an Israelite man, Elimelech, led to a threat to the life of promise, but a Gentile woman, Ruth, acted to preserve the line.

Therefore, we can observe that the first section of the genealogy, from Abraham until David, is particularly focused on the preservation of God's promises in the Abrahamic covenant and culminates with the birth of David, the king.[34] Through the intervention of Tamar, Rahab and Ruth, Gentile women all, Israel's God kept his promises to preserve the line of Abraham and bring them into the Promised Land. Moreover, the culmination of this section with the birth of David reminds us that the Abrahamic promises were focused not simply on the multiplicity of offspring, but also on a particular line, from Judah's tribe, that would bear the responsibility and privilege of bringing those covenant promises to the nations in a unique way.[35]

The prominence of Abraham in this section coupled with the inclusion of these Gentile women make it likely that Matthew was, even in the first lines of this Gospel, pointing forward to the proclamation of the good news to the nations at the end of the book in 28:17–20.[36] But the inclusion of the Gentile women is more than simply a hint at the great commission.

These three Gentile women are not only the ancestors of the Messiah, but also point forward to him in their work of preserving God's covenant line and rescuing his people from imminent destruction. In other words, they are themselves saviours of Israel.[37] While interpreters who see the Gentile women in the genealogy foreshadowing the commission to the Gentiles in Matthew 28 are correct, this foreshadowing is found not only in their Gentile identity, but also in their direct actions that preserve

---

[34] Morris 1992: 24.

[35] Matthew, like other early Jewish writers, likely emphasized the messianic promises through the lens of Jacob's blessing for Judah in Gen. 49:8–12. See Hood 2011: 72–74.

[36] Contra Nolland's assertion that 'it is probably a mistake to find any hint of good news for the Gentiles on the basis of the wider reach of the promises to Abraham' (2005: 72).

[37] This argument is similar to the one made by Hutchison, who concludes that in each episode the three women and Bathsheba demonstrate 'extraordinary faith in contrast to Jews, who were greatly lacking in their faith' (2001: 153).

the line of promise.[38] Thus in the first section of the genealogy Matthew highlights that through these three saviour figures – Gentile women no less – God keeps his covenant promises to Abraham.

David to exile

The second major figure in Matthew's chiastic genealogy is King David. Just as the first section corresponds to one major covenant in Israel's story (Abraham), the second act in Israel's history corresponds to another covenant. In this section Matthew focuses primarily on the promises to David and his offspring and so highlights the covenant with David (see Table 2.2).[39] Moreover, the additional information that appears in this section is different from what we see in the first triad. Rather than

Table 2.2 David to exile

Character	Description
David	Father of Solomon, *whose mother had been Uriah's wife*
Solomon	Father of Rehoboam
Rehoboam	Father of Abijah
Abijah	Father of Asa
Asa	Father of Jehoshaphat
Jehoshaphat	Father of Jehoram
Jehoram	Father of Uzziah
Uzziah	Father of Jotham
Jotham	Father of Ahaz
Ahaz	Father of Hezekiah
Hezekiah	Father of Manasseh
Manasseh	Father of Amon
Amon	Father of Josiah
Josiah	Father of Jeconiah *and his brothers at the time of the exile to Babylon*

[38] This conclusion is consistent with Brown's conclusion that the women demonstrate 'how God uses the unexpected to triumph over human obstacles and intervenes on behalf of His planned Messiah' (1977: 73–74). However, he neither distinguishes between the named and unnamed women nor makes the connections with the Gentile theme in Matthew in the way we are observing here.

[39] As others have observed, most notably Gentry and Wellum, the covenant with David is an administration of the covenant with Abraham (2012: 423–427).

including references to key persons (Gentile women) who preserve the line of promise, Matthew gives greater attention to two particular events closely related to the covenant with David and, perhaps, other covenants with Israel.

Because of this shift it is likely that the focus has moved from individuals who preserve the promises to events that disrupt and delay the fulfilment of these covenants. The section that begins with so much promise ends with the beginning of the exile as Matthew traces a direct line from David's sin with Bathsheba and Israel's exile. That is to say, these events explain the broken chiasm discussed above. However, we must again consider briefly the content of the covenant promises that frame this section in the OT.

Abrahamic and Davidic covenants

In Genesis 17:6 the Lord promises Abraham that he will be the father of nations and kings. Moreover, these promises are directed both to Abraham and his offspring. Presumably, if the covenant promises are directed to Abraham's descendants and at least some of those descendants were to be kings, then the focus of these promises would be directed to this royal offspring. This connection is confirmed in Jacob's blessing for Judah in Genesis 49:8–12. The sceptre would be in the hands of Judah's offspring; that is, the kings in Abraham's line would be from the tribe of Judah, and these kings would rule the nations (see Ps. 72:17). Thus, Eloff rightly observes in his comparison of the covenant promises to Abraham and David:

> the similarities between these two promises are striking indeed. In both the recipient is promised a great name and rest/blessing. In both a place and rest/blessing for Israel is secured ... In both the idea of establishment is present, with Abraham in terms of blessing for the nations; with David in terms of God's presence (the temple) and mediated rule.[40]

The Davidic covenant also required the king to remain faithful. In the very institution of the covenant in 2 Samuel 7 the Lord warns David that when he and his descendants are unfaithful, the Lord will

---

[40] Eloff 2004: 81.

discipline them (v. 14).[41] In the history of Israel this discipline culminates with the exile. This middle section of Matthew's genealogy begins with a reference to David's sin with Uriah and Bathsheba and ends with the exile in Babylon. That is to say, the focus in this section is the trajectory of unfaithfulness that marked the entire span of the Davidic monarchy.

Most Matthew scholars assume that Matthew's reference to Bathsheba has the same function as the three named Gentile women in the first section. Hood supports this argument by noting that 'the components of SIS passages work together as a unit'.[42] However, Matthew shifts from personal names in the first part of the genealogy to the more allusive *tēs tou Ouriou* in verse 6. It is possible that he is emphasizing that Bathsheba's husband was a Gentile, Uriah the Hittite. Given the emphasis on exile in this second section, it is more likely that Matthew is flagging for his readers that his attention is not on Bathsheba, but rather on Uriah and the events surrounding his tragic death at David's indirect hand.[43] Matthew has no interest in singling out Bathsheba or shifting blame from David to her.[44] Rather, the focus is on David's failure, which then sets a course from which none of his descendants were willing or able to deviate. We might call this the 'original sin' of the Davidic monarchy. Therefore, unlike the women in the first section, Matthew's attention is not on Bathsheba per se but rather on David's failure and the unfaithfulness of his royal descendants, culminating in the exile.

Although some generations are omitted in order to maintain the fourteen-generation narrative shape of the genealogy, Matthew continues uninterrupted until the end of this second section.[45] With the reference

---

[41] 2 Sam. 7:14 says, 'When he does wrong, I will punish him with a rod wielded by men, with floggings inflicted by human hands.' The Hebrew preposition *b* is typically translated 'when', with the assumption that the king will commit iniquity; this could also be considered a conditional. The phrase is rendered *ean elthē* in the LXX, a third-class conditional clause in Greek, commonly considered the more probable future condition, though it is probably better to see it as less certain than the first-class conditional (see Köstenberger et al. 2016: 443). In any case, the history of Israel makes it clear that this condition was indeed realized.

[42] Hood 2011: 88.

[43] Nolland reaches a similar conclusion; however, he also argues that Matthew includes each of the named women in the first section for a distinct purpose (1996: 75–77). While each makes a distinct contribution to the story of Israel, Nolland does not carefully consider the unity of the first three in contrast to the reference to Bathsheba.

[44] As is the case in the description of this event in 2 Sam. 11 – 12, while others are forced to endure the consequences of this sin, the blame falls squarely on the shoulders of David alone.

[45] While it is difficult to know for certain, the best explanation of Matthew's thrice-repeated fourteen-generations shape is that it emphasizes the Davidic Messiah through gematria, for

to Josiah's fathering Jeconiah and his brothers in verse 11, the second 'series' in Israel's history comes to an ignominious end with the deportation to Babylon. It is likely that Judah's reign over his brothers in verse 2 and Jeconiah's reign with his brothers in verse 11 mark out the tragic move from the hopeful promise of the Davidic king to the tragic end of the Davidic monarchy in the exile.[46] In Matthew's genealogy this event becomes the fulcrum of Israel's history. It is the inevitably tragic outcome of the path that David's sin with Bathsheba had marked out. The story of Israel's kings in Matthew's genealogy is a story of failure that leads to tragedy.

Any reader familiar with the OT will recognize that the broken covenant with David alone does not account for the exile in Babylon. In fact, the exile is typically linked more closely with the blessings and curses of the law covenant, especially those found in Deuteronomy. When the law covenant was reiterated in Deuteronomy, it included the threat of exile from the land if Israel were to be unfaithful to their God (Deut. 28 – 30). Among the most prominent texts that point to the connection between the law covenant and the exile is Deuteronomy 28:36–46. While on the verge of entering the Promised Land, the Lord warns Israel that continuing infidelity to the law will result in their removal from the land.

A closer link between the law covenant and Matthew's genealogy might be found in Deuteronomy 17:14–20. In this text the nation is given permission to instal a king after settling in the land. However, the king is warned not to acquire excess wealth or wives (vv. 16–17) and exhorted to study and keep the law (vv. 18–20). The Davidic kings, especially David's heir, Solomon, were abject failures with respect to these instructions. Nonetheless, Matthew's genealogy does not directly allude to this or other instructions from the law.[47] In fact, Matthew omits any direct mention of the law covenant in his genealogy. Given Matthew's many references to

---

the Hebrew letters for David (*dwd*) add up to fourteen. Davies and Allison's suggestion of a link to the seven weeks of years in Daniel 9:24–27 may also play a role (1988: 161).

[46] Hood sees the reference to Jeconiah as fundamentally positive (2011: 80–83). However, if the contrast between the first and second triads is hope versus tragedy ending in exile, this is unlikely. Thus his further suggestion that both Judah and Jeconiah sacrifice themselves for the sake of their brothers to prefigure the Messiah does not quite fit. He is correct to see Matthew's hinting at figures who prefigure the Messiah, but these hints are linked to the named Gentile women in the genealogy.

[47] Hays observes that Matthew's 'narrative strategy of beginning with the genealogy has the effect of highlighting Jesus' identity as messianic king rather than as lawgiver' (2016: 111).

Moses and the law covenant in the rest of the Gospel, we must be careful not to overstate the significance of this omission. Regardless of whether it has a significant role in the genealogy, Israel's failure to keep the law covenant looms large in the rest of Matthew. But the focus here remains on the Davidic covenant as the background of the deportation to Babylon, and the implicit hope for the Messiah is that he will be a king fully able to enact the instruction of Deuteronomy 17.[48] In Deuteronomy itself the direction of the king with respect to Deuteronomy 17 determines the direction of the nation with respect to Deuteronomy 28 – 30. As the king goes, so goes the nation. Thus, the second chapter in Israel's history ends on a dark note, with the nation entering exile in Babylon.

As much as the first section of Matthew's genealogy is hopeful, high-lighting the preservation of God's people and promises, the second section is dark, with the shadow of exile looming over the Davidic monarchy almost from its inception. But Israel's story does not end in Babylon, for while it included a threat of discipline for infidelity, the covenant with David also included the promise of an enduring kingdom (2 Sam. 7:13). This promise of an enduring kingdom frames the continuing story of Israel in the third section of Matthew's genealogy.

Exile to Messiah

The third period Matthew highlights stretches from the beginning of the exile until the birth of the Messiah, Jesus (see Table 2.3). As noted above, 'after the exile to Babylon' (*meta de tēn Babylōnos*) in 1:12 refers to the beginning of the exile but not its completion. It is telling that the end of the exile does not seem to be in view at all here: the noun *metoikesia* means 'deportation', but does not connote return.[49]

The historical narratives in the OT inform us that the Jews did indeed return to the land during the lifetime of Zerubbabel and others (see Ezra 2:2; 3:2; Neh. 7:7; Hag. 1:1; Zech. 4:9). Yet Matthew mentions only the beginning of the exile and continues the genealogy as if the remaining generations continue in this state of exile. In fact, from the beginning of the exile until the generation just before the Messiah, this third section of the genealogy provides no additional information. It includes no references

---

[48] For an overview of the development of Deut. 17 as a messianic hope in the OT, see Goswell 2017: 169–181. Goswell concludes that 'the portrait of the king in Deut 17 is interpreted as providing a model for future kingship that is properly classified as messianic' (ibid. 180).

[49] BDAG, s.v. '*metoikesia*'; see also Piotrowski 2015: 194.

Table 2.3 Exile to Christ

Character	Description
Jeconiah	Father of Shealtiel
Shealtiel	Father of Zerubbabel
Zerubbabel	Father of Abihud
Abihud	Father of Eliakim
Eliakim	Father of Azor
Azor	Father of Zadok
Zadok	Father of Akim
Akim	Father of Elihud
Elihud	Father of Eleazar
Eleazar	Father of Matthan
Matthan	Father of Jacob
Jacob	Father of Joseph
Joseph	*Husband of Mary, and Mary was the mother of Jesus who is called the Messiah.*

to the return from Babylon, the rebuilding of the temple, the Maccabean revolt or any other events from the nation's history during this period. In contrast to the first two sections that provide us with additional clues along the way, this third section indicates that Israel's circumstances were essentially unchanged from the beginning of the exile until the birth of the Messiah.

However, this does not mean we are completely in the dark about Matthew's understanding of this season of Israel's history, for the continued existence of the line of promise itself is a significant clue. As noted above, the Davidic covenant included a promise that God would 'establish the throne of his kingdom for ever' (2 Sam. 7:13). Coupled with this, the promise of the new covenant in Jeremiah 31:31–34 and similar texts indicate that, no matter how dark its circumstances, the history of Israel was fundamentally optimistic, for Israel's God had promised to fulfil his covenant promises to Abraham and the world.

This hope provides the foundation for Matthew's third section, which in many ways serves as a bridge to the last chapter in Israel's history, the place where Matthew picks up and advances this history. Waetjen sees Jesus as the transitional figure to a 'fourth epoch' of Israel's history. He argues:

The genealogy ... may be divided into three parts according to 1:17, but that is not its real extent or scope. At least a fourth section is implied; and since the table presents essentially a history of Israel it may be assumed that this is the fourth period.[50]

As John Mark Jones highlights, the exile itself assumes Israel's covenantal failure: 'Matthew provides ... an answer to the problem of Israel's apostasy: the birth of Jesus, who "will save his people from their sins"' (1:21).[51] Therefore, it is during this implied fourth period of Matthew's genealogy that the exile will come to an end and the new-covenant promises will be fulfilled. In the chapters following his genealogy Matthew tells Israel's story again, in a manner of speaking. It is no coincidence that after his birth in Judea, Matthew's narrative follows Jesus to Egypt and back (2:13–15), through the waters (3:13–17) and into the wilderness (4:1–11).[52] Unlike Israel's sojourn in the wilderness, however, Jesus remains faithful to the Lord and in so doing succeeds where Israel have failed.[53]

Conclusion to Matthew's genealogy

Matthew's genealogy is a story of unexpected salvation to preserve the line of promise and keep God's covenant commitments. These covenants include both the covenant blessings promised to Abraham and David and the covenant curses for those who were unfaithful. Admittedly, much lies below the surface in Matthew's genealogy. But at key points portions of this background break the surface enough for us to make sense of Matthew's emphases throughout this section. Moreover, as the Gospel unfolds, the covenantal background of the genealogy helps makes sense of Matthew's telling of the fourth act in Israel's history – an act that expands the boundaries of Israel's identity.[54]

Therefore, as we reconsider Matthew's broken chiasm, we see the exile as the central narrative problem in this SIS. It is the exile (and

---

[50] Waetjen 1976: 212.

[51] Jones 1994: 264.

[52] Waetjen even includes Mary in this formulation, arguing that Matthew 'interprets her maternity in the light of the OT idea of the corporate motherhood of Israel giving birth to the Messiah' (1976: 229).

[53] Hays observes, 'At the end of his time in the wilderness, Jesus has rightly embodied the covenant faithfulness Israel was meant to render to God – and he has done it, in Matthew's elegant narration, simply by reciting the very Scriptures through which that covenant faithfulness was originally defined and commanded' (2016: 120).

[54] We will examine the identity of Israel in greater detail in chapter 5 below.

all of its theological implications) that is the lingering barrier to the Abrahamic and Davidic covenants finally finding their fulfilment. Thus, Piotrowski is correct to observe that the exile 'is the inhibiting factor for the fulfillment of Yahweh's Davidic and Abrahamic promises'.[55]

The goal of Matthew's genealogy is to summarize the history of Israel with a particular emphasis on the inevitability of the coming of the Messiah, in spite of obstacles to the contrary. In the first section Matthew hints at the role of particular women (Tamar, Rahab and Ruth) to overcome obstacles to the preservation of the line of promise. In the second section the genealogy points to two events – the failure of the Davidic monarchs and the resulting exile – as potential obstacles to the fulfilment of the covenant promises. In the final section while the shadow of the exile does not fade, neither does the surety of the covenant promises. In the darkness of a displaced people and overthrown monarchy the promises to Abraham and David remain. And Matthew's Gospel begins by proclaiming that the fourth chapter of Israel's history in which the exile will end has begun. As the genealogy ends, we find ourselves with another threat to the line of promise, this time from King Herod. Yet once again, through the decisive actions of a band of unlikely heroes – Mary, Joseph and the Gentile magi – God preserves the line of promise. A woman in a surprising circumstance becomes the means by which the line of promise reaches its climax. With the birth of the Messiah, the climax of Israel's history has begun and the exile is finally coming to an end. As Matthew's Gospel moves forward, the coming of God's kingdom at the end of the exile is highlighted throughout, and the story of Israel plays a prominent role.

The context of the parable of the tenants

As we have observed, Matthew seems to have taken special care to fold retellings of Israel's story into both the forest and the trees of his Gospel. However, while the story of Israel frames the structure of

---

[55] Piotrowski 2015: 200. Eloff rightly concludes, 'Matthew is stating that the problem of the exile and the consequent nonfulfillment of the promises to the Patriarchs, to David, and thus for Israel, are only finally resolved with the coming of Jesus' (2004: 83).

Matthew's Gospel, we do not have a record of Jesus' telling Israel's story in quite the same way that we observe in the speeches in Acts. Yet we do find something near to this in the parable of the tenants (Matt. 21:33–44).[56]

This parable is certainly not the first reference to Israel's history since the genealogy in the first chapter. The Gospel of Matthew is permeated with this story. Throughout his life and public career Jesus himself is re-enacting the history of the nation. However, this parable is the most complete retelling of the story since the genealogy, and it is in this parable that we see some of the clearest connections to the OT. In it we see Matthew's concern to provide an interpretation of Israel's history. But, more than that, we see that this concern was born out of the teaching of Jesus himself.[57]

Therefore, although this parable appears in all three Synoptic Gospels (see e.g. Mark 12:1–12; Luke 20:9–19), our aim will be to discuss this parable with an emphasis on how it fits into the overall structure of Matthew. We need not assume Matthean priority for the parable, yet the structure of Matthew makes this parable a particularly useful window into how Jesus himself told the story of Israel.[58]

Although it is different in many ways, the parable of the tenants in Matthew tells essentially the same story of Israel that we saw in the genealogy. God's covenant people repeatedly failed to keep his covenant and consequently were sent into exile. Jesus retells the story of Israel so that God's people may remember that they were warned often about the consequences they were facing. However, this parable focuses especially on the loss of the fundamental covenant blessing: God's dwelling among

---

[56] Therefore, we need not rehearse the arguments for and against the quest for this historical Jesus (whatever one means by 'quest', 'historical', or, for that matter, 'Jesus'). Nevertheless, we cannot ignore the question of how Jesus understood the story of Israel without ignoring the testimony of the Gospels themselves.

[57] Snodgrass makes a compelling case for the authenticity of the parable (see 1998: 108–109). While some have doubted the authenticity of the parable because of its unrealistic storyline, this argument largely ignores the OT foundations of the parable. The Song of the Vineyard in Isaiah was not 'realistic' in a narrow sense, yet this does not affect our assessment of its authenticity. In any case, regardless of whether some features are exaggerated, Lee is correct to conclude, 'The basic story reflects well the tensions between owners and tenants in the ancient world' (2005: 158).

[58] For an argument for the Matthean priority of the parable, see Snodgrass 1998: 57–71. Also, while some scholars argue that the parable's earliest form was preserved in the *Gospel of Thomas*, we will focus our attention on the Synoptic Gospels, for our goal in this study is to understand the SIS in the NT canon. See also Snodgrass 1998: 193–194.

them. The SIS in this parable is that of a tragic story, but not one without hope.

The parables of the two sons and the wedding feast in the near context may tell aspects of the same story, but are not SIS per se. Also, Matthew tethers the parable of the tenants most directly to the OT, so it is fitting that we focus on this parable as a story of Israel's history.[59]

Finally, as we approach the parable in Matthew, it is important to recognize the prominence of the temple theme throughout in the immediate context.[60] The parable is part of the last narrative-discourse section in Matthew's Gospel, which is largely set in or focused on the temple. Moreover, it is likely that the entirety of Matthew 21 – 25 is in some way oriented towards the temple. In Matthew 21 itself the temple plays a prominent role. In verses 12–13 Jesus 'cleanses' the temple. In verses 14–17 Jesus heals and teaches in the temple. And in verses 18–22 Jesus curses the fig tree, which is probably a picture of Israel, and then likely points to the temple mount, saying that through faith the temple will be upended (a further reference to coming judgment).[61] Finally, the parable of the tenants is included when Jesus 'entered the temple courts' (v. 23). Read in this context, the story of Israel in the parable of the wicked tenants must be heard, both literally and figuratively, in the shadow of the temple.

However, while we will highlight the temple imagery throughout this section, we must also remember this caution from George Brooke: 'In the parable of the vineyard in whatever canonical form we read it, we are dealing with mixed metaphors, all gloriously intermingled.'[62] This makes interpreting the parable a complex task. Therefore, as we enter into discussion of the parable, we must recognize that there are layers of symbolism that overlap at several points.

---

[59] See also Wright 1996: 232. Some interpreters have given pride of place to the agricultural metaphors and their likely reception by the original audience of the parable; however, this is a wrong starting place. Rather, the OT imagery must shape our interpretation of the parable. For more on the self-evident references to Israel throughout the parable, see Pennington 2012: 200–202 and the literature cited there.

[60] For a broader sense of the function of the temple in the story of redemption, see Beale 2004.

[61] The chapter moves from temple judgment (vv. 12–17) to fig-tree judgment (vv. 18–22) and back to the temple (vv. 23–45). In this context a reference to a mountain would most likely refer to the temple mount.

[62] Brooke 1995: 282–283.

The content of the parable
of the tenants (Matt. 21:33–46)

Matthew's version of the parable and its aftermath has three basic moves. First, Jesus tells the parable itself (Matt. 21:33–39), drawing heavily from OT imagery, and especially Isaiah 5. The second part focuses on Jesus' interpretation of the parable (Matt. 21:40–44). This provides the interpretative key and proper response to the parable, as seen through the lens of Psalm 118:22–23 and Daniel 2:34–35. Finally, we hear the response of Israel's leaders, who, when seen in the wider context of Matthew's Gospel, may represent any Israelites who reject the Messiah (Matt. 21:45–46).

The details of the parable itself are straightforward. The master of a house built a vineyard with a fence surrounding it, a winepress and a tower. He then leased it to tenants and went on a journey (v. 33). Given the verbal connections to Isaiah 5 here, it is highly unlikely that the first audience of this parable would have missed the connections.[63] To an audience of chief priests, Pharisees and elders (vv. 23 and 45), the echoes would be quite clear: Jesus was telling the story of Israel. However, in order to get a better sense of the way Jesus, the apostles and the Jewish leaders would have understood this parable, we will briefly return to Isaiah, where the prophet tells Israel's story in a unique way.[64]

Isaiah 5

Like the parable in Matthew 21, the structure of the song in Isaiah 5 is straightforward.[65] The Lord plants a vineyard and builds a wall, a tower, a winepress, and so on (v. 1). Then he awaits the harvest. However, rather than producing good fruit, the vineyard produces wild grapes (MT) or thorns (LXX). In response the vineyard keeper asks what else he can do for his vineyard.[66] The assumed answer is, of course, nothing (v. 4). Consequently, he will take away its hedge, leave it to run wild and even call

---

[63] Ps. 80:8–16 may also be part of the OT background. However, there are more direct parallels to Isa. 5. Also both Isa. 5 and Matt. 21 are prophetic announcements of Israel's failure and coming judgment.

[64] See Hester 1992: 34–40. However, Hester later concludes that the meaning of the parable in the Gospels has been detached from its original intent and reinterpreted in an allegorical sense (ibid. 31–33).

[65] For a more detailed analysis of the literary structure (including a chiasm), see Motyer 1993: 68.

[66] The word 'wait' (*qwh*) occurs three times in the song (vv. 2, 4, 7).

down drought upon it (vv. 5–6). Then, in verse 7, we hear the interpretation of the song: the vineyard of the Lord is the house of Israel, and it has become desecrated. As Kidner helpfully translates this verse, 'Did he find right? Nothing but riot! Did he find decency? Only despair.'[67]

The parallels between Isaiah 5 and Matthew 21 are clear. Both contexts include a vineyard, winepress, wall and tower. While neither Matthew nor Jesus himself likely quoted directly from Isaiah 5, it is almost certain that his audience would have heard the connections to the Lord's vineyard.[68]

On several fronts the parable functions in Matthew in much the same way that it functions in Isaiah.[69] In both accounts we hear the story of God's people and their failure to keep his covenant. In both accounts we see in vivid Technicolor the insanity of what it looks like for God's people to turn away from his grace and good gifts. Therefore, when commentators on the parable question whether the original audience would have considered the beatings and murder of the servants and the son to be a plausible scenario, it seems they are missing the point.[70] In both Matthew and Isaiah the point is that God's people are not acting rationally. Thus, Motyer's summary of the main point of the song in Isaiah equally applies to Matthew's parable: 'What can now be done for the people of God when a total work of grace has been lavished on them and yet they remain as if grace had never touched them?'[71]

However, we should not assume the imagery in Isaiah and Matthew is identical in every respect. Many commentators recognize the parallels between them while also glossing over the differences between the two stories.[72] In Isaiah the vineyard is explicitly identified as the house of Israel or the men of Judah (v. 7). Therefore, some commentators assume that the vineyard in Matthew must represent Israel as well.[73] On closer examination, however, this is not quite correct. As Iverson observes in his analysis of the parable in Mark,

---

[67] Kidner 1994: 637.
[68] Note, however, that in Matthew the order is planting, raising the fence, digging the winepress, building the tower; in LXX the order is raising the fence, digging the trench, planting, building the tower, digging the winepress.
[69] Blomberg notes, 'The account in Isaiah is remarkably similar to Jesus' story' (2007: 71).
[70] See e.g. Morris 1992: 542.
[71] Motyer 1993: 68.
[72] See Davies and Allison, who casually observe, 'The transparent use of Isa 5.2 means that we have an allegory: as in Isaiah "the vineyard of the Lord of hosts is the house of Israel" (Isa 5.7), and the owner must be God' (2004: 179).
[73] Nolland 2005: 871.

the tenants – not the vineyard – are judged for their wicked behavior, and stewardship of the vineyard is granted to 'others' ... Isaiah's account ends with judgment against the vineyard, whereas Mark's parable concludes with the condemnation of the tenants and the productivity of the vineyard unquestioned.[74]

The same observation applies in Matthew. The judgment is focused on the tenants; the productivity of the vineyard itself is not part of the failure. Therefore, if the vineyard in Matthew's parable is not Israel per se, what does it represent?

Without giving a full taxonomy, other options for the vineyard include God's election and its privileges,[75] the kingdom,[76] the Mosaic tradition and authority[77] or the covenant community.[78] None of these interpretations are necessarily mutually exclusive, for the imagery could overlap in several ways. The citizens of the kingdom are elect, heirs of the Mosaic tradition and members of the covenant community. However, it seems that the temple imagery surrounding this parable should lead us to consider the implications of the temple for our understanding of the parable in more depth.

Early Jewish interpretation

To get a better sense of how other early Jewish readers of Isaiah's vineyard song understood this chapter, we can first note one key change in the early translation from Hebrew to Greek. Along with changing the person of the verbs so that the entire song is in the first person,[79] for our purposes the most significant change to observe in the Greek translation is found in verse 6 (see Table 2.4).[80]

---

[74] Iverson 2012: 310–311.

[75] Snodgrass adds, 'to interpret the vineyard as Israel only creates problems. How can Israel be taken away and given to others?' In response to this problem, he suggests, 'The basic image, however, is to the *people* as the possession of God, and often this is limited to the remnant (Psalm 80,9–20; II Kings 19,30; Isaiah 3,14; 27,2f.; 37,31; Jeremiah 6,9; Hosea 14,6–9). The metaphorical vineyard in the Old Testament does not designate the nation so much as the elect of God and all the privileges that go with this election' (1998: 75; emphasis original).

[76] Iverson 2012: 312–313; Hagner 1995: 620.

[77] Horne 1998: 114–115.

[78] Osborne 2010: 786.

[79] While the verbs in the MT shift from first person in v. 1 to third person in v. 2, back to first person in vv. 3–6, and then to third person again in v. 7, in the Greek OT the verbs remain in first person throughout the Song.

[80] For more on the differences between the MT and the Greek OT, see Weren 1998: 7–8.

Table 2.4 Isaiah 5:6a MT and LXX

Isaiah 5:6a MT	Isaiah 5:6a LXX
wa'ăšîtēhû bātāh	kai anēsō ton ampelōna mou
And I will make it a waste . . . (our tr.)	And I will leave my vineyard . . .

Whereas the MT speaks of the owner's (God's) destruction of the vineyard, in the Greek translation God departs from the vineyard. The vineyard in this translation still refers to Israel. However, the song envisions God's covenantal presence departing from his people.

In this understanding of Isaiah the removal of God's presence is almost certainly a reference to the exile. The threat of exile hangs over the whole book and one of the fundamental threats of the exile is the removal of God's presence.[81] Elsewhere in the OT the vineyard and garden theme are commonly linked with God's covenantal presence, specifically in the temple. Perhaps the best-known example of this phenomenon is the connection between the Garden of Eden and the temple.[82] Therefore, when we see garden imagery in the OT in connection with God's relationship with his people, we should expect to find the temple as well. The translators of Isaiah, while not making this connection explicit, hint at a link between the vineyard and the temple.

In other early Jewish texts we can see similar links between the vineyard and God's covenantal presence, specifically in the temple. In the Aramaic Targum of Isaiah 5:2 the vineyard is closely associated with the sanctuary and the altar, both symbols of the temple. In verse 5, according to the Targum, the Lord says that he will remove his presence and that he 'will break down the place of their sanctuary'. The reference to the destruction of the sanctuary certainly refers to the destruction of the temple, in either the sixth century BC exile or AD 70, or possibly both. Also, while the change is not quite as stark as the Greek translation discussed above, the first clause in verse 6 says, 'I will make them [to be] banished', another reference to exile.[83] Therefore, it seems that the Targum

---

[81] One of the main points of Isa. 6 is that the sin of the people will continue to multiply until the judgment of exile comes; this sin prevents them from entering the presence of God.

[82] Both Beale and Walton, among others, have made a compelling case linking the Garden of Eden and the temple. See Beale 2004: 32 33; Walton 2006: 123–127.

[83] Tr. from Chilton 1990: 11; emphasis original.

saw a close association between the temple and the vineyard of Isaiah 5, and the judgment on that vineyard is a reference to the exile.

4Q500 1 also ties the vineyard and the temple closely together. It speaks of the vineyard (line 7) as the place where God has planted 'the stream of [his] glory' (line 5) and 'the branches of [his] delight' (line 6) at the 'gate of the holy height' (line 4).[84] Again this is temple imagery. The stream of God's glory likely refers to the most holy place where God's presence dwells, the branches point to the lampstand outside the holy place, and the gate refers to the entrance to the temple. George Brooke is thus correct to conclude, '4Q500, therefore, almost certainly uses the Isaiah 5 vineyard material in interpretative association with a description of the temple.'[85]

Isaiah 5 in Matthew 21

As we return to Matthew we can observe a clear appropriation of the Isaianic vineyard theme, applied to Jesus' audience.[86] Jesus and Matthew may also stand in line with the interpretation that ties the temple and the vineyard closely together, for the temple theme permeates this section. The removal of God's presence from the temple is one of the fundamental curses of the exile; therefore, as was the case in his initial retelling of Israel's history in the genealogy, the exile may be in view here as well. If the temple and exile imagery play a role in Matthew 21 the point of the vineyard parable in Matthew would roughly parallel the pattern of Israel's history that we observed in the genealogy above:

1 God entrusted his covenantal presence and blessings to Israel and worked to preserve those covenant promises.
2 The specific focus of these covenant promises and responsibilities belonged to Israel's leaders; however, they failed to uphold their covenant obligations.

---

[84] For more on the OT backgrounds and import of each of these phrases, see Brooke 1995: 269–272. Other texts, such as *Tg. Jon.*, Isa. 5.2 and *Sukkah* 3.15, indicate that the temple is in view here.

[85] Brooke 1995: 272.

[86] Ellis describes the exegetical use of Isa. 5 in this parable as a form of midrash. Like other 'midrashic' uses of the OT in the New, Ellis sees the parable built around an initial text (in this case Isa. 5), followed by an exposition linked to the initial text by a catchword (*lithos*), and one or more concluding texts, also linked to the catchword (Ps. 118:22–23; Dan. 2:34, 44; 1977: 205). While we think the word 'midrash' may raise more problems than it solves, Ellis's observations about the general structure of the parable are correct. However, Ellis does not comment on the connections between the 'rock' motif and the temple.

3 When the prophets, such as Isaiah, warned them of judgment, rather than repenting they rejected those prophets and the result was exile.

While this exile continued, the greatest rejection of God's prophets was imminent from the perspective of the parable, for the people had already rejected the son. Because of this, the covenant blessing would be taken from unfaithful Israel. The covenant and its concomitant blessings would be given to those who remained faithful. However, we will also consider the other OT citations in this parable (Ps. 118 and Dan. 2) to get a better sense of how exactly this was to happen.

Psalm 118

The Greek text of Psalm 118 quoted by Matthew is an essentially word-for-word equivalent with most manuscripts of the Greek OT. Of the three OT references in the parable, this one is the most explicit quotation. However, many scholars doubt the historical authenticity of the quotation from Psalm 118:22–23. Admittedly, this quotation may seem out of place in our context. Yet if the vineyard is a symbol for the temple or, more precisely, the covenant blessing of God's presence localized in the temple, the use of this psalm makes good sense as a capstone to Israel's history.[87] Moreover, this citation from Psalm 118:22–23 fits with a wider 'stone' motif that appears throughout the NT.[88]

The psalmist recounts thanksgiving to God for delivering him from his enemies. One could even say that, in a sense, Psalm 118 also recounts the history of Israel, moving from the retelling of the Lord's deliverance in the exodus in verses 11–16 to the arrival at Mount Zion for those who sang the song on their ascent to the temple mount.[89] Moreover, we see in verses 22–23 that, as was the case so often in the nation's history, the threat to

---

[87] Beale suggests that Matt. 16:18 may 'anticipate' the stone references in Matt. 21 (2004: 187). Similarly, Wright notes, 'The idea of the "stone" is closely linked with the idea of the new eschatological Temple' (1996: 499).

[88] Bruce wrote that this motif 'appears in so many strata of the New Testament that it must be recognized as unusually primitive' (1969: 65).

[89] See esp. v. 5 (the Lord's response to his people's anguish) and vv. 10–14 (deliverance from nations who surrounded Israel). The psalmist also seems to echo both the exodus and the return from exile, while continuing to pray that the Lord may save his people (v. 25). See also Kidner 1973: 412. Dahood observes 'several striking verbal similarities' between Ps. 118 and Exod. 15 (1970: 156).

Israel came from within. The stone that the builders themselves rejected has become the capstone.[90]

Psalm 118 in Matthew 21

When considering Matthew's use of Psalm 118, Blomberg is correct to observe, 'Here is classic Davidic typology or, if one thinks the psalm originally referred to Israel as a nation, one may see the continuance of Matthew's theme of Jesus recapitulating the experience of Israel.'[91] The psalm tells the story of Israel as one of unexpected victory over the enemies of God through the discarded stone, and in Matthew the stone is the Messiah himself. Therefore, the climax of Israel's history was to be found in the rejection of the Messiah, who would then be vindicated and established as the cornerstone.

When read as the climax of the parable of the wicked tenants, the use of the psalm makes good sense. The history of Israel was marked by the failure of its leaders, who rejected the prophets time and again. After they rejected the Messiah, he became the cornerstone of God's renewed covenant people, who become the living stones of the renewed temple, if we may use Petrine imagery (see 1 Peter 2:4–6). To see the final layer of this story, however, we must turn our attention to Daniel 2.

Daniel 2

While Isaiah 5 is clearly the driving OT beat and Psalm 118 the concluding note, an allusion to Daniel 2 in verses 43–44 may round out the OT resonance in this parable. In Daniel 2 we find the well-known dream of Nebuchadnezzar. In it he saw an image representing five kingdoms that would reign for a time but eventually would be struck by a stone, broken in pieces and swept away like chaff (vv. 34–35). This stone then 'became a huge mountain and filled the whole earth' (v. 35). We then see that the stone represents the kingdom that will 'be established for ever' (v. 44, LXX). Moreover, given the common reference to the Lord as a 'Rock' in the OT, the stone motif may also point to the presence of God himself in this worldwide kingdom.[92]

---

[90] As Kidner notes, the 'ring of foes' in v. 10 symbolizes 'the builders themselves, the men of power in Israel' (1973: 415). Whether the stone itself is a 'cornerstone' or 'capstone' is irrelevant for our purposes.

[91] Blomberg 2007: 74.

[92] Lucas 2002: 74. For the 'stone' theme, see 2 Sam. 22:2–3; Pss 18:2; 42:9; 71:3; Isa. 44:8; Hab. 1:12.

Some may question an allusion to Daniel 2 in Matthew's version of the parable.[93] Yet the ready availability (and familiarity) of this text to Jesus' audience combined with clear thematic resonance make a reference to Nebuchadnezzar's dream in the parable likely.[94] There is a strong conceptual parallel between Daniel 2:34–35 and Matthew 21:44, in that both texts refer to the stone that represents God's kingdom crushing those who resist it. However, the most striking parallel between the two texts is the reference to the kingdom being removed and given to another nation. In Daniel the kingdom 'will not pass to another people' (*hautē hē basileia allo ethnos ou mē easē*; v. 44), but in Matthew 'the kingdom of God will be taken away from you and given to a people who will produce its fruit' (*arthēsetai aph' hymōn hē basileia tou theou kai dothēsetai ethnei poiounti tous karpous autēs*; 21:43). The texts initially appear to be making opposite points, and we will return to this tension below. For now, it is sufficient to observe that they share thematic and even verbal parallels.

Daniel 2 in Matthew 21

As he finishes his explanation of this parable, Jesus shifts the focus of the imagery slightly from the temple to the kingdom (v. 43). The context in Matthew and the connections between the vineyard and the temple highlight the temple themes here; the emphasis on the kingdom at this point helps us recognize that the kingdom and temple are ultimately synonymous. In other words, to answer the question of whether the vineyard refers to the temple or the kingdom, the answer is yes it does.

With Daniel 2 in the background of this reference, this shift makes good sense. While the stone in Daniel 2 differs in significant ways from the cornerstone of Psalm 118, they are likely referring to the same basic image. Daniel's stone is a kingdom, established by God himself, that becomes a mountain that fills the whole earth. In the OT the 'mountain of the LORD' and the temple are closely connected (e.g. Isa. 2:2–3; Mic. 4:1–2).[95]

We observed one significant difference between Daniel 2:44 and Matthew 21:43–44 above. In Daniel the mountain kingdom 'will not pass to another people'. However, Matthew seems to make just the opposite

---

[93] Hartman claims, 'The only possible allusion to the stone of Daniel 2 [in the NT] is in Luke 20:18' (1978: 150).

[94] We allude here to Richard Hays's seven criteria for biblical allusions (1989: 29–32).

[95] For a fuller explanation of the links between Dan. 2 and the temple, see Beale 2004: 144–153.

statement: the kingdom will be 'taken from you'. This shift highlights the fundamental point that the parable is making: Israel's history would culminate with the establishment of God's kingdom, as this audience was expecting, but membership in the kingdom was dependent on connection and submission to the cornerstone of this mountain kingdom. No Israelite could be included in this everlasting kingdom while continuing to reject God's messengers and God himself. That is to say, the everlasting kingdom belongs (and only belongs) to those who are connected to the Rock/ Cornerstone.

Therefore, given the verbal and thematic parallels to Daniel, when we see the kingdom brought into the equation, it is likely that this reference to the kingdom of God is linked to the stone/mountain of Daniel 2. We could call this an ironic use of the OT in which Jesus is correcting his audience's wrong perceptions of God's covenant presence in the temple and ultimately in the kingdom.[96] The kingdom is the place where God's covenantal presence will dwell universally and eternally, but only for those who do not reject the true cornerstone of God's kingdom.

Conclusion to the parable of the tenants

Given what we have seen to this point, Beale is correct to argue that the key link between Isaiah 5, Psalm 118 and Daniel 2 is the temple image.[97] As we noted above, there was a significant link between temple themes and the vineyard in the OT and early Judaism. In 4Q500 and other early Jewish texts the vineyard is the temple. When the context of this parable is seen in concert with the temple imagery in Daniel 2 and Psalm 118, the most plausible conclusion is that the vineyard itself is closely linked to the temple. Thus, we are certainly not the first to see the connections between the vineyard and God's covenantal presence in the temple. In fact, many of our observations are quite close to Beale's observations on this parable. The vineyard, which represents God's covenantal presence, is taken away from unfaithful Israel and rebuilt on the foundation of the Messiah, Jesus. In this telling of Israel's story Jesus is the Psalm 118 cornerstone of the new temple, which is also the Daniel 2 stone foundation of the temple-kingdom that will fill the whole earth.

---

[96] Beale describes the ironic use of the OT as those cases when 'clear OT allusions are used with the opposite meaning from the OT' (2012: 92). In this case Jesus would be using Dan. 2 ironically to persuade his audience to see its wrong understanding of the text.
[97] Beale 2004: 186.

However, the parable of the wicked tenants is not just a way of explaining what was to become of the temple. This parable summarizes the story of Israel as Jesus himself told it. In the parable of the wicked tenants we have the story of Israel told in its most tragic form. Therefore, the story of Israel in the parable of the wicked tenants is this: God entrusted his people, Israel, with the covenantal blessing of his presence. However, when God's prophets held the people accountable to keep their covenant obligations, they failed time and again. Finally, God sent his son, the Messiah, Jesus, to the tenants. When they rejected and killed him, this was the final straw. The vineyard, God's covenantal presence, would be taken from them and given to others (v. 43) by means of a new temple, built on the foundation of the rejected cornerstone.

The irony of this transferral could not have been missed by Matthew's readers. The Gospel begins by highlighting the narrative tension of the exile in Israel's story. Here, as we approach the end of Matthew, we find that just when the kingdom is being established, we could say that unfaithful Israel is sent into exile yet again, for the presence of God in the person of Jesus is being taken from them and any claim to a temple and land will be decisively removed in the judgment of AD 70. Thus, while Matthew's genealogy is shaped to inform us that the end of exile comes through the Messiah, the parable of the tenants informs us that for those who continue to reject the Messiah, the experience of exile is only intensified.

As we consider the other images in the parable, of course the vineyard's owner is God the Father and the Son is Jesus.[98] We have seen that the vineyard and its accompanying blessing is God's covenantal presence, localized in temple. While most scholars argue that the tenants are Israel's leaders (the chief priests, scribes and elders), we have to consider this claim in the light of the wider context of Matthew and Israel's history as a whole.

Certainly this judgment would fall resoundingly on Israel's leaders. However, we cannot assume that the judgment is limited to them alone. In his discussion of Mark's version of the parable Iverson also notes that the culpability for Jesus' death belongs not just to the leaders but to the people in general.[99] The same could be said of Matthew's Gospel, and perhaps even more so. Regardless of one's view on the timing and referent

---

[98] Apart from a few interpreters, this view is nearly universal.
[99] Iverson 2012: 321–325.

of the judgment in Matthew 24, it seems difficult to deny that Jesus' prophecy speaks, at least in part, of the destruction of the temple as a judgment on the city (and the nation) more broadly. Moreover, when given the choice between Jesus and Barabbas, the whole crowd who was present called for Jesus' crucifixion (Matt. 27:23).

However, we must not misconstrue this story. As is clear from elsewhere in Matthew, where the disciples are the foundation of the new community in chapter 16, and the rest of the NT, where the earliest Christian leaders were all Jewish, this in no way excludes ethnic Israelites from salvation or leadership in God's new-covenant people. Rather, the community where God's presence dwells is no longer limited to a single nation. Therefore, the reconstituted community, the church, is the 'other' to whom God now entrusts his covenantal presence, and there is a pointer towards the multinational character of the church here.

The earliest Christians understood that God's covenant was a blessing that came with obligations – and the foremost obligation is loyalty and submission to the Messiah, Jesus, and they learned this from Jesus' own retelling of Israel's story. This is a sobering and significant story, but if we are to be faithful to the witness of the NT, it is one we must not ignore when considering how the earliest Christians tell the story of Israel. It is sobering because it is a story of judgment on Israel because of their failure to keep their covenant obligations consistently throughout the nation's history. Jesus read the story of Israel as a story in which the nation itself would face judgment but then would be reconstituted in and through the son, the rejected cornerstone, who is the stone that becomes a mountain that will fill the whole earth.

Reading Israel's story with Matthew

For Matthew, Israel's story is incomprehensible apart from the coming of the Messiah, Jesus. The covenants with Abraham, Israel and David stand in the background of this story as a substructure of sorts, and Matthew invites his readers to enter into this continuing story. Moreover, the shaping of the Gospel of Matthew implies that Jesus not only is the culmination of Israel's history and covenants, but also repeats Israel's history in his own life, death and resurrection.

Matthew's second telling of Israel's story in the parable of the tenants reveals why it is necessary for Jesus to embody Israel's mission. As God's vineyard keepers, Israel's leaders were to cultivate the fruit of God's kingdom-temple-vineyard. However, they failed to do this, and so judgment came. This tragic story also stands behind the genealogy. Without arguing for precise parallels between them, in both accounts God's work both establishes and sustains Israel, Israel's leaders fail to remain faithful to their responsibilities and, as a result, judgment comes on the nation – first in the exile (Matt. 1:11) and finally in the judgment of Israel's leaders and all who continue to break the covenant (Matt. 21:41). This judgment was later fulfilled through the destruction of the temple and later Jerusalem itself. Because Israel, and specifically their leaders, failed to keep God's covenant, it was necessary for the Messiah to embody Israel's mission to fulfil its vocation as its truly faithful king. As Wright asks and answers the question, '[W]ho did Jesus think he was? The first answer must be: Israel-in-person, Israel's representative, the one in whom Israel's destiny was reaching its climax'.[100]

Thus, in both his genealogy and in the parable of the tenants Matthew displays that the story of Israel as a whole was inevitably and relentlessly driving towards the coming of the Messiah. However, the constituent parts of that story, including the figures, symbols and very mission of Israel, point us forward in a more direct way to the Messiah because he is to be found not simply at the end of the story but in the details of the story as well.

Yet Matthew's understanding of Israel's history does not end with the coming of the Messiah, for in both the genealogy and the parable of the tenants the kingdom of God and reign of the Messiah point forward and outward to the Gentile nations. As noted above, in the first section of the genealogy three Gentile women are both progenitors of the Messiah and also directly point forwards to his saving work. From the very beginning the Gentiles were a part of God's redemptive plan. Regardless of how one sees Israel's national destiny, it is difficult to deny that the parable of the tenants points forwards to the significant role of the Gentiles in the kingdom of God. After the Messiah is rejected and vindicated, the kingdom that fills the whole earth is then given to the whole earth.

Given that Matthew sees the Gentiles throughout Israel's story, it should not be surprising that the Gospel ends with an eye towards the

---

[100] Wright 1996: 538.

nations.[101] Therefore, before we move on from Matthew's Gospel, we will make several observations from Matthew 28:18–20 that help us see the great commission as a continuation of Israel's story in Matthew.

The great commission and Israel's story in Matthew's Gospel

Matthew reads the OT as the story of Israel; however, he does not read the OT as the story of Israel without remainder. Rather, through its represent-ative and king the story of Israel would continue as the good news of his reign goes to the nations. And so, in the well-known great commission that ends Matthew's Gospel the risen Christ calls his followers to continue the story of Israel in the mission of his church. While we will not examine Matthew 28:18–20 in any detail, the inclusion of Gentile women in the genealogy of Matthew and pointer to Gentile inclusion in the parable of the tenants help us see that Matthew's retelling of Israel's story inevitably leads to the proclamation of the good news of the Messiah, Jesus, to the nations.[102]

Moreover, Jesus' claim in verse 18 'all authority has been given to me' likely alludes to more of the story of Israel than may appear at first blush. Hays argues that Daniel 7:14 lies in the near background of Matthew 28:18–20. In Daniel 7 the son of man receives authority so that all the nations will be under his never-ending rule. While the verbal parallels are limited, the authority to rule over an eternal kingdom that includes 'all nations' (*panta ta ethnē*) strengthens a link between Daniel 7 and Matthew 28.[103]

As others have noted, in Daniel 7 the 'one like a son of man' (v. 13) first receives authority to rule over an everlasting kingdom (v. 14). Sub-sequently, the 'holy people of the Most High' receive the kingdom and possess it for ever (v. 18). Therefore, in some sense the son of man figure represents the saints. If indeed Daniel 7 is in the background of the great commission, then Jesus, the triumphant Son of Man who has received authority over all nations, extends this authority to his closest followers

---

[101] For more on the theme of Gentile inclusion, rooted in the OT, found throughout Matthew, see Hays 2016: 175–183.

[102] For a detailed examination of the links between the genealogy and the great commission, see Hood 2011: 142–156.

[103] See Davies and Allison 1988: 683.

as they continue his mission – and the story of Israel – by taking the good news of his kingdom to the nations. Thus, Hays rightly concludes, 'Matthew is portraying the risen Jesus as the triumphant Son of Man figure – representing Israel – who exercises *exousia* over all the nations of the world in a kingdom that will not pass away.'[104]

The contribution of Matthew's summaries

Jonathan Pennington observes Matthew's Gospel presents a 'redefinition of the people of God as based on faith-response to Jesus rather than ethnicity'.[105] Therefore, Matthew's Gospel continues the story of Israel by insisting that this story is both retrospectively and prospectively centred in the Messiah, Jesus. As Wright concludes:

> Until the great day of redemption dawned, Israel was still 'in her sins,' still in need of rescue. The genealogy then says to Matthew's careful reader that the long story of Abraham's people will come to its fulfilment, its seventh seven, with a new David, who will rescue his people from their exile, that is, 'save his people from their sins.' When Matthew says precisely this in 1:18–21 we should not be surprised.[106]

To this we might add that the entire Gospel speaks to the fulfilment of this great story. The genealogy reminds us that Israel's history from the beginning was intended to climax with the life and mission of the Messiah; the parable of the tenants reminds us that the story of Israel continues in and through the Messiah, along with those who have faith in him.

We can make three additional observations that are closely linked to the continuing story of Israel in Matthew. First, God's covenants with Israel shape this story. The covenants with Abraham and David are primary in the genealogy. However, the Mosaic covenant and the promise of the new covenant are implicit in the story as well, for the exile and return are impossible to understand without covenant blessings and

---

104 Hays 2016: 184.
105 Pennington 2017: 95.
106 Wright 1992: 385–386.

curses that are bound up in both the Mosaic and new covenants; the new covenant is fundamentally a promise of the end of exile. In the parable of the tenants the same covenant blessing and curse structure are implied. Without this, the parable is incomprehensible. The major turning points and trajectory of the story revolve around God's covenant promises to Israel.

Related to this, the second contribution we see in Matthew is that the covenant structure of Israel's story helps us perceive that for Matthew the story is not complete. The genealogy indicates that with the coming of the Messiah the fourth chapter of Israel's history has only just begun. This is confirmed through the commission found in the last few lines of the Gospel, where the story continues into the present. If we are to read this story with Matthew and Jesus, we must read it as an incomplete story, a story that continues even into the present. We will return to the implications of this later in this study.

Finally, in the story of Israel as Jesus told it in the parable of the tenants we see that the plot of Israel's story leads inexorably towards the tragedy of the exile and beyond. The presence of God would be removed from God's people and Israel would be reconstituted on the foundation of the rejected cornerstone that would become a mountain to fill the whole earth. Thus, the exile is the fundamental tension in the plot of Israel's story, and that tension is resolved through the Messiah, Jesus. This parable portrays the judgment on Israel's leaders and all in the nation who reject the Messiah while also implying the multinational character of the covenant community in this new chapter of Israel's story. As the rejected cornerstone, Jesus becomes the foundation of the reconstituted people of God, which now extends beyond the boundaries of Israel.

Conclusion

Though often in unexpected ways, the trajectory of Israel's story was always moving towards the climactic appearance of the Messiah, and is full of patterns and persons who foreshadow the Messiah. The genealogy obviously highlights Jesus' Davidic lineage. As we noted, it also seems to portray several Gentile women as saviour figures who prefigure the Messiah but also foreshadow the multinational character of the new-covenant messianic community. The parable of the tenants presents the messianic Son as the culmination of a series of prophetic messengers whom the Father sent to Israel, only to see them rejected. This final rejection then becomes the means by which the last chapter of Israel's history begins, as the rejected Messiah is installed as the reigning Davidic king.

In what follows we will continue to trace the way that the apostles and other early Christians read and proclaimed the story of Israel. In our next chapter we will move to the SIS in Luke's Gospel and Acts. In Stephen's speech in Acts 7 and Paul's speech in Acts 13 we will find many of the same themes enhanced and expanded and several new themes that emerge, giving us a fuller picture of how best to learn to read the story of Israel with the earliest Christians.

3

Luke, Acts and the climax
of Israel's story

Apart from what we have observed in Matthew, the canonical Gospels include few, if any, unique SIS. While it is true that both Mark and Luke include Jesus' parable of the tenants, their versions are essentially the same as Matthew's. Moreover, they make the same theological claims about Israel, Jesus and the nascent church, so we will not give them further attention here. However, the Gospel of Luke lays the groundwork for Acts, which includes two of the clearest and most significant stories of Israel in the NT: Stephen's speech in Acts 7 and Paul's sermon at Pisidian Antioch in Acts 13.

In this chapter we will follow the same basic structure as the previous chapter. However, before examining the context for each of the SIS in Acts, we will briefly consider their prequel in the Gospel of Luke. After providing context for each summary, we will analyse the content of each story, highlighting its unique emphasis and contribution to the overall goals of Acts. Finally, at the end of the chapter we will summarize the contributions of the stories of Israel in Acts and the unique emphases of Luke's biblical theology on display in this book.

We will see that the overall structure and individual characters in the stories of Israel in Acts inevitably lead us towards Jesus as the climax of Israel's history. Stephen's and Paul's SIS in Acts 7 and Acts 13 both assume a covenantal substructure that informs the overall shape and climax of the story. This covenantal substructure explains, at least in part, the emphases and plot points in each of these summaries. Not only do these retellings of Israel's story help us to understand the plot, but they also help us to understand better the characters in Israel's story, particularly the rejected yet vindicated servants who prefigure the Messiah, Jesus. As we will see, both of these stories emphasize this theme to some degree, but it is particularly prominent in Stephen's speech. Moreover, while the roles of David and the Davidic covenant that lead to Christ are highlighted in both summaries, they are particularly prominent in Paul's sermon. Before we consider these stories, however, we will begin in the Gospel of Luke.

The context: the Gospel of Luke

Unlike Matthew, who tells a story of Israel in his genealogy, Luke's genealogical record does not include the same signs of narrative shaping. This is not to say Luke's genealogy does not have a narrative focus; rather, his genealogy does not tell the story of Israel as such. However, we should not conclude that Luke has little interest in Israel's history, for the very first verse of his Gospel speaks of the things that 'have been fulfilled' (*peplērophorēmenōn*); presumably, this fulfilment is linked to the story of the OT.[1] In an episode that will be echoed later in Paul's synagogue sermon in Acts 13, Jesus' first recorded teaching in Luke takes place in a synagogue in Nazareth. After reading from Isaiah 61:1–2, he proclaims that this text had been 'fulfilled' in their hearing (*peplērōtai*; Luke 4:21).[2] In both Luke and Acts Jesus' ministry is directly linked to the fulfilment of the OT. Thus, from the outset Luke's Gospel account weaves together OT references in both its narrative structure and especially in its account of Jesus' teaching.[3]

As noted above, all three Synoptic Gospels include the parable of the tenants. Luke's version of the parable is quite similar to Matthew's. He places the parable in substantially the same place as Matthew, just after Jesus enters Jerusalem and cleanses the temple in response to questions about his authority (see Luke 20:9–18). Therefore, Luke's version of the parable plays much the same function as it does in Matthew.[4] Near the end of Jesus' ministry he sums up Israel's history and interprets the

---

[1] See Thompson 2011: 21–22.

[2] Chris Bruno elsewhere argues that Jesus and Luke are likely drawing together a number of OT themes related to the biblical year of Jubilee. See Bruno 2010: 81–101.

[3] See Kimball 1994, *passim*.

[4] Marshall argues that this parable in Luke 'contains some allegorical reference to the history of Israel and the rejection of God's messengers by its leaders, although this element is much less prominent in Lk. than in Mk. and Mt.' (1978: 726). If this is the case, it is consistent with Luke's pattern of hinting at the story of Israel in the Gospel and making it explicit in Acts.

rejection of the Messiah as consistent with an observable pattern in Israel's story. Israel, and especially its leaders, has rejected God's revelation through his prophets. Therefore, at the climax of their history Israel have also rejected the Messiah, Jesus. In Matthew the rejection of the son is part of an overall pattern of rejecting God's prophets in Israel's story. This is present to some degree in the third Gospel; however, Luke's version of the parable foreshadows a more explicit presentation of this theme in the apostolic speeches in Acts.

While the Gospel of Luke does not include any additional stories of Israel that fit our criteria, he includes what we might call a story of a story of Israel in Luke 24. In the well-known account of Jesus' walking with his disciples on the road to Emmaus Luke records Jesus' teaching about the necessity of the Messiah's suffering and subsequent glory by telling the story of Israel (Luke 24:27). For Luke and presumably for Jesus himself the climax of Israel's story is the suffering and exaltation of the Messiah as the fulfilment of the OT promises. Later in the chapter Jesus again points to his own role as the climax of Israel's story (v. 44) and explains the necessity of his death and resurrection as the fulfilment of the OT (v. 46). However, he also adds another component or, to use the same metaphor we did when considering Matthew, he speaks of a new, forthcoming chapter in this story: the proclamation of forgiveness of sins in his name to all nations (v. 47). Thus, Alan Thompson rightly argues that Acts continues the story of Luke, which in turn continues the story of Israel in the OT.[5]

Like Matthew, Luke presents Jesus as the culmination of Israel's story. Like Matthew, Luke hints at the inclusion of the Gentiles in his description of the birth and earliest days of Jesus (Luke 2:31–32).[6] Like Matthew, he portrays Jesus' lamenting the consistent pattern of Israel's and their leaders rejecting God's messengers, culminating in the Messiah (Luke 19:41–44). Unlike Matthew, however, Luke's Gospel hints at these themes but does not often make them explicit. Yet he picks them up more directly as the apostles and their associates both explain the significance of Jesus as the climax of Israel's story and consider the fulfilment of that story in the book of Acts.

---

5 Thompson 2011: 22.
6 Jeska 2001: 215. For a discussion of Gentile inclusion in the Gospel of Luke, see Morgan-Wynne 2014: 158–160.

The context: Acts

Luke and Acts were almost certainly intended to be read in succession. The themes that were set up in Luke are picked up in different ways in Acts, for, as Marshall concludes, 'The first volume was likely written with at least one eye already on the sequel.'[7] However, it is best not to think of them as a single book ('Luke-Acts') but rather as a two-volume series.[8] One might say they are less *Lord of the Rings* and more *Chronicles of Narnia*. Therefore, without ignoring the significant continuity and connection between the two books, we need not attempt to create an elaborate structure to combine the two nor draw direct lines between Luke and Acts at every point.

Rather, as we seek to interpret the stories of Israel's history in Acts, we can consider the structure of Acts as a discrete unit. As we do so, we will observe that Luke includes stories of Israel's history near key turning points in the book that point to the structure of the book and his theological agenda in the narrative. From this we will be able to draw conclusions about the biblical-theological method of Luke, Stephen and Paul and their application of Israel's story to the present.[9]

Structure of Acts

A geographic outline of Acts, if not the only feasible structure for the book, remains one of the clearest.[10] Jesus' charge to his disciples to be his witnesses first in Jerusalem, then in Judea and Samaria, and finally to the ends of the earth fits the continuing plot of the book (Acts 1:8):

Jerusalem (chs. 1 – 7) → Judea and Samaria (chs. 8 – 12) →
Ends of the earth (chs. 13 – 28)

---

[7] Marshall 1993: 176–177.

[8] For discussion of the relationship of the books, see Marshall 1993: 163–182.

[9] Our assumption is that Luke is faithfully presenting the main content of the sermons and speeches found in Acts. Therefore, they represent the theological perspective of the speakers faithfully. However, without distorting their intent or content, Luke summarizes and shapes his presentation of the speeches. Therefore, they also represent a theological perspective of Luke, which essentially overlaps with the original speakers. For a good overview of arguments for and against Luke's use of sources for the speech (as well as a mediating approach), see Keener 2013: 1338–1342. Our view is closer to that of Bock, who sees this and the other speeches in Acts as faithful summaries of the original content (2007: 20–23).

[10] A good representative of this understanding of the structure is found in Schnabel. While he includes a more detailed structure, Schnabel follows this basic outline (2012: 46–53).

At the outset of each of these geographic sections Luke records an apostle (Peter, Paul) or a close associate of the apostles (Stephen) proclaiming the Messiah, Jesus, as the fulfilment of the OT story. Significantly for this study, in the transition from a focus on Jerusalem (Acts 1 – 7) to Judea and Samaria (Acts 8 – 12) we find a lengthy recounting of Israel's history in Stephen's speech (Acts 7). Also, in the transition from the mission to Judea and Samaria (Acts 8 – 12) to the mission to the end of the earth (Acts 13 – 28) Luke again includes a summary of Israel's history in Paul's sermon at Pisidian Antioch (Acts 13). As we observe the details of each of these accounts, we will also consider their place in the overall structure of Acts. From this we will gain a window into Luke's biblical-theological presuppositions and method for reading the story of Israel.

Peter's sermon (Acts 2)

While it is near the beginning of the first geographical section, Peter's sermon in Acts 2 is not, strictly speaking, a SIS. Therefore, we will not give it detailed attention here. However, we will highlight Peter's understanding of how his ministry relates to the rest of Israel's story, for this sermon serves a similar purpose in the first section of Acts to those of Stephen's and Paul's recitations of Israel's history later in the second and third parts of the narrative.[11]

As Peter stood up to address the crowds gathered in Jerusalem for the Day of Pentecost who had witnessed the outpouring of the Spirit, he announced that they were witnessing the events that Joel 2 had said would take place 'in the last days' (Acts 2:17). That is, Joel's prophecy looks forward to the days of the new covenant, when God's saving promises to Israel will reach their climax.

The inauguration of this new-covenant era, Peter argues, was accomplished through the rejection, death, resurrection and ascension/reign of the Messiah, Jesus. He proclaimed that the words of Psalm 16:8–11 find their fulfilment in the resurrection of Jesus. This psalm expresses a strong hope and expectation that God will be faithful to his covenant promises. Reading the text with 'messianic and resurrection logic', in which the pinnacle of God's covenant-keeping is seen in the life, death, resurrection

---

[11] Kistemaker notes similar features in the three speeches (1990: 37). However, he does not relate them to the narrative structure of Acts.

and reign of Jesus, Luke and Peter read the psalm consistently with the messianic trajectory that we observed in Matthew's Gospel.[12]

Jesus is the son of David who will not see corruption because God raised him from the dead, exalted him as the ruling king and gave him the new-covenant promise of the Spirit (vv. 32–33). As was the case in Matthew's reading of Israel's history, God's covenant promises find their surprising climax in the rejection and vindication of his own son.

Peter's conclusion to the sermon underlines this point. Just over a month before the Day of Pentecost the Jewish leaders, with the consent of the gathered crowds, had handed Jesus over to the Romans to be crucified. This rejection, though a great evil, became the very means that God used both to keep his promises to David and to launch the new-covenant era. As we will observe below, these covenant promises lie under the surface of the SIS in Acts; even here, however, we can see Peter's assuming God's commitment to keeping his covenants as the culmination of Israel's story.

One could make a case for Peter's next sermon, in Acts 3:12–26, as another candidate for a story of Israel. Howard Clark Kee rightly observes that in Peter's sermon 'the significance of Jesus is placed within the framework of the history of Israel'.[13] Peter also highlights significant covenantal turning points with references to Abraham, Isaac and Jacob (v. 13), Moses (v. 22) and Samuel (v. 24), who looms large in the establishment of the Davidic covenant. However, this speech does not trace the story of Israel in a narrative sequence; rather, it demonstrates the Messiah, Jesus, as the fulfilment of God's commitment to keep his covenant promises found in this story (v. 25).

Moreover, in the structure of Acts this commitment to keep his promises results in the expansion of the gospel from Jerusalem to Judea to Samaria to the ends of the earth. However, it begins in Jerusalem with the outpouring of the Spirit and the inauguration of the new covenant. Salvation is indeed from the Jews, but as God keeps his promises to Israel the good news of Jesus' death, resurrection and exaltation must inevitably reach the Gentiles. As we examine Stephen's speech in Acts 7 and Paul's summary in Acts 13, we will see these themes clarified and expanded. As is the case throughout this study, our primary goal in this section will be to observe the

---

[12] The phrase is from Harriman 2017: 256. Harriman rightly observes that the psalm highlights 'God's inexorable loving faithfulness, the covenant, and God's justice' (ibid.).
[13] Kee 1993: 57.

biblical-theological method of the NT writers, not to compare Luke's recitations of Israel's history to other early Jewish stories of Israel.[14]

The context of Stephen's speech

While some may debate its historicity and background, few can dispute that Stephen's speech in Acts 7 and its aftermath play a crucial role in the unfolding narrative of Acts. The 'great persecution' (8:1) that followed on the heels of this speech becomes the impetus for the spread of the gospel message to Judea and Samaria and the reason for Saul's journey to Damascus, which was interrupted in a rather significant way (Acts 9:1–30). Thus, it serves as a narrative hinge for Acts to move from Jerusalem to Judea and then Samaria, which finally leads to the gospel reaching the end of the earth.

Some scholars may agree with Richard Pervo's assessment that the speech 'contains little more than an indubitably partisan review of biblical history up to the construction of the first temple, followed by a brief but sharp attack on the auditors'.[15] However, we believe this window into the earliest Christians' understanding of Israel's story is of great value for our own reading and understanding of the OT.[16] Yet a careful examination of every part of Stephen's speech would require a monograph-length treatment.[17] Since our goal is to comprehend Stephen's retelling of Israel's story as representative of the earliest Christians, we will touch on those points that help us see how Stephen put his Bible together, so to speak. To do this, we will examine the structure of the speech and the key themes that help bind the structure together. From there we will make several observations about how Stephen's reading of Israel's history (and Luke's presentation of it) help us best understand the biblical theology of the earliest Christians.

---

[14] This type of comparison is the primary goal of Jeska (2001). Moreover, we are assuming that the author of both Luke and Acts was the same man, Paul's travel companion, whom the church has for centuries consistently identified as the author of these books.

[15] Pervo 2008: 174.

[16] In a recent study of Acts 7:2–16 Whitenton has compared Stephen's account of Abraham and the patriarchs with those found in the LXX, *Jubilees*, Philo's *On the Life of Abraham* and Josephus's *Jewish Antiquities* (2012: 149–167). However, by reading Stephen's speech through the lens of these other writings, Whitenton has perhaps unintentionally overcomplicated the background material. While we should not ignore parallels with other early Jewish literature, our best starting point is considering how the speech fits into the overall framework of the OT.

[17] Monographs of this sort include Kilgallen 1975; Matthews 2010; and Penner 2003.

In short, we will observe that Stephen's speech in Acts 7, while compatible with some Greco-Roman rhetorical forms, points us to the covenantal substructure that shapes Israel's history and climaxes with Christ. In his recitation of Israel's story Stephen considers three key eras: the era of Abraham and the patriarchs (vv. 2–16), the era of the exodus and conquest (vv. 17–45a) and the era of David and Solomon (vv. 45b–47). In so doing Stephen highlights the covenantal structure of the OT narrative, which is built around the covenants with Abraham, Israel and David, respectively. As we examine Stephen's key emphases as recorded by Luke, we will observe that, while God's people continued in covenant infidelity, God himself designated key individuals to represent his people as covenantal intercessors and representatives, not unlike the Gentile women in Matthew's genealogy. In Acts, however, these became the very means of advancing the redemptive plan, often through their rejection and subsequent vindication. This line of righteous sufferers then culminates in the coming of 'the Righteous One', Jesus (v. 52), who brings the history of Israel and God's covenantal promises to their climax.

Rhetorical structure

When considering the structure, many interpreters follow Jacques Dupont's rhetorical outline of Stephen's speech: *exordium* (v. 2a), *narratio* (vv. 2b–34), transition (v. 35), *argumentatio* (vv. 36–50) and *peroratio* (vv. 51–53).[18] While Dupont's standard rhetorical outline of the speech includes a transition to the *argumentatio* in verses 36–50, Fearghus Ó Fearghail is likely closer to the mark in arguing that the *narratio* continues until verse 50, followed by a conclusion in verses 51–53.[19] Given the focus on Moses in verses 35–41, this proposal makes good sense.

While we will not attempt to undermine a rhetorical reading of this text, in this study we also will not analyse the speech through the lens of Greco-Roman rhetoric.[20] Rather, we will consider its place in the structure of Acts and as a story of Israel. In truth, these approaches are not mutually

---

[18] See Dupont 1985: 153–167. Scholars who follow Dupont include Mittelstadt 2004: 106; Bock 2010: 277; and Keener 2013: 1332–1333.

[19] Ó Fearghail 1988: 106, 108.

[20] Most scholars affirm both a rhetorical structure and a biblical outline to Stephen's speech. However, Peterson correctly observes, 'Observations about the rhetorical character and structure of Acts 7 are helpful as far as they go. But a detailed analysis of the argument, with its highly selective use of Scripture, repetition of key words, and progressive development of important themes, suggests . . . [a] literary and theological structure' (2009: 246).

exclusive. For example, although Craig Keener uses rhetorical analysis in his exposition of the speech, he also notes the similarity between Stephen's speech and several OT prophetic narratives.[21]

While there is no consensus on the structure of Stephen's speech with reference to Israel's history, Schnabel is correct to observe that most interpreters see a 'biographical focus' to the structure.[22] That is to say, Stephen tells Israel's history by moving from Abraham (vv. 2b–8) to Joseph (vv. 9–16) to Moses (vv. 17–43). However, this biographical focus breaks down in the last part of the speech, when the focus shifts to the temple and the prophets (vv. 44–50).

Longenecker hints at a structure that highlights 'the three great pillars of popular Jewish piety': land (vv. 2–36), law (vv. 37–43) and temple (vv. 44–50).[23] These themes are certainly present, but this seems to minimize the biographical focus that dominates the first part of the speech. Schnabel, among many others, rightly emphasizes that the main character of the speech – and consequently of Israel's history – is God himself.[24] Therefore, he suggests six divisions in the speech:

(1) God and Abraham (vv. 2b–8); (2) God and Joseph (vv. 9–16); (3) God and Moses (vv. 17–43); (4) God, the tabernacle, and the temple (vv. 44–50); (5) an indictment of Israel and the reality of Israel's need for salvation (7:51–53); (6) an explication of Jesus' identity (v. 56).[25]

While Schnabel is indeed correct to shift the focus towards God as the main character in Israel's history, he does not consider fully the important role the covenants play in God's relationships with his people and the unfolding covenantal structure in Israel's history.

As noted above, the threefold geographical structure from Acts 1:8 provides a good starting place for understanding the narrative. As the gospel advances in Jerusalem in the wake of the outpouring of the Spirit at Pentecost, the authorities begin to take notice. The apostles were performing signs and wonders and defying the ruling council (Acts 4:19–20), and the

---

[21] Keener points to parallels with Deut. 1 – 4; 1 Sam. 12:8–11; Isa 5:1–2; and Ezek. 16 (2013: 1333).

[22] Schnabel 2012: 355. For an argument for this basic outline, see Bock 2010: 276.

[23] Longenecker 2017: 198, 337–339; See also Peterson 2009: 245.

[24] Schnabel 2012: 362. See also Keener 2013: 1329.

[25] Schnabel 2012: 362.

rulers in Jerusalem were clearly displeased with what was happening in their city. In addition to this, among the many who became followers of the Messiah 'a large number of priests became obedient to the faith' (Acts 6:7). In response, when Stephen began performing signs and wonders, some of his fellow Jews challenged him. When these 'could not stand up against the wisdom' the Spirit gave Stephen, they accused him of speaking against the temple and the law (Acts 6:10, 13).

These twin accusations, speaking against 'this holy place and against the law' (Acts 6:13), are the occasion for Stephen's defence; as Bock summarizes the charges, 'the query is whether Stephen is unfaithful to the basic tenets of the faith and is encouraging others in Israel to think likewise'.[26] Since the story of Israel in large measure orbits around the temple and the law, it is appropriate for Stephen to answer their accusations with a SIS.

The agenda of the speech is not a dispassionate recitation of Israel's history (as if that were possible). Rather, it is meant to provide an answer to the charges levelled at Stephen while also providing a cogent defence of Jesus' role in Israel's history. Within this story of Israel a covenantal substructure is present as well. While he is not explicitly arguing for it, Stephen is presupposing an understanding of Israel that is built around the major covenants, and their respective covenantal promises.

The content of Stephen's speech (Acts 7)

Some scholars debate that Stephen's speech was not a meaningful defence against his accusers.[27] However, it would be a mistake to assume that Stephen's speech was designed to be a defence of the sort that would get himself 'off the hook', so to speak.[28] Rather, his goal was to get the ruling council 'on the hook'. Their misunderstanding of the law and the temple

---

[26] Bock 2010: 281.

[27] Pervo comments, 'The relationship between the speech and the charges of 6:11–14 is Lucan and shrewd' (2008: 179). He goes on to say that Luke has 'fashioned an iron glove for the fist of Paul' (ibid.). That is to say, the speech has no real historical connection with the charges. Fitzmyer is a bit softer, arguing, 'It does purport to answer the charges brought by the "false witnesses," suborned by diaspora Jews resident in Jerusalem . . . At least it so begins, but further analysis shows that its purpose is to accomplish something else' (2010: 361). We would not say it is intended to accomplish something else, but rather something *more*.

[28] Gaventa notes, 'Contemporary readers who anticipate a traditional defense speech, in which a defendant or an attorney itemizes charges and rebuts them in explicit detail, necessarily find Stephen's speech puzzling, to say the least' (2003: 119).

is part of a larger problem that had plagued the nation since the days of the patriarchs. Yet in God's sovereign purposes this problem became the very means God used to move his covenant promises forward.

Thus, Stephen's primary goal in the speech was to emphasize that God had kept his covenant promises to his people through the Messiah, Jesus, and he often used the rebellion of his covenant people and their rejection of his chosen servants to further those promises. As noted above, the main character in Stephen's recitation of Israel's history is not Abraham and the patriarchs, Moses or David and Solomon, but God himself.[29] God's interaction with those figures becomes the basic framework for Stephen's account of Israel's history. Keener correctly notes that in this history 'Stephen develops both the theme of God's fulfillment of his promises (e.g., 7:17) and the theme of the opposition to agents of promise that appear in each generation (e.g., 7:9, 27–28, 35–37).'[30] Yet we can go one step further to say that the advance of God's covenantal promises is accomplished through the opposition to his agents of promise.

It is no surprise that the speech begins with Abraham, for God's covenant with Abraham is foundational for Israel's history. Moreover, it is instructive to note which aspects of the Abrahamic covenant Stephen mentions in his speech. He first highlights the promises to Abraham in verses 2–8, yet he does so in a way that underscores the presence of God in a number of places outside the borders of the Promised Land. While it is a stretch to say that there is anti-temple polemic built into this version of the Abraham narrative, Stephen is clearly emphasizing that during the period of the Abrahamic covenant, there was not a centralized location for the worship of the Lord.[31] Instead, 'the God of glory appeared . . . in Mesopotamia' (v. 2).[32] Nevertheless, the focus of Stephen's attention in this section is oriented towards Joseph, not against the temple. Had he wished to drive home an anti-temple message, he could have said much more about the patriarchs and God's presence among them. Rather, he turns

---

[29] Parsons notes that God (*theos*) is the subject of seven of the eight main verbs in Acts 7:2–8a. The word appears seventeen times throughout the speech in four of the five Greek cases (only the vocative is excluded; 2008: 90–91; see Gaventa 2003: 121). See also Kim 2007: 353; Whitenton 2012: 151.

[30] Keener 2013: 1330.

[31] Pervo argues that Stephen intends to emphasize that 'no theophanies are associated with the temple' (2008: 181).

[32] For a discussion of the apparent differences between the Hebrew OT, the LXX and Stephen's speech, see Bock 2010: 282–283. For more on Stephen's treatment of the patriarchs, see Kim 2007: 341–360.

his attention to Joseph because it is not just in spite of, but through the rejection and subsequent vindication of, Joseph that God kept his covenant promises.

Therefore, when Stephen cites Genesis 15:13–14 in verses 6–7, he does so with an eye towards Joseph. This then becomes the focus of Stephen's attention during the patriarchal – or Abrahamic – era. In so doing he emphasizes that the patriarchs' rebellion and betrayal of Joseph was the means by which God kept his promises. Through this rebellion he raised up Joseph to deliver his people. It was not simply in spite of his enslavement and subsequent imprisonment that Joseph rescued the line of promise. Rather, God used the rejection of his righteous servant to accomplish his covenant purposes. Bock rightly points out that unlike the Qumran account of this incident, which condemns Joseph's brothers (CD-A 3.4–6), 'Stephen's version keeps the focus on God and his goal of saving his stubborn people.'[33]

Again, while he alludes to temple-worship ('afterwards they will . . . worship me in this place', v. 7), the focus is on Israel's covenant-keeping God and the means by which he has kept his covenant promises: the rebellion of his people and the rejection of his righteous representatives.[34] God's covenantal faithfulness lies under the surface of the speech.[35]

The narrative continues in verses 17–34 with a shift to events surrounding the exodus from Egypt. Unsurprisingly, both God's promises and the unexpected means by which he keeps those promises permeate this section. While Stephen refers to Joseph's virtues only indirectly,[36] he refers often to Moses' positive features, praising his beauty (v. 20) as well as his might in word and deed (v. 22).[37] As Loader correctly observes, Stephen is 'picturing Moses' calling as God's prophet par excellence as

---

[33] Bock 2010: 287.

[34] Though Bock argues that 'in this place' is 'more general', given the centrality of the temple in this section, the temple is a more likely referent (see ibid. 285).

[35] Though it is not entirely clear why Stephen includes Shechem here, Gaventa may be correct that this reference 'may anticipate the Samaritan mission in Acts 8' (2003: 124).

[36] Stephen mentions that God 'gave Joseph wisdom and enabled him to gain the goodwill of Pharaoh king of Egypt' (v. 10). However, he does not comment on Joseph's personal worthiness to receive that goodwill and wisdom.

[37] For more on the connection between Moses' beauty and the coming redemption of God and its reception history, see Loader 2011: 913–922. Loader notes, 'A closer look at verse 20 reveals that the beauty of the infant is enhanced over against both the Tanach and the Septuagint. He is not only beautiful, he is divinely beautiful' (ibid. 916).

well as Stephen's recourse to the often recurring motif of God's beauty in the Old Testament'.[38] In the OT and in Stephen's reading of Israel's history there was evidence that Moses was a fit leader and deliverer for Israel even from his birth.

Stephen mentions the rejection of Joseph only in passing, but gives significantly more attention to the rejection of Moses, devoting almost as much space to the episode with the Egyptian taskmaster as the OT itself does.[39] Yet even in his description of the Egyptian's death, Stephen's portrayal of Moses is unflinchingly positive. Moses defended and avenged his oppressed brother (v. 24). He assumed that his fellow Hebrews would recognize that 'God was giving them salvation by his hand' (v. 25).[40] But, like the patriarchs, they did not understand. In other words, they rejected the one through whom God intended to save them.

But it was through this rejection and Moses' subsequent exile that God himself appeared to Moses (outside the Promised Land) and told him of his intent to deliver his people from Egypt (vv. 30–34). Again we see the covenantal substructure of the speech emerge, as God reiterates his promises to Moses in verses 32–34. While the people of God did not understand or recognize his means of saving them, God himself remained committed to doing just that.

As God kept his covenantal promises to Abraham through the rejected Joseph, here he used a rejected leader as a way of moving his promises forward. In verse 35, when Stephen declares that the rejected Moses was made ruler and deliverer, he is assuming this story in which God is committed to keeping his promises to his people. The righteous messenger rejected by Israel is later vindicated and honoured by Israel's God.

In verses 36–50 Stephen continues to emphasize God's covenant faithfulness. Throughout this section he refers often to the glory that was given to Moses, who led Israel, doing wonders and signs (v. 36) and received the 'living words' (v. 38) of the law itself.[41] Thus, as we also can see in Acts 6:11 and 13, Moses and the law were inseparable. To speak ill of Moses was to speak ill of the law and vice versa. But also, to

---

[38] Ibid.

[39] The LXX version of the Egyptian's murder and the aftermath in Exod. 2:11–15 contains 138 words. In Acts 7 the story is 108 words.

[40] This comment begins the explicit connections to Jesus that will come later in the speech.

[41] While the law is not called 'living words' elsewhere in the NT or the LXX, Rom. 3:2 refers to it as 'the oracles of God' (*ta logia tou theou*).

misunderstand Moses was to misunderstand the very purpose of the law covenant.

This misunderstanding is why Stephen also notes that Moses pointed beyond himself. In verse 37 Stephen alludes to Deuteronomy 18:15, where Moses speaks of a coming prophet who will supersede and complete Moses' ministry.[42] Even as God was keeping his covenant promises through his rejected servants, there was a clear indication that greater promises (and greater fulfilments) were yet to come.[43] Along with this, however, is the not-yet-stated assumption that those greater promises may yet be accompanied by another rejection of God's chosen servant. Again the rejection and subsequent vindication of God's servants remains a central theme in Stephen's recitation of Israel's history.

As Stephen increases the pace of his summary in the later part of the speech, it becomes increasingly clear that the rejection of Moses and Joseph was not merely a rejection of God's servants. When they rejected his servants, they were rejecting God himself. In verse 39 Stephen says that Israel will not obey Moses, and this rejection is in fact a return to Egypt 'in their hearts'. Once they returned to Egypt in their hearts, their actions in the golden calf incident followed closely behind. And this pattern continued throughout Israel's history. They turned away from God and he 'gave them over' to worship their idols (v. 42). Thus, Stephen can move quickly from the golden calf incident to a reference to the exile in Amos 5:25–27 (vv. 42–43).[44] The prophet's condemnation is paradigmatic for the history of the nation. From Sinai to the exile Israel's idolatry was rooted in continuing rejection of God's rule over them.

Implicit as well in verses 44–50 is the forward motion of God's covenantal promises. In verse 46 David's favour before God is a clear reference to the Davidic covenant. Unlike Matthew's genealogy, Stephen's reference to David is exclusively positive. And in the fulfilment of the Davidic promise when Solomon built the temple, the promise to Abraham that Stephen had alluded to in verse 7 was fulfilled. The temple was 'this place' in which Israel was to worship God. Thus, through their rejection of

---

[42] This prophecy of a coming prophet is well attested in other early Jewish writings. See 4Q175; 4Q375; and *Aristobulus* 2.4. Whether it was read messianically in these texts is less clear.

[43] So Jeska 2001: 191.

[44] The quote from Amos 5 demonstrates that 'the consequences of the rejection of Moses reach all the way to the Exile' (Gaventa 2003: 127).

Joseph and Moses, which in reality point at their continued rejection of God's rule over them, God maintained his commitment to keep his covenant promises and even used the disobedience and rejection of his people to accomplish these purposes, as can be seen in the subsequent vindication of God's servants. Moreover, Stephen is assuming a connection between the Abrahamic and Davidic covenants. It was through the fulfilment of the promise to David that the promise to Abraham was also fulfilled.

In spite of God's faithfulness to his promises, Israel still failed to see and submit to the Lord's rule over them. In the climax of the *narratio* Stephen points to Isaiah 66 as a summary of Israel's failures (vv. 49–50). In quoting from Isaiah 66:1–2 Stephen does not intend to criticize the temple per se, as is often argued.[45] Rather, his point is that just as Israel rejected God's redeemers and rulers, they also failed to see God's transnational covenantal purposes. The temple in Jerusalem was insufficient to be 'his house and nowhere else'.[46] As the Lord revealed himself outside the Promised Land, he was reminding his people of his lordship over all the earth. Peterson rightly notes, 'God's self-revelation was not confined either to the promised land or to the temple.'[47] As the covenant with Abraham unfolded, his descendants should have expected the nations to be blessed along with them (Gen. 12:3). Yet they rejected God's redeemers, which was in truth a rejection of God himself, so they failed to fulfil the Abrahamic covenant and bless the nations. This includes their failure to see the international purposes for the temple.

Thus, Schnabel is correct to observe that the reference to the Most High in verse 48 'underlines his transcendence and sovereign rule over all things, which cannot be contained in a structure made by human beings'.[48] However, the worldwide rule of God is also implied in the temple itself and the covenant with Abraham. Even though Israel failed to see the international purposes of the temple, God was still committed to his promises to Abraham to bless all nations. Thus, we ought to expect that in the climactic fulfilment of God's promises we would see both a rejection of his chosen redeemer/servant and a continued push towards his international purposes.

[45] See Pervo 2008: 191 and Schnabel's helpful response in his 2012 work (385).
[46] The phrase is from Bock 2010: 303.
[47] Peterson 2009: 248.
[48] Schnabel 2012: 385.

As he nears the climax of the speech, Stephen pulls together the threads of his history that also coincided with the charges against him. In his final indictment of Israel's leaders Stephen, to make two key points that connect back to the initial charges against him, again hints at the covenantal substructure of Israel's story. Israel failed to remember that the temple and law pointed beyond themselves. They forgot that the temple was part of a covenant story that included the international blessing of Abraham (vv. 49–50). This was due in large part to their failure to submit to God's chosen messengers, beginning with Moses, and to God himself (vv. 51–52a). A fourth covenant, the new covenant, emerges here, if only in passing. It is in the new covenant that all of God's promises find their fulfilment. Through the Righteous One, Jesus, the promises to Israel from beginning to end reached their culmination. But when the Righteous One came, they rejected him as well (vv. 52b–53).[49]

Yet it was through this rejection that God's new-covenant promises were inaugurated, and his vindication and exaltation to the right hand of the Father once again demonstrate God's commitment to his promises (v. 55). Surprisingly, Jesus himself and Stephen are the only two people in the NT to call the Messiah 'Son of Man' (v. 56). Perhaps alluding to texts such as Psalms 8:4–5, 110:1 and Daniel 7:13, Stephen and Luke see the exaltation of Jesus as the climax of the story of Israel. The son of man figure in Dan. 7 embodies, fulfils and supersedes the promises of the Davidic king's reign, which are ultimately fulfilled in the new covenant.[50] The exalted Messiah is a divine figure, receiving the prayer of his servant Stephen. This is indeed an early and high Christology.[51]

---

[49] Shepherd also points to the influence of Nehemiah in the close of the speech: 'The conclusion to Stephen's exposition in Acts 7:51–53 follows that of Neh 9:29–31. He calls his accusers "stiff-necked" (*sklērotrachēloi*, cf., *esklērynan ton trachēlon autōn* [LXX Neh 9:16–17, 29]) and "uncircumcised in heart" (Deut 30:6; Jer 4:4). He says that they have resisted the Holy Spirit and are the sons of the prophets' persecutors (cf., Neh 9:30). They are the murderers of the righteous one and have not kept the law (cf., Neh 9:29, 34)' (2013: 84).

[50] Many have noted that in Stephen's vision Jesus is standing rather than sitting, vis-à-vis Ps. 110:1. Whether this posture indicates that Jesus is prepared to welcome Stephen, execute judgment on unbelieving Israel or (perhaps most likely) both does not affect our understanding of the story of Israel here. See Peterson 2009: 267.

[51] Pelikan observes, 'For Stephen to commit his spirit to the Lord Jesus when the Lord Jesus himself has committed his spirit to the Father was either an act of blatant idolatry or the acknowledgment of the *kyrios Iēsous* as the fitting recipient of the dying prayer of Stephen – and the fitting recipient of the spirit of the dying Stephen – because he was one with the Father (John 10:30), "one in being with the Father" (*homoousios tō patri*), as the Council of Nicea confessed in 325' (2005: 107).

When Stephen had concluded his speech, the Sanhedrin responded just as he likely expected them to respond. In short, the reason why Stephen's speech provoked a violent reaction was because it made the same essential claim that Jesus did about Israel's history; moreover, he made the same claims about Jesus that Jesus himself had made.

> Other Jewish sects or visionaries challenged the temple, but most of them did so privately or from a distance, such as the wilderness sectarians of Qumran. The early Christian leaders, however, were vying with the temple authorities for the leadership of Jerusalem's Jewish faith, a conflict that would ultimately lead to Stephen's martyrdom as it had led to that of Jesus.[52]

Although he begins by acting as his own defence lawyer, by the end of his speech Stephen has assumed the role of prosecutor, suggesting that many in Israel have become like the Egyptians, Philistines or Babylonians. Yet God used these very enemies to advance his own covenant purposes unwittingly. In the same way Stephen argues that for much of Israel's history this is exactly the role many of its people played; for as they rejected and killed his servants and prophets, God was indeed advancing his covenantal promises.

Summary of Stephen's speech

In the covenantal substructure of Israel's history Stephen assumes three key eras: the era of Abraham and the patriarchs (vv. 2–16), the era of the exodus and conquest (vv. 17–45a) and the temple (the era of the Davidic covenant, vv. 45b–50). In so doing Stephen is referring us back to the covenantal structure of the OT narrative, which is built around the covenants with Abraham, Israel and David, respectively (see Table 3.1). While God's people continued in covenant infidelity, God himself designated key individuals to represent his people as covenantal intercessors and representatives, culminating in 'the Righteous One', Jesus (v. 52). In short, Stephen reads (and preaches) the OT as a story of the covenant faithfulness of Israel's God in the face of the people's continuing rebellion.

---

[52] Keener 2013: 1330.

Table 3.1 Covenantal substructure in Acts 7

Covenant	Rejected servant
Abrahamic (vv. 2–16)	Joseph
Law (vv. 17–45a)	Moses
Davidic (vv. 45b–50)	David
New (vv. 52b–53)	Christ

As we consider the place of the speech in the structure of Acts, it stands as an introduction to the movement of the gospel from Jerusalem to Judea and Samaria, and subsequently from Judea and Samaria to the end of the earth. Thus, Stephen's underlying emphasis on the universalistic aspects of the covenant with Abraham are unsurprising. Stephen's speech is not only a recitation of salvation history in the past, but also of the foundation for the continued story of God's saving acts.[53] Once again, although Israel's leaders rejected God's messenger and servant, this very rejection became the means for God's purposes to advance. Those purposes included taking the gospel to the Gentiles, particularly in Samaria, and to the end of the earth.

The temple and law were always intended to point beyond them-selves – to the Messiah, Jesus, and to the worldwide mission that he would launch, all in fulfilment of God's promises to Abraham – and to his com-mitment to the creation from Genesis 3 onwards. As we look forward in Acts, it is no mistake that the martyrdom of Stephen leads to the scattering of the church, which in turn leads to the advance of the gospel to the nations.[54] As Keener notes, 'He [Luke] suggests that the Spirit pushes God's people to what we could describe as an international, multicultural vision and that tradition that holds people back from such a vision is not serving God's purpose.'[55]

---

[53] Jeska rightly argues that the reference to Abraham (and, we might add, the speech as a whole) is best interpreted not simply in the light of the charges against Stephen but in the light of Luke's view of history (2001: 198–199).

[54] Smith concludes, 'Luke thus uses a speech to explain and validate the movement of the larger narrative, and he marks the significance of this speech both by its length and by the violent interruptions that highlight and terminate Stephen's words' (2012: 227).

[55] Keener 2013: 1329.

The context of Paul's sermon

The other significant retelling of Israel's story in Acts is found in Paul's sermon at Antioch of Pisidia in Acts 13:16–41.[56] As was the case with Stephen's speech, in the unfolding narrative of Acts this speech comes near a transition in the geographical structure of the book. The triumph of the gospel in Samaria and Judea is evident in Cornelius the Gentile's receiving the new-covenant gift of the Spirit as the gospel goes to the nations (ch. 11) and Peter's miraculous escape from prison followed by the subsequent death of Herod, both of which demonstrate the authority of Jesus over the ruling powers of Judea and Samaria (ch. 12). With this demonstration of the power of the gospel and the authority of Jesus, the third section of the book begins as the gospel begins to reach the ends of the earth. Like Peter's sermon and Stephen's speech, Paul's sermon functions as a hinge in the geographic structure in Acts. The remainder of the book is focused on the spread of the gospel to the ends of the earth, namely, the imperial capital of Rome (Acts 28:14–31).

Acts 13 traces the beginning of this movement to the end of the earth as the church in Antioch sends Paul and Barnabas to proclaim the gospel in Asia Minor. After travelling from Antioch in Syria to Cyprus, where the proconsul in Paphos came to faith (vv. 4–12), they landed in Asia Minor, moving from Perga to Antioch in Pisidia (vv. 13–14). Both before and after this account, Paul's custom was to preach first in the synagogues of every city they entered, but here Luke gives us a window into what his message typically included and what their experience in the synagogues typically entailed.[57]

---

[56] As is the case with every speech in Acts, many scholars argue that this one is not historical and is inconsistent with other pictures of Paul in the NT and early Christianity. While we could spend a considerable time debating the 'Lukan Paul', the 'Deutero-Pauline Paul' and the 'real Paul', for our purposes we will limit our discussion to Paul's view of Israel's story. As we will observe below and in the chapters on Romans and Galatians, there is considerable unity to Paul's presentations of this story in Acts and his epistles. Many of the key themes that we will observe below, including the nature of God's covenant promises, Jesus as the Davidic Messiah and the continuing story of the OT, appear in Paul's epistles (Gal. 3 – 4; Rom. 9 – 11).

[57] Schnabel observes, 'Paul's sermon in the synagogue of Antioch is the first, and the last, missionary sermon that Luke relates for Paul' (2012: 564). Some might argue for Acts 17 as a missionary sermon. The context and content of Paul's oration there is quite different from a synagogue sermon. Regardless, while the sermon in Acts 13 was specific to Pisidian Antioch, it is also representative of the content of the synagogue sermons that Paul had preached in the other cities during this journey. The paradigmatic nature of this account, however, does not mean that it 'exhibits no interest in concrete history ... depicting the historical significance of Paul's labors' (Pervo 2008: 344). There is no need to create a false dichotomy here.

The contexts of Stephen's and Paul's speeches differ in both setting and occasion. Stephen, facing a hostile audience, to use Greco-Roman rhetorical categories, stands up to deliver a forensic, judicial defence that essentially turns into an indictment of Israel's leaders. Paul's audience was not hostile, at least in the way that Stephen's was, but many were curious about his teaching (though some became hostile after hearing his message).[58] While his sermon may share features with Greco-Roman rhetoric, it is better to understand it as a sermon in the vein of Peter's sermon in Acts 2. Therefore, our analysis below will largely exclude rhetorical categories.[59] Rather, Paul's speech is a synagogue sermon, addressed to a gathering of curious Jews and God-fearers (v. 16). Also, perhaps because his oration is a synagogue sermon rather than a semi-formal apologetic and defence, Paul directly quotes OT texts more frequently than Stephen does in Acts 7. Given the number of direct OT references in the sermon, we will not be able to devote extended attention to all of them. While it is necessary to consider each citation to some degree, in our examination we will limit our observations to those features that are most important for understanding the use of each citation in Acts 13.

The content of Paul's sermon (Acts 13:16–41)

If we were to limit our discussion strictly to Paul's recitation of the story of Israel, our analysis would end at verse 25. However, the rest of the sermon further explains the continuing significance of Israel's story and its fulfilment in Jesus; therefore, we will consider the sermon as a whole. Moreover, most scholars identify three divisions in Paul's sermon: the history of Israel (vv. 16–25), the gospel message that announces Jesus' fulfilment of that history (vv. 26–37), and an appeal to respond to this gospel proclamation (vv. 38–41).[60] These divisions make good sense, for Paul, in addressing his audience, begins each section with a vocative.[61]

---

[58] Kee calls Paul's sermon 'a much gentler version of this thesis of Stephen about Israel's history' (1993: 59).

[59] E.g. those in Kennedy 1984: 124–125.

[60] Morgan-Wynne 2014: 62–68; also Schnabel 2012: 571–572. Other commentators differ slightly, but most affirm these general divisions.

[61] *Andres Israēlitai kai hoi phoboumenoi ton theon* in v. 16; *andres adelphoi hyiou genous Abraam kai hoi en hymin phoboumenoi ton theon* in v. 26; *andres adelphoi* in v. 38.

However, there is also a subdivision between verses 31 and 32 within the second section. The kerygma itself ends with the ascension of Jesus in verse 31. In verse 32 Paul begins to explain that this gospel message is the fulfilment of the OT. While the gospel events and their explanation from the OT are inseparably linked, it is helpful to recognize the distinction between the gospel events and their interpretation.[62] Moreover, for the purposes of our study, the close link between the events of Israel's history, the events of Christ's life and ministry, and Paul's interpretation of these events are all essential parts of understanding the story of Israel in Paul's Pisidian Antioch sermon.

Covenantal substructure

Unlike many other stories of Israel, Paul does not begin his summary of Israel's history with an explicit reference to Abraham.[63] He does, however, ground the whole story in the election of the patriarchs, with possible allusions to Exodus 6:6–7 and/or Deuteronomy 4:37.[64] Both of these texts reflect on the occasion when God 'chose our ancestors' (*exelexato tous pateras hēmōn*; Acts 13:17). Israel's very existence and history are a result of this divine action.

As a result of his choice of the patriarchs, God brought Israel out from Egypt and into the Promised Land. The OT itself is clear that the events of the exodus were rooted in God's faithfulness to the covenant with Abraham (see Exod. 3:15). Thus, God's promises to Abraham are not far from the surface in Paul's recitation of the exodus. God chose Abraham's family and then exalted them during their sojourn in Egypt (v. 17b). This concept is reminiscent of God's promise to make Abraham's name great (Gen. 12:2). Moreover, he brought them into the place that he had first promised to Abraham so that they might inherit the land (v. 19). Thus, as in Acts 7, the covenants provide a substructure for Paul's understanding of Israel's history in Acts 13.

While he neither focuses on the rejected servants of the Lord nor Abraham and Moses as covenant representatives, Paul points to the link

---

[62] Morgan-Wynne considers this division between vv. 31 and 32 but ultimately dismisses it because of the close link between events and interpretation (2014: 66).

[63] Schnabel also notes that the sermon begins with a reference to the election of the patriarchs and concludes in v. 47 with God's commitment to bring his covenantal blessing to the end of the earth; thus, while it is not explicit, the entire sermon hangs on the Abrahamic covenant (2012: 575).

[64] Ibid.

Table 3.2 Covenantal substructure in Acts 13

Covenant	Representative
Abrahamic (vv. 17a)	N/A
Law (vv. 17b–19)	N/A
Davidic (vv. 20–22)	David
New (vv. 22–25)	Christ

between David and Christ and their respective covenants (see Table 3.2). After the nation had settled in the land, God set judges over them, culminating in Samuel (v. 20). Although God gave them Saul when they first asked for a king, he then removed King Saul to establish David as the rightful monarch. While much could have been said about the nature of Saul's kingship or the idolatry of the people in rejecting God's authority when asking for Saul, Paul quickly moves to the next major covenant in Israel's history: God's covenant with David.[65] Paul alludes to earlier covenants, for some understanding of those covenants is necessary for understanding Israel's history; however, the covenant with David is the primary focus of Paul's sermon. Bock rightly observes:

> This speech develops Israel's history in detail, phase by phase, until it reaches David. It then leaps over one thousand years of Israel's history to go directly to the promise of a son of David who will deliver the nation. This is Paul's point in the speech.[66]

Paul cites both Psalm 89:20, which highlights God's own covenant faithfulness and election of David, and 1 Samuel 13:14, which speaks of David's own fidelity to the covenant as a 'man according to [God's] own heart' (*andra kata tēn kardian*). Some dispute the meaning of this phrase in 1 Samuel 13:14, but Paul clarifies his understanding of the phrase with a likely allusion to Isaiah 44:28: 'who will do all my will' (*hos poiēsei panta ta thelēmata mou*; v. 22; our tr.). This phrase in Isaiah 44 refers to King Cyrus as the instrument through whom God will accomplish his new-covenant promises. Cyrus, whom Isaiah calls the Lord's anointed

---

[65] In Luke and Acts the emphasis on David can be traced back to Gabriel's promise to Mary in Luke 1:32–33 (see Morgan-Wynne 2014: 150).

[66] Bock 2010: 453.

in the following verse (Isa. 45:1), fills out the picture of the Davidic Messiah.[67]

Therefore, as he considers the Davidic covenant, Paul not only has God's covenant faithfulness in view, but also the faithfulness of the Davidic king himself, for the covenant fidelity of the king is essential for the fulfilment of the covenant. This aspect of the covenant, then, explains the move directly from David to Jesus. As we will see in more detail below, for Paul the obedience of David foreshadows that of his greater son, Jesus.

The promise to which Paul refers in verse 23, therefore, is the promise of the Davidic covenant, which is rooted in the previous covenants with Abraham and Israel. In this way Paul's sermon presents Jesus the Messiah as the culmination of Israel's history. The earlier covenants were designed to be fulfilled in and through the Messiah, Jesus, who inaugurated God's new-covenant promises.

As Paul announces in verses 24–25 that Jesus has fulfilled all of God's covenant promises, Luke once again highlights Jesus as the rejected and vindicated servant of the Lord par excellence. John the Baptist, as the last of the old-covenant prophets, announced Jesus' impending arrival (vv. 24–25).[68] While John's arrest and subsequent execution are not explicit here, Paul alludes to John's rejection as 'completing his work' (v. 25). However, John's vindication is found not in his own release or resurrection, but rather in Jesus' messianic ministry.

The climax of the story

As the second section of the sermon begins, Paul shifts away from the story of Israel proper to the recitation of Jesus' life, death and resurrection (vv. 26–31), and the interpretation of these events (vv. 32–37). In short, these are the gospel events that have been announced throughout the book of Acts. Jesus was rejected by his own people because they rejected the voice of the prophets. They did not perceive that he was the culmination of God's saving plan, though this very failure fulfilled the words of the prophets. Therefore, even though they could find no cause to condemn him to death, they asked Pilate to execute him. Yet this rejected servant

---

[67] Schnabel 2012: 577.

[68] Pervo notes, 'In this speech, the prophetic era extends from Samuel to the Baptizer.' He notes that an echo of Mal. 3:1–2 may be present here as well (2008: 336–337).

was vindicated when God raised him from the dead, as many witnesses had testified (v. 31). His death was the necessary sacrifice for sin. As Paul presents the interpretation of these events in verses 32–37, he summarizes the climax of Israel's history, which then sets the stage for his call for the proper response to this climax in verses 38–41. Peterson rightly observes, 'Linked with the offer of the forgiveness of sins through Jesus (vv. 38–39), this suggests that his death was the vicarious atonement which made possible the inauguration of the New Covenant.'[69]

In his interpretation of the gospel events, Paul cites three OT texts that explain the nature of Jesus' life and ministry and support his proclamation of Jesus' resurrection as the fulfilment of the Davidic covenant (Ps. 2:7; Isa. 55:3; Ps. 16:10). While these texts are explicitly quoted, it is also likely the Davidic promises in 2 Samuel 7 are in the near background, as they have been through much of the sermon; some even suggest that this text was read in the synagogue before Paul's sermon.[70] In 2 Samuel 7:12–16 God promises that David's kingdom will be permanently established, that David's offspring will 'build a house for my Name' and that God himself will 'establish the throne of his kingdom for ever' (v. 13).

In what follows, Paul's interpretation of the Davidic covenant parallels Peter's exposition in Acts 2:27–31.[71] Using what is commonly classified as a *gezerah shewa* interpretation, 'where two texts can be exposited together if they share a term or a related form of a word',[72] Paul cites three OT texts to explain these Davidic promises further. The three OT references work in concert to demonstrate how God has fulfilled the Davidic covenant both through his covenant fidelity and through the faithfulness of Jesus, the greater David. We will briefly consider how each contributes to Paul's recitation of Israel's history and so connects with the larger covenantal substructure behind this history that culminates in the Davidic Messiah. From there we will be able to summarize the sermon's unique biblical theological content as a story of Israel.

---

[69] Peterson 2009: 391.
[70] Schnabel theorizes that Deut. 4:25–46 and 2 Sam. 7:6–16 were the readings for the day (2012: 574). Morgan-Wynne observes, 'In general terms, 2 Sam. 7 is behind the whole sermon and the verb ἀνίστάναι is exploited for its potential to refer to resurrection from the dead, while specifically Ps. 2.7; Isa. 55.3 and Ps. 16.10 are quoted to explain the significance and meaning of the resurrection of Jesus' (2014: 147–148).
[71] See Pervo 2008: 339.
[72] Bock 2010: 457.

Psalm 2:7

Psalm 2:7 is one of the most often cited OT texts in the NT and could be seen as one of the definitive statements of Jesus' messianic identity.[73] In its context the Son of God in verse 7 is also the king in verse 6 whose throne God establishes in Zion. Paul's citation of Psalm 2:7 here is consistent with its use elsewhere in the NT: it indicates that Jesus has been enthroned as the promised Davidic king, the Son of God who reigns in Zion. In Acts 2:34–35 Peter's proclamation of the resurrection and reign at the Father's right hand is grounded in Psalm 110:1; in Acts 7:56 Stephen makes a similar proclamation. Paul's reference to Psalm 2:7 in Acts 13:33, as Morgan-Wynne observes, grounds the resurrection and ascension as Jesus' 'coronation . . . Through resurrection, Jesus enters upon a never-dying, eternal reign.'[74]

Isaiah 55:3

Unlike the citations from the Psalms, Isaiah 55:3 appears only here in the NT. Beyond this, the meaning of the verse in both the Hebrew and Greek OT is debated. The key question is how best to translate the phrase *ta hosia Dauid ta pista* (*ḥasĕdê dāwid hanne'ĕmānîm*, MT).[75] The NIVUK is typical of most English versions, reading the Greek OT as an objective genitive: 'the holy and sure blessings promised to David' (Acts 13:34). H. G. M. Williamson defends a similar understanding of the Hebrew text, concluding that the subject of covenant loyalty (*ḥsd*) must be God.[76] Moreover, he argues for a connection to God's covenant with David in 2 Samuel 7 that indicates we should understand David as the object of God's covenant loyalty here. On this reading, God is faithful and David is the beneficiary of his faithfulness.

However, Peter Gentry has demonstrated that the grammatical evidence likely indicates the genitive noun *Dauid* is a subjective genitive.[77] On this reading, David himself is said to be faithful to the covenant. The difficulty of this reading is in understanding how David, a human king, could fulfil the stipulations of an 'eternal covenant' (*diathēkēn aiōnion*, LXX).

---

[73] Along with the allusions to it in the NT (Acts 4:25–26; 13:33; Heb. 1:5; 5:5; Rev. 2:26–27; 12:5; 19:15), *Pss Sol.* 17.26 also appears to read Ps. 2 as a prophecy of the Messiah.

[74] Morgan-Wynne 2014: 146.

[75] Acts 13 and the LXX are identical here.

[76] Williamson 1978: 31–49.

[77] Gentry concludes, 'Linguistic usage demands, then, that the first notion to enter the mind of the native reader is to construe the free member as subject' (2007: 281).

Gentry also notes that in the verses that follow the reference to this covenant, the emphasis is placed squarely on David's covenantal fidelity.[78] Thus, he concludes, 'The blessings do come to the nations . . . because a new David who is an obedient son succeeds in bringing Yahweh's Torah to all humans.'[79] This reading makes good sense in Acts 13, for it provides a proof that the Messiah, Jesus, has kept the stipulations of the Davidic covenant and has therefore been vindicated in his resurrection.

Psalm 16:10

The third OT reference Paul cites, Psalm 16:10, has already appeared in Acts. As noted above, Peter cited Psalm 16 as proof for the resurrection of Jesus, the promised Messiah. Paul's use of the psalm here is more or less identical.[80] In the Psalm David expresses his hope that God will remain faithful to the covenant.

When coupled with his previous two OT citations, Paul is arguing that, as a result of Jesus' faithfulness to the covenant, Jesus received the blessings promised in the covenant with David. One of these blessings, according to Psalm 16:10, is the resurrection. That Jesus, and not his ancestor David, is the proper recipient of these promises is clear in verses 36–37. In short, David's body was laid in the tomb to decay. Not so with Jesus. Through his rejection and subsequent vindication, God has fulfilled the covenant promises to David.

From our brief consideration of these three texts, we can observe that Paul is particularly focused on Jesus as the fulfilment of the Davidic covenant in his retelling of Israel's history. His references to the patriarchs, the exodus and the conquest, along with the implicit presence of the covenants with Abraham and Israel, are all moving towards the climax of the story. In this account of Israel's story the climax is found in the Davidic covenant as fulfilled through Jesus the Messiah, which then leads to the new-covenant era.

The continuing story

In the last section of the sermon, verses 38–41, Paul calls for a response from his audience. Through the Messiah, Jesus, complete forgiveness of

---

[78] Ibid. 294.
[79] Ibid. 298.
[80] Morgan-Wynne suggests, 'The brevity of the quotation from Ps. 16 might be due to Luke's having already used it extensively in Peter's speech on the day of Pentecost in Acts 2' (2014: 212).

sins was available to all within his hearing. In anticipation of what we will observe in our discussion of Galatians below, Jesus was able to do what the law could not do.[81] Though some label this a 'Deutero-Pauline' conception of forgiveness, there is nothing here that is inconsistent with any of Paul's epistles.[82] Rather, as we will observe below, Luke's presentation of Paul's understanding of the covenants and Paul's own writings show remarkable consistency.

In any case, even in his proclamation that Jesus has done what the law cannot, Paul has not left the OT behind. Paul cites three OT references to explain the significance of Jesus' resurrection; in the conclusion of the sermon and its aftermath he quotes two further OT prophetic texts that connect his ministry to the continuing story of Israel. With the inclusion of these texts we have a fuller window into Paul's understanding of Israel's story.

Habakkuk 1:5

Paul concludes the sermon with a reference to Habakkuk 1:5 as a warning to his hearers to avoid the judgment promised to those who continue to resist God and act unjustly. In its OT context Habakkuk is calling his hearers to respond rightly to God's work in salvation history. The immediate appeal in Habakkuk's day was to see God's hand in the coming invasion from the Chaldeans; for Paul, the appeal is to see God's hand in the death and resurrection of Jesus. While the original context was the Lord's faithful covenant-keeping judgment, and Paul's appeal was the Lord's faithful covenant-keeping blessing, both contexts include essentially the same warning: if you do not respond rightly to God's gracious covenant-keeping, then you will face judgment. Thus, Robert Wall's summary of the continuity between Habakkuk 1 and Acts 13 is fitting: 'Even as the prophecy issues God's warning of imminent destruction to an unfaithful Israel, its use in Acts appeals to a later generation of Israel to believe this new report of God's work.'[83]

Like Stephen, Paul appears to be placing himself in the line of OT prophets who warned God's people about impending judgment if they did

---

[81] 'The forgiveness that God provides through Jesus is total forgiveness, an acquittal from everything, without exception, that separates sinners from a righteous God' (Schnabel 2012: 584).

[82] See Pervo 2008: 340.

[83] Wall 2000: 250. As Schnabel puts it, 'The consequence of refusing God's gracious offer is a disaster' (2012: 584–585).

not repent of their refusal to recognize and submit to God's unexpected work in salvation history. In the overall narrative of Luke and Acts this line of course includes Jesus himself, who proclaimed the climax of God's saving purposes in history. Thus, the parallel between Jesus in Luke 4 and Paul's sermon here has a deeper significance in simply introducing the preaching ministry of both men. Rather, Luke is framing the ministries of both Jesus and Paul as eschatologically significant and the fulfilment of God's purposes. Pervo rightly notes that both sermons came immediately after Satan's defeat (Acts 13:6–12).[84] Moreover, just as was the case for Jesus, many of those gathered did heed this warning and follow Paul's teaching (v. 43).

The following Sabbath, however, many more gathered to hear Paul's teaching, including many Gentiles. As a result of this, many of the Jews who had gathered resisted Paul and Barnabas and attempted to contradict their teaching because they were filled with jealousy (v. 45).[85] In response to this opposition, Paul announces one more chapter of Israel's story that includes an unexpected twist in the new-covenant era. However, to careful readers of Acts this twist is not unexpected.[86] Rather, this new chapter of Israel's story also coincides with the structure of Acts we observed above. While God's servants continued to face opposition, the gospel is extending to the ends of the earth. Moreover, like Stephen, Paul not only announced the pattern of rejected and vindicated servants, but also embodies it himself in a significant way. Through Paul's last Scripture citation in the account of the sermon, the theme of the rejected servant of the Lord is explained more clearly.

Isaiah 49:6

Paul and Barnabas responded to the Jews who opposed them by appealing once again to Israel's story. Assuming they followed their normal practice of Paul's being the primary speaker, he informed the Jewish audience that they had rejected the word of God, and thus proved or judged themselves to be unworthy of eternal life (v. 46). Because of this the gospel was then

---

[84] Pervo 2008: 331.

[85] Intriguingly, here Jewish jealousy leads to Gentile salvation, yet that is not the end of the story. As we will observe below, in Rom. 11 Paul expected Jewish jealousy to lead back to Jewish salvation.

[86] Contra Pervo, who argues, 'The first twelve chapters have not laid the ground for this radical claim [that Christ has fulfilled the OT and invites Gentiles]' (2008: 341).

to be proclaimed to the nations. Grounding their claim in Isaiah 49:6, Paul and Barnabas do not see the proclamation of the gospel to the Gentiles as a repudiation of Israel's history, but rather as its climax as Paul himself in some way continues the ministry of Jesus, the Isaianic servant, as a light to the nations.

In Isaiah 49 the prophet seems to shift from a corporate identity for the servant (v. 3) to an individual who will gather Jacob and Israel back to him (v. 6, LXX). This shift indicates that the servant in some way *represents* Israel through this section of Isaiah. As Michael Bird observes, 'A striking pattern emerges in Isaiah 40–55 where the servant, as the representative of Israel *par excellence*, is Yahweh's chosen instrument to extend salvation to the outer parts of the earth.'[87] For the writers of the NT, it was self-evident that this servant figure refers to the Messiah. For example, elsewhere in Luke and Acts the servant prophecies are clearly applied to Jesus (Luke 2:32; Acts 26:23). However, in Paul's sermon he presents himself and Barnabas as the fulfilment of Isaiah's prophecy of the servant.

Most interpreters of Acts 13 recognize the questions that Paul's use of Isaiah 49 raises. We cannot enter into all of the hermeneutical issues that surround Paul's use of this text; however, for our purposes it is important to consider how the ministry of the servant fits within the overall story of Israel in the OT. In brief, as we have observed already in this study, the earliest Christians saw themselves as the heirs of the continued story of Israel and the community of the new covenant. Moreover, Michael Lyons argues that Isaiah 56 – 66 itself hints that the new-covenant community will share in the experience of the servant, concluding 'the Servant creates a community (the "servants"/"offspring") that suffers righteously and is vindicated like him'.[88] If the servant of Isaiah 40 – 55 represents and creates the new-covenant community, and the Lord's directive for that community is that it must be a light to the nations, then it should not be surprising to see Paul's continuing this mission.[89]

Many of the Jews, particularly the leaders in the synagogues, rejected Paul's message about Jesus the Messiah; consequently, Paul turned to the

---

[87] Bird 2006: 123.

[88] Lyons 2013: 352. Lyons also demonstrates that 'the author of Luke-Acts understands Jesus as the Servant and his followers as his servants, the community who shares in his sufferings and carries out his mission' (ibid. 353–354).

[89] Schnabel 2004: 942–944; for an overview of research on this question, see Lyons 2013: 346–350.

Gentiles. However, this does not imply a decisive break with all Jews, for in Acts 14:1 Paul and Barnabas continue their pattern of going first to the synagogue. Also, the response to Paul's sermon creates a template repeated several times in Acts (18:5–7; 19:8–9; 28:25–28).[90] Bird is therefore correct to conclude:

> The point of the statement is not to imply a rejection of the Jews or the cessation of a Jewish mission, but rather, that in the same way that Christ went to his people (i.e. Israel, Acts 13:26), Christ also has a mission to the Gentiles, and the point is that this two-pronged mission guided Paul's missionary endeavours.[91]

However, just as it was for the original audiences of both Isaiah and Habakkuk, those in Israel who hear and reject the message about the Messiah face God's judgment. As Gentiles are grafted into the covenant community, they too begin to share in the identity and mission of the servant, who continues the story of Israel.

Summary of Paul's sermon

As we noted above, Luke ends his Gospel with a summary of Jesus' teaching about the Messiah in the OT. In Luke 24:46–47 Jesus claimed that the OT itself teaches that the Messiah will suffer, rise and then be proclaimed to the nations. In the sermons in Acts the ministry of the suffering and vindicated servant from Isaiah becomes a key OT theme to support this claim.[92] As we have observed throughout this chapter, the structure of Acts is built around the expansion of the gospel to the end of the earth, as Jesus commands his followers to take the good news of his death, resurrection and reign from Jerusalem to Judea and Samaria and finally to the end of the earth. Here in Acts 13 Paul's SIS ends with his announcing that he and Barnabas are now embodying the ministry of the servant.

While Stephen's speech hinted at the unity between the Messiah and his people through their shared suffering and subsequent vindication,

---

[90] Wall notes, 'Paul's prophetic preaching of the gospel sharpens the intramural conflict within Israel between those who define the covenant by Moses and those who define it by Messiah' (2000: 252).

[91] Bird 2006: 127.

[92] Beers 2015.

Paul's claim in Acts 13:47 makes this unity all the more explicit. In short, as they continue the mission of the Messiah, the history of Israel continues through the ministry of the apostles, and Paul in particular, in the latter part of Acts. Paul's reading of Isaiah 49:6 is consistent with the proclamation of Jesus in Luke 24:47, for the proclamation of the Messiah to the nations is a part of Israel's story. In other words, when Paul summarizes the history of Israel, he is not standing outside a completed story but instead is standing in a later part of the story rehearsing its earlier events. His ministry is part of the continuing story of Israel.

Paul reads Israel's history much the same way that both Stephen in Acts 7 and Jesus himself in the parable of the tenants did. The story is not yet complete; however, it has reached its climax. Everything is now interpreted in the light of the coming of the Messiah, the Righteous One. The majority of the ethnic Jews hearing this message rejected it. Like the citizens of Jerusalem and their rulers, they did not recognize or understand the prophets (cf. v. 27). Therefore, Paul and Barnabas turned to the ends of the earth.

Neither Paul nor Luke has abandoned the covenantal substructure that we observed in Acts 7. The ministry of the Isaianic servant, embodied by Jesus and continued by Paul, is inseparable from the new covenant. Before Isaiah speaks of the salvation of the Lord reaching the ends of the earth (Isa. 49:6), he speaks of the restoration and regathering of Israel (v. 5). Throughout Isaiah 40 – 66 and in the rest of the prophetic writings the new covenant and the restoration of Israel are simply two ways of speaking of the same reality.[93]

As noted above, the formal structure of Stephen's speech and Paul's sermon are different. Nevertheless, the material content of their summaries of Israel's history is much the same. Israel's history is one that is marked by the tragedy of the obstinacy of God's people. Time and again they rejected the word of the Lord and his prophets. However, Israel's history is also supported and carried forward by God's unrelenting commitment to his covenant promises. Like Stephen, Paul also has a biographical focus, particularly in the rise of the monarchy and the lives of Samuel, Saul and David. It is noteworthy that David is the only character

---

[93] See e.g. Jer. 31:8, 10, which in close proximity with the most explicit 'new covenant' reference in the OT, Jer. 31:31–33, speaks of the regathering of God's people.

who plays a prominent role in both Acts 7 and Acts 13.[94] However, in Paul's sermon the Davidic covenant is central, for God's action to fulfil the Davidic covenant through the Messiah, Jesus, is the culmination of God's covenant promises to his people.

Unlike other near-contemporary stories of Israel that are oriented towards Greco-Roman philosophy or fundamentally shaped by a reaction to what Kee calls 'aggressive pagan culture', the stories of Israel in Acts have a different focus.[95] They are rooted in God's faithfulness to his covenant promises, which are the substructure that gives Israel's history its coherence. They also provide the hope that when God's righteous servants suffer, they will be vindicated. Beyond this, the story of Israel, and especially the covenants that are the backbone of that story, also become the backbone of the mission of the apostles in Acts. As the story of Israel continues through the suffering and vindicated apostles, who take the good news to the end of the earth, God's faithfulness to his covenant promises is on full display.

The contribution of Luke's summaries

The SIS in Acts instruct us about the story's climax in the life, death, resurrection and reign of Jesus. Yet this story is not over, for God is continuing to fulfil his covenant promises to his people. Moreover, since the purpose of the book of Acts is to recount the continuing work of Jesus in the world, Luke is drawing a connection between the story of Israel and the ministry of Jesus, his apostles and his church.

Building on this summary observation, we can draw attention to three additional contributions from our overview of these stories in Acts. First, God's covenants frame the story of Israel and are a necessary component for making sense of the story. This concept was evident in Matthew, but it is even clearer in Acts. In Peter's speech in Acts 2 the continuing story of God's people is founded on the fulfilment of his new-covenant promises, which were in turn a fulfilment of the promises to David. Stephen's speech is structured around the three major eras that correspond to the covenants with Abraham, Israel and David, respectively. While he briefly alludes to the covenants with Abraham and Israel in his retelling of Israel's story,

---

94 Jeska 2001: 227.
95 Kee 1993: 64.

Paul's focus is primarily on the covenant with David and its subsequent fulfilment in and through the Messiah, Jesus. This covenantal structure drives their understanding of Israel's story, and this story climaxes with the ministry of the Messiah.

Second, while the covenants shape the plot of Israel's story, the stories of Israel in Acts highlight the individual characters in this story, particularly as Stephen emphasizes the rejected and vindicated servants of the Lord. This pattern culminates in the rejection and vindication of Jesus the Messiah, but it does not stop there. Instead, the speakers themselves, along with Luke's account of them, indicate that Stephen and Paul continue this pattern. The rejection and vindication of God's messengers, both before and after the climactic ministry of the Messiah, are not simply an incidental part of the story of Israel, but instead are the very means that God uses to advance the plotline of the story.

Third, Paul's sermon singles out the fulfilment of the covenant with David as the climax of the story of Israel. To segregate Christ from the story of Israel and the Davidic covenant is to fail to understand the goal of this story. Unlike Matthew's genealogy, both Stephen and Paul emphasize David's positive role in the story, yet even David was not able to bring the story to its resolution. This requires a greater David, the Messiah, Jesus. Thus, Israel's story reaches its climax with the coming of the Messiah and his subsequent life, death and resurrection. Every part of Israel's story is leading to this climax, and nothing in the story is ultimately complete apart from these gospel events.

Conclusion

Many of the details and emphases in Israel's story differ from one another, yet the overall picture of what we observed in the Gospel of Matthew matches the story in Luke and Acts. As Stephen and Paul rehearse the continued rejection of God's servants, this covenantal structure of Israel's story leads inevitably to the exile of Israel from the Promised Land. But in the decisive return from exile accomplished by the messianic servant to fulfil the new covenant the boundaries of the people of God have shifted. No longer is the message of God's covenant faithfulness limited to ethnic Israel; rather, in fulfilment of the OT promises, this message is reaching the nations. While this does not amount to a full-scale rejection of the Jewish people, it does lead to the inevitable conclusion that when individual Jews finally rejected Jesus as the Messiah, they confirmed their status as 'permanent exiles' who are under God's judgment.

In Matthew's genealogy the Messiah brings the exile to a close, launching the era of new-covenant fulfilment and continuing Israel's story as God decisively fulfils his covenant promises. In the parable of the tenants the rejected son, who stands in a long line of rejected servants, brings judgment on the covenant community with the result that its boundaries shift to include the nations. The climax of Israel's history, the covenant faithfulness of Israel's God, the rejection of God's servants and the inclusion of the Gentiles all loom large in the stories of Israel in Luke and especially Acts.

The story of Israel is a story that is only properly read as a story about God's work to fulfil his covenants in and through the Messiah, Jesus. Thus, there is continuity between the stories of Israel in the Gospels and Jesus and the stories of Israel found in Acts. As we move into the epistles of the NT we will find a similar picture to what we have already observed as the Messiah, Jesus, marks the climax of Israel's history. In the following chapters we will observe further aspects of Israel's story that are only understandable in the light of the coming of Jesus Christ, beginning with the place of the law in Israel's story in Galatians 3 – 4.

4
Galatians and Israel's law

In this chapter we move beyond the narrative literature of the NT to the epistles, but we have not left the story of Israel behind. We have seen that Matthew and Luke narrate the story of Israel as a history that finds its climax in Jesus Christ and the continuing life and mission of the church. Now we will see the apostle Paul tell the story in a similar way, arguing that Christ is the 'seed' of Abraham to whom the covenantal promises were made (Gal. 3:16) and those who belong to Christ are Abraham's seed as well (Gal. 3:29). Some Pauline scholars view the apostle's argument in Galatians 3 – 4 as a rejection of Israel's story or salvation history.[1] But the apostle's argument is no more of a rejection of Israel's story than are the genealogy or the parable of the tenants in Matthew, which find their climax in the Messiah. We must not forget that the Messiah/Christ is a major part of *Israel's* story in Scripture.[2] And this story is a major part of Paul's argument in Galatians 3 – 4 in which he focuses on the divinely intended role of the law.

Following the pattern established in the introduction, we will begin this chapter with an explanation of the historical and literary context of Galatians 3 – 4. These chapters contain a series of polemical arguments against certain people who were trying to compel the Gentile Christians in Galatia to be circumcised. Each argument supports Paul's claim that a person is not justified by works of the law but by faith in Christ (Gal. 2:16). And three of the arguments are biblical-theological, summarizing the

---

[1] For a helpful description of the 'anti-*Heilsgeschichte* Paul' as presented by Martyn and de Boer, along with a nuanced response that has influenced our discussion, see Maston 2012: 90–103. Longenecker argues similarly to Martyn and de Boer that in Galatians 'Paul attempted to sever an organic relationship between Israel's story and that of Christians' (2002: 74), although he qualifies this statement by observing that Paul does not completely separate the story of Israel and Christians (ibid.).

[2] Hooker makes the same point in response to Longenecker, finding it significant that Paul does not identify 'Jesus' as the seed of Abraham but as 'Christ' (Gal. 3:16; Hooker 2002: 90–91).

story of Israel from Abraham to the law to Christ (3:6–14; 3:15 – 4:7; 4:21–31).[3] Our study of the context will help us understand the content of the story, which is characterized by the distinctive element of repetition or recapitulation. Paul tells the story of Israel three times in Galatians 3 – 4. This repetition allows him to make several arguments from Israel's story while keeping his audience fixed on the Abraham narratives and the question of circumcision. After examining the content of these stories in detail, we will be in a position to consider the contribution that Galatians 3 – 4 makes to our study of apostolic biblical theology.

We will see that the story of Israel in Galatians 3 – 4 teases out the implication of the climactic role of Christ for one of Israel's most important institutions, the law. Answering those who promote circumcision and law-keeping among Gentile believers in Christ, Paul argues that Israel's law was never meant to be the climax of the story. Rather, God intended the law to play a secondary, negative, temporary and preparatory role.

The context of Paul's summary

Paul's biblical theology in Galatians was hammered out in the midst of a heated response to certain people who were stirring up trouble among the churches of Galatia (Gal. 1:7; cf. 5:10, 12). Specifically, they were pressuring Gentile believers in these churches to be circumcised (6:12; cf. 2:3) and probably to keep the rest of the law, since Paul laments that the Galatians had already begun to keep the calendar laws (Gal. 4:10). These troublemakers were like the Jewish believers who came to Antioch and taught Gentile believers that 'Unless you are circumcised, according to the custom taught by Moses, you cannot be saved' (Acts 15:1), and those at the Jerusalem Council who argued that '[t]he Gentiles must be circumcised and required to keep the law of Moses' (Acts 15:5).[4] Paul's

---

[3] One might argue that only Gal. 3:15 – 4:7 is properly a SIS. The allegorical comparison of Isaac and the Galatians in Gal. 4:21–31 reads somewhat like Paul's comparison of Adam and Christ in Rom. 5:12–21, a passage we have decided not to include in this study because it lacks historical progression. The difference is that Gal. 4:21–31 is in the immediate context of a clear telling of Israel's story (Gal. 3:15 – 4:7). Thus, it seemed to us that Paul is appealing again to the plotline and chronology of the OT in Gal. 4:21–31 (as well as in Gal. 3:6–14).

[4] Most scholars agree that the troublemakers in Galatia thought of themselves as Christians. Paul says they were proclaiming a different 'gospel' (1:6), which shows that they claimed to be preaching the Christian message (Barclay 1987: 86; Moo 2013: 21). Moreover, it is likely that they were Jewish-Christians, because Paul identifies them in 6:13 as 'circumcised' (Martyn 1997: 121).

response to this argument is remarkably pointed. He chastens the Galatians for giving them a hearing (1:6; cf. 3:1–5), says the troublemakers are 'trying to pervert the gospel of Christ' (1:7), proclaims God's curse on anyone who would preach such a thing (1:8–9),[5] impugns their motives (4:17; 6:12) and warns the Galatians that if they undergo circumcision 'Christ will be of no value to you at all' (5:2). Why such a pointed response?

Paul makes it clear that the problem as he saw it was not merely whether Gentile believers should be circumcised. Twice he says that circumcision and uncircumcision are matters of indifference (Gal. 5:6; 6:15; cf. 1 Cor. 7:19).[6] Nor was it simply that people were *pressuring* Gentile believers to be circumcised (6:12; cf. 2:3), a problem to be sure but not the main issue Paul highlights in his response.[7] Rather, *the issue at stake among the churches of Galatia in Paul's view was how both Jews and Gentiles are justified before God* (Gal. 2:15–16).[8] The question about whether Gentile believers must be circumcised was the surface issue revealing the deeper question about whether a person is righteous before God by works of the law or by faith in Christ.[9] This deeper question about the law and Christ is the one Paul addresses with the story of Israel in his response to the troublemakers.

Paul's response formally begins in Galatians 2:15–21, a passage that commentators regularly identify as the main point of the letter.[10] He couches it in a narrative about how he responded to Peter in a similar situation at Antioch, when Peter had stopped eating with the Gentile

[5] Cf. 2:4, where he speaks of those who pressure Gentiles to be circumcised as 'false believers' (literally, 'false brothers', *pseudadelphoi*).

[6] According to Acts 16:1–5, Paul had Timothy circumcised, a story that confirms Paul's repeated insistence that circumcision is a matter of indifference.

[7] Contra Sanders, who recognizes the soteriological problem that accepting circumcision was 'acting as if faith in Christ was not sufficient', but still argues that the main problem was that they were *compelling* Gentiles to be circumcised (2015: 496).

[8] The allusion in Gal. 2:16 to Ps. 143:2 ('no one living is righteous before you') shows that Paul's concern was with the means by which one is righteous *before God* (cf. 'justified before God' in Gal. 3:11; so Barclay [2015: 375]).

[9] Readers unfamiliar with Greek should note that the verb 'justify' (*dikaioō*; Gal. 2:16 [3×], 17; 3:8, 11, 24; 5:4), the noun 'righteousness' (*dikaiosynē*; Gal. 2:21; 3:6, 21; 5:5) and the adjective 'righteous' (*dikaios*; Gal. 3:11) are from the same word group and all refer to 'justification' in Galatians.

[10] E.g. Betz and Longenecker, using rhetorical analysis, both identify Gal. 2:15–21 as the *propositio*, or propositional statement, unpacked in the following arguments of the letter (Betz 1979: 114; Longenecker 1990: 82–83).

believers and was in effect pressuring them to observe the food laws (Gal. 2:11–14).[11] There Paul confronted Peter publicly and said:

We who are Jews by birth and not sinful Gentiles know that a person is not justified by the works of the law, but by faith in Jesus Christ. So we, too, have put our faith in Christ Jesus that we may be justified by faith in Christ and not by the works of the law, because by the works of the law no one will be justified.
(2:15–16)

According to Moo, the 'key point' of 2:15–21 is found in verse 16, where Paul reminds Peter that both Jews and Gentiles are not justified before God by 'works of the law' but by 'faith in Jesus Christ'.[12] Unfortunately, the meaning of these two phrases is highly debated by Pauline scholars. For the purposes of this chapter, we can only state our position and point readers to resources for further study.

We understand the phrase 'works of the law' to refer to all the works required by the law.[13] Advocates of the new perspective on Paul have argued that this phrase refers only (or primarily) to circumcision, Sabbath and food laws, the 'boundary markers' that divided Jews from Gentiles.[14] As we have observed, the question of whether Gentile Christians must be circumcised is the immediate issue Paul confronts in this letter. However, Paul sees the immediate issue of circumcision pointing to a deeper problem: 'I declare to every man who lets himself be circumcised that he

---

[11] Paul uses the same verb *anankazō* of Peter and the troublemakers in Gal. 2:14 ('force') and 6:12 ('compel'). He also observes that both Peter and the Judaizers were motivated by fear of persecution (Gal. 2:12; 6:12).

[12] Moo 2013: 153.

[13] The OT does not contain an exact equivalent of Paul's phrase 'works of the law'. But it does use the verb 'to work' and the noun 'law' when calling Israel to do what the law requires (e.g. Deut. 27:26, which Paul quotes in Gal. 3:10). An exact equivalent of Paul's phrase in Hebrew has been found in a document at Qumran, which gives its reader 'some works of the Torah' so that he may rejoice at the end of time and that it may be reckoned to him as 'righteousness' (4QMMT C26–31). This goal of righteousness and eschatological rejoicing by means of works of the law provides a nice example of what Paul is arguing against in Galatians. For discussion, see Gathercole 2002: 92–95. For a 'new perspective' take on 4QMMT, see Dunn 1997.

[14] E.g. Sanders argues, 'When Paul writes "not by works of the law" (three times in [Gal.] 2:16), only one point of the law is at issue: circumcision, the entry rite to Judaism' (2015: 513). He later expands his definition to include Sabbath and food laws (ibid. 562). Dunn says that in principle 'works of the law' refers to everything required by the law, but in practice it refers specifically to circumcision and food laws, the test cases that divided Jews and Gentiles (1993: 136–137).

is required to obey the whole law' (Gal. 5:3); that is, to obey the whole law in order to be righteous before God. Thus, when Paul says 'by the works of the law no one will be justified' (Gal. 2:16c), he is referring to human inability to keep the requirements of the law and be justified.[15]

'[A] person is not justified by the works of the law, *but* by faith in Jesus Christ' (Gal. 2:16a).[16] Many Pauline scholars in recent decades have argued that this phrase and the similar *ek pisteōs Christou* in Galatians 2:16b should be translated 'by the faithfulness of [Jesus] Christ'.[17] The two Greek phrases are ambiguous in that Christ could be taken as either the subject of *pistis* ('faithfulness of Christ') or as its object ('faith in Christ'). If Christ is taken as the subject of *pistis*, then Paul argues here that justification comes about through Jesus' own faithfulness to the point of death. This view fits Paul's emphasis in Galatians on the sufficiency of the cross for justification, which is really the reason he emphasizes the sufficiency of faith.[18] However, in our view it is simply not the best translation of the phrases in Galatians 2:16, for Paul refers unambiguously to Christ as the object of faith in the clause 'we, too, have put our faith in Christ Jesus'. This unambiguous reference should lead us to translate the ambiguous phrases *dia pisteōs Iēsou Christou* and *ek pisteōs Christou* in the same way.[19] Sinful human beings cannot be justified before God by works of the law, but can be counted as righteous in his sight by faith in Jesus Christ.

---

15 For a classic overview of 'works of the law' in Pauline scholarship that has been very influential on our thinking see Schreiner 1991. It should be observed that in Paul's allusion to Ps. 143:2 he substitutes 'no flesh' (*ou . . . pasa sarx*) for 'no one living' (*ou . . . pas zōn*). The phrase *pasa sarx* is a common way to refer to humanity in the LXX and NT (noted by Silva 2007: 790), but it is likely that Paul uses *sarx* purposely to refer to the sinfulness and mortality of humanity, as he does in places such as Gal. 5:16–26 and Rom. 7:5–6 (cf. Isa. 40:6–7). Dunn may be correct that 'flesh' also refers to those who are circumcised in the flesh (see Dunn 1993: 140–141).

16 The conjunction *ean mē* is most likely adversative ('but') rather than introducing an exception. This is a common use in Greek literature, and Paul clearly contrasts works and faith in Gal. 2:16b and 3:2, 5 (see Hunn 2007). All emphases in Scripture quotations in this volume are our own.

17 This change in understanding these phrases came about through the influential dissertation of Hays 2002 (originally published in 1983).

18 We owe this insight to Moo, who observes that it is 'Paul's conviction about the utter adequacy of *Christ* that engenders his insistence on the adequacy of *faith*' (2013: 193; emphases original).

19 So Hansen 1989: 103. Those who argue for the subjective genitive ('faithfulness of Christ') would respond that translating the phrases in the same way leads to redundancy in Paul's argument (see many examples of this charge in Matlock 2007: 175). But it is clear that Paul is repeating himself for rhetorical reasons in Gal. 2:16 (ibid. 199). For a recent summary of the *pistis Christou* debate from an advocate of the 'faithfulness of Christ' translation, see Kugler 2016.

Thus, Paul's response to Peter in Galatians 2:15–21, and his response to those compelling the Gentiles in Galatia to be circumcised, is that a person is not justified before God by observing the law but by faith in Jesus Christ. Paul realized that these Gentile believers were considering the step of circumcision in order to be righteous before God: 'You who are trying to be justified by the law have been alienated from Christ; you have fallen away from grace' (5:4). This is why he speaks of the troublemakers' view as 'different gospel' (1:6), a perversion of the true gospel of Christ, or a setting aside of the grace of God given in Christ. 'I do not set aside the grace of God, for if righteousness could be gained through the law, Christ died for nothing!' (Gal. 2:21). One is either justified by doing the law or by the grace God gives to believers in Christ. And, as Paul reminded Peter, they both knew that 'a person is not justified by the works of the law, but by faith in Jesus Christ' (Gal. 2:16).

Galatians 3 – 4 contains a series of arguments in support of this statement. In these chapters Paul uses the prepositions *ek*, *dia* and *en* to identify faith and Christ, not the law and works, as the instrumental cause of justification or equivalent blessings.[20] Two of his arguments are based upon the Galatians' own experiences (3:1–5; 4:12–20), but three are exegetical, rooted in the story of Israel (3:6–14; 3:15 – 4:7; 4:21–31).[21] The first relies heavily on citations from OT Scripture (3:6–14). The second focuses on the chronology or history of Israel (and the Gentiles; 3:15 – 4:7). And the third is an allegorical interpretation of Abraham's two sons as a foreshadowing of Israel's later history (4:21–31). But all three arguments from the OT are rooted in the same plotline of Abraham to the law to Christ. In fact, the long argument from Israel's history in 3:15 – 4:11 repeats the law-to-Christ sequence several times (see Table 4.1).[22]

---

[20] Cosgrove suggests that these prepositions speak of the law or faith as the *instrument* of justification but not its evidential basis (or cause; 1987: 658, 660). But a distinction between instrument and basis cannot be maintained in the light of Phil. 3:9, where Paul speaks in the same breath of righteousness 'through faith in Christ' (*dia pisteōs Christou*) and 'on the basis of faith' (*epi tē pistei*). The prepositions *ek*, *dia* and *en* indicate the means of justification that is also its cause, or the 'instrumental cause', of justification.

[21] Martyn rightly calls Gal. 3:6 – 4:7 and 4:21 – 5:1 Paul's 'exegetical arguments' (1997: 25–26). Note that he and other commentators see the argument in 4:21–31, as including the transition verse in 5:1.

[22] Bruno has previously described the three retellings of Israel's story as three salvation-historical contrasts (2013: 163–171). While it is correct to observe a salvation-historical contrast between the law covenant and the promises to Abraham, this contrast is built into the story of Israel, so these passages can also be described as SIS.

Table 4.1 The story of Israel in Galatians 3 – 4

Arguments/references	Plotline of Israel's story
Argument from Scripture[23]	
(3:6–14)	Abraham's blessing → the law's curse → Christ's redemption
Argument from history	
(3:15–22)	Abraham's promise → the law → the seed of Abraham
(3:23–29)	under the law as guardian → the coming of faith/Christ
(4:1–7)	under the law/the elements → the sending of God's Son
Argument from allegory	
(4:21–31)	Abraham's children → the law covenant → the new covenant

These exegetical arguments repeatedly come back to the Abraham narratives, which probably reflects the troublemakers' own appeals to these narratives in order to convince the Gentile believers to be circumcised.[24] But it also demonstrates the importance of Abraham in Paul's own understanding of biblical theology; in particular his understanding of how Jews and Gentiles are righteous before God (cf. Rom. 4).[25] Paul's exegetical arguments, his biblical-theological arguments, indirectly address the immediate question of circumcision by directly addressing this deeper question about justification.

The content of Paul's summary (Gal. 3 – 4)

As we have observed, each of Paul's three exegetical arguments begins the story with Abraham. His argument from Scripture begins with God's initial blessing of Abraham (Gen. 12), his argument from history begins

---

[23] Our labels for Paul's arguments are based loosely on Schreiner's outline of Galatians (Schreiner 2010: 58–59).

[24] Barclay sees 'Paul's repeated references to Abraham' as good evidence that one of 'the opponent's line of arguments, which we may again see reflected in Paul's reply, was an appeal to Scripture, and in particular the Abraham narratives' (1987: 87). It is hard to imagine that they did not appeal to Gen. 17, the foundational text on circumcision and the covenant.

[25] 'Being in Abraham's family, in other words, *matters*' (Wright 2013: 573; emphasis original).

with God's covenant or promise to Abraham (Gen. 15, 17) and his argument from allegory focuses on Ishmael and Isaac, the two sons of Abraham (Gen. 16 – 21). The conclusion that Paul comes back to again and again in these arguments is that Gentile believers in Christ are the children of Abraham or the children of God (children of Abraham: 3:7, 29; children of God: 3:26; 4:7, 28, 31). This conclusion rests on a view of Abrahamic sonship that understands it not only as a physical but as a theological category. Abraham's children are the children of *God*, because they are inheritors of God's blessing and promise to Abraham. In other words, Abraham's children are those who are justified before God. This theological understanding of Abraham's offspring is deeply rooted in the OT and was something Paul presumably held in common with his Jewish-Christian opponents.[26] Where he disagreed with them was on the role of the law in obtaining God's blessing to Abraham. Paul argues that Gentiles cannot experience this blessing by the law but only by faith in Jesus Christ.

Argument from Scripture (Gal. 3:6–14)

Paul's initial argument relies heavily on OT quotations and may be his weightiest one.[27] The Abrahamic blessing of justification comes by faith, for, instead of blessing, the law actually brings a curse! Paul sees a tension in Israel's history between the blessing of Abraham and the curse of the law, a tension that has been resolved in the cross of Christ. In his first telling of the story the apostle seeks to prove that the Abrahamic blessing comes by means of faith in this crucified Christ.

Abraham enters Paul's argument as the father of those who believe and are blessed. Paul is concerned both with Abraham's faith and his father-hood, because Abraham's faith is the basis upon which his fatherhood is established. Faith has become, in the memorable words of Hays, the 'family resemblance' of Abraham and his children, the joint means by which they inherit the blessing together.[28] And this blessing for Paul is

---

[26] Hansen's study concludes that '[m]ost of the references to Abraham in the OT outside of Genesis are reminders of God's covenantal promises to Abraham' (1989: 178). This theological understanding of Abraham's offspring also underlies the claim in John 8 that Abraham is the father of the Jews (v. 39) and therefore God is their Father (v. 41).

[27] Gal. 3:6–14 contains one of the most concentrated series of OT quotations in all of his letters. Comparable passages are found only in Romans (3:9–18; 9:1 – 11:36; 15:7–13).

[28] Hays 1989: 108. Silva rightly observes that 'the apostle's point is not simply that we should believe as Abraham believed ... but that those who believe become the recipients of the redemptive blessings associated with the patriarch' (2007: 793).

none other than the blessing of justification, because the words 'blessing' and 'justification' occupy the same place in his argument. Scripture announced the good news that the Gentiles would be *blessed* in Abraham because it foresaw that God would *justify* the Gentiles by faith (Gal. 3:8).[29]

Abraham's faith and consequent justification are established in the first verse quoted from the OT in Galatians: 'So also Abraham "believed God, and it was credited to him as righteousness"' (Gal. 3:6, quoting Gen. 15:6). The importance of Genesis 15:6 for Paul's biblical theology can hardly be overstated.[30] Not only does it open his argument from Scripture in Galatians, but it is also the key verse for Paul's discussion of Abraham in Romans 4. There Paul expounds the verse at length within its context of Genesis 15 and 17. Here, however, he simply quotes the verse, demonstrating that, according to Scripture, Abraham was justified by faith. The introductory 'so also' (*kathōs*) links Abraham's faith with the faith of the Galatians described in Galatians 3:1–5,[31] and Paul exploits this link in the next verse, concluding that Abraham's fatherhood is based upon his faith-righteousness. 'Understand, then, that those who have faith are children of Abraham' (Gal. 3:7). As we have observed, Abrahamic fatherhood for Paul is not simply a physical but a theological category referring to those who receive God's blessing. Paul reasons, on the basis of Genesis 15:6, that if Abraham received God's blessing by faith, then those who receive the blessing, his children, are those who believe as Abraham did (cf. John 8:39).[32]

Further, Paul argues that *Gentile* believers are included as Abraham's believing children. He sees this point in the very first statement of the Abrahamic blessing: 'Scripture foresaw that God would justify the

---

[29] We are taking the participle 'foresaw' (*proïdousa*) as indicating cause, meaning 'because it foresaw' (so Burton 1921: 160).

[30] Gen. 15:6 also stood out to Philo, another first-century Jew, for he highlights Abraham's faith in God as his possession of the 'queen of the virtues' (*On Abraham* 262–274; for a comparison with Paul's reading, see McFarland 2012). Contrast this with Josephus, who in writing a history of the Jewish people some decades after Paul recounts Gen. 15 without ever mentioning Abraham's faith or righteousness (*Jewish Antiquities* 1.183–185).

[31] *Kathōs* should be taken with its normal comparative force ('just as'), pointing to Abraham as an example to follow, just as Paul uses it four times in 1 Cor. 15:6–9 with reference to Israel in the wilderness as an example not to follow (contra Betz, who suggests it is a shortened form of Paul's citation formula 'as it is written' [1979: 140]).

[32] Hunn argues that Paul's proof is based upon a concept of 'metaphorical family relationship' seen throughout the Bible (2016: 505–510). This is similar to our position, except that we think Paul's understanding of Abrahamic fatherhood is unique to what God promised specifically to Abraham. Thus, Abraham's family is better understood not simply as a metaphorical but as a *theological* (or biblical-theological) category.

Gentiles [*ta ethnē*] by faith, and announced the gospel in advance to Abraham: "All nations [*ta ethnē*] will be blessed in you"' (Gal. 3:8, quoting Gen. 12:3).[33] Paul's citation changes the word 'tribes/peoples' (*mišpĕḥōt* in the MT; *phylai* in the LXX) to 'Gentiles/nations' (*ethnoi*), assimilating the first statement of the blessing in Genesis 12:3 to its later repetitions that use the word 'Gentiles/nations' (Gen. 18:18; 22:18; 26:4). This is likely a purposeful change to show more clearly that Scripture foresaw from the very beginning of Abraham's story in Genesis 12 that believing Gentiles would be blessed with their father Abraham.[34]

Paul's conclusion in Galatians 3:6–9 draws together insights from both Genesis 15:6 and Genesis 12:3: 'So those who rely on faith are blessed along with Abraham, the man of faith' (Gal. 3:9). The influence of Genesis 15:6 is seen in Paul's identification of Abraham as 'the man of faith', the basis of his fatherhood. And the influence of Genesis 12:3 is seen in the slight adjustment Paul makes as he rewords his initial conclusion in Galatians 3:7 to include the idea of blessing. Although the subject of both Galatians 3:7 and 3:9 is 'those who have/rely on faith' (*hoi ek pisteōs*),[35] the predicate changes from 'are children of Abraham' in 3:7 to 'are blessed along with Abraham' (3:9). Paul interprets Scripture's good news that the Gentiles will be blessed 'in' Abraham (*en soi*; Gen. 12:3) as a reference to their participation with him (*syn . . . Abraam*; Gal. 3:9). Together Abraham the believer and his believing Gentile children receive God's blessing by faith.

But if Paul associates Abraham's chapter of the story with divine blessing by faith, he associates the law's chapter with a curse! 'For all who rely on the works of the law are under a curse' (Gal. 3:10a). The opening

---

[33] We have changed the NIVUK's 'through you' to a more literal translation 'in you' (*en soi*) in order to show how Paul interprets this phrase in Gal. 3:9 in terms of participating 'along with' Abraham. There is debate about whether the Hebrew verb *nibrĕkû* in Gen. 12:3 should be understood to mean that the nations will be blessed by God (passive) or will invoke Abraham to bless themselves (middle/reflexive). Mathews observes that the passive translation found in the LXX and Paul fits the context of Gen. 12:1–3, in which God is the source and Abraham the conduit of divine blessing (cf. 'you will be a blessing' in Gen. 12:2; 2005: 117).

[34] Stanley agrees that Paul's use of *ethnos* is likely purposeful, since the word is so important to his argument (1992: 237). It seems likely that Paul is simply assimilating Gen. 12:3 to later repetitions of the blessing rather than joining the verse specifically to Gen. 18:18 (as argued by Schreiner [2010: 194]) or to Gen. 22:18 (as argued by Longenecker [1999: 101]).

[35] This Greek construction is partitive, indicating members of this group (see BDAG, s.v. '*ek*', use 3.b; cf. 'those who belonged to the circumcision group', *hoi ek peritomēs*, in Gal. 2:12). But because of Paul's use of the preposition *ek* with the objects *pistis* and *nomos* to refer to the instrumental cause of justification throughout Gal. 2:16 – 5:12, it seems likely that *hoi ek pisteōs* refers to those seeking to be justified by means of faith.

word 'for' (*gar*) indicates that Paul is continuing to explain the Abrahamic blessing; namely, that it does not come by works of the law. The law brings a curse instead.[36] Paul's argument is stated as a general principle applying to 'all who rely on works of the law' for justification (*hosoi ex ergōn nomou*).[37] But he is also appealing to Israel's history, since he establishes the principle with a quotation from the curses threatened in the end of Deuteronomy against Israel.[38] The curse of the law is a highly debated topic in Pauline theology, but we dare not ignore it here, for Paul uses the language of cursing not only to explain the role of the law (*kataran* in 3:10a; *epikataratos* in 3:10b) but also the significance of the cross in Israel's story (*kataras* in 3:13a; *katara* in 3:13b; *epikataratos* in 3:13c).

As proof of the law's curse, Paul cites Deuteronomy 27:26, the final and summative curse that the Levites were to shout to Israel as a warning against those who would disobey the law: 'as it is written: "Cursed is everyone who does not continue to do everything written in the Book of the Law"' (Gal. 3:10b). Most interpreters have understood Paul's proof to rely on the unstated premise that no sinful human being can obey the law completely; thus all who rely on it are under this curse.[39] But many modern scholars have been hesitant about this interpretation because it rests on an unstated premise, and because this premise itself seems unlikely given that the law made provisions for atonement and that even Paul viewed himself as having been 'faultless' under the law (Phil. 3:6).[40]

---

[36] As Moo observes, the *gar* in 3:10 'introduces the following verses as an explanation of an implied negative counterpart to v. 9: "Those who are of faith" inherit the Abrahamic blessing *and not "those who are of works of the law"* because . . .' (2013: 201; emphasis original). See also Wright's paraphrase of the connection with v. 9: 'this is further proved by the fact that works of Torah, so far from providing blessing, hold out curse instead' (1991: 142).

[37] Like the similar phrase 'those who have/rely on faith' (*hoi ek pisteōs*) in Gal. 3:7, 9, *hosoi ex ergōn nomou* indicates members of a group but in the context of Galatians it likely refers specifically to those who are seeking to be justified by means of works of the law.

[38] Wright lucidly brings out the Deuteronomic background of Paul's argument, although he wrongly pits Israel's corporate sin and experience of the curse against the individual's sin and experience of the curse (1991: 146).

[39] Moo notes that this interpretation is found in Ambrosiaster, Chrysostom, Luther, Lightfoot and Burton (2013: 202). Luther's explanation of Gal. 3:10 is complex, but he clearly sees Paul's argument resting on the premise that no one can keep the law as Moses demands (*LW* 26: 257, 260; although the believer with the Spirit is the true 'doer of the law'; ibid. 259–260). Jerome, in his commentary on Gal. 3:10, likewise observes that 'no one could fulfill the law and do everything that was commanded' (Jerome 2010: 133).

[40] For these two objections, see Wright 1991: 145. Matlock observes that the provision of atonement and Paul's statement in Phil. 3:6 are the main reasons scholars object to the traditional reading (2009: 155–157).

The alternative proposals, however, also rest on unstated premises.[41] And there are good reasons to believe that Paul assumes human inability to obey the law.

First, Paul chose to quote from the LXX, which unlike the MT contains the word 'all' calling for obedience to the entire law: 'Cursed be any person who does not remain in *all* the words of this law to do them' (Deut. 27:26, NETS).[42] Paul apparently wanted to emphasize that every person under the law must obey it entirely. Second, Deuteronomy itself prophesies that Israel will not be able to keep the law and will experience its curse in exile (Deut. 29:4; 30:1–4; 31:14 – 32:43).[43] Third, Paul also says that the law could not bring life because of human sinfulness or inability to obey (Rom. 8:3; Gal. 3:21–22). Fourth, Paul warns the Galatians that if they attempt to be justified by circumcision, they will be obligated to obey the *entire* law (Gal. 5:3). Fifth, Paul says that even the opponents do not obey the law (Gal. 6:13). Thus, it seems likely that Paul rests his argument for the law's curse on the unstated premise that no one can keep the entire law.[44] Therefore, 'all who rely on the works of the law are under a curse' (Gal. 3:10).

This is where Christ enters the story of Israel, as the redeemer from the curse of the law: 'Christ redeemed us from the curse of the law by becoming a curse for us, for it is written: "Cursed is everyone who is hung on a pole"' (Gal. 3:13).[45] By means of his vicarious death ('for us') Christ

---

[41] Matlock surveys the alternative explanations and concludes that '*Any* reading of these verses will have to contend with gaps in Paul's argument, however it is construed' (ibid. 176; emphasis original; see 157–176 for his survey). This is true of Hunn's recent proposal as well, for she argues that Paul relies on the implied premise that the law either justifies or condemns (2015).

[42] The MT does speak of 'all' the commandments in similar verses in this context (28:1, 14–15, 58; 29:29), so the LXX of Deut. 27:26 is in harmony with the context of the MT even though it does not have the exact wording of the MT.

[43] It is also striking that Deut. 27 contains only a list of curses and not blessings.

[44] What then did Paul mean when he said that he was 'faultless' as to the righteousness of the law (Phil. 3:6)? This comment represents Paul's pre-conversion way of thinking that he abandoned in order to gain Christ (see Phil. 3:7–11). Compared to his contemporaries he had been 'faultless' (cf. Gal. 1:14), an evaluation of his careful obedience to the law, which likely included making use of the means of atonement. But after his conversion Paul did not think such blamelessness qualified him to escape the curse, for he saw that '*all* who rely on the works of the law are under a curse' (Gal. 3:10a). Hunn argues that the Galatians would not accept this premise that no one can keep the entire law (2015). But she fails to see that Paul is not simply assuming this premise as common ground in Galatians but actually making arguments in favour of it through his use of 'all' in 3:10 and his explicit statements in 5:3 and 6:13.

[45] We will not discuss Paul's citations of Hab. 2:4 and Lev. 18:5 in Gal. 3:11–12, because these verses establish theological principles and do not really advance Israel's story.

purchased release or freedom from the law's curse.[46] Paul proves his point by citing Deuteronomy 21:23, a text that pronounces God's curse on a body hung on a tree. But he explains the meaning of the cross through this text in a way that ties it into the larger curse of the law, for he changes the LXX's *kekatēramenos* to *epikataratos* (both mean 'cursed') in order to match the curses of Deuteronomy 27, and especially its summative curse in verse 26.[47] The law had placed Israel under God's curse (3:10), but Christ took this curse upon himself in the cross (3:13).[48]

Paul states the purpose of Christ's work in the next verse, a statement that implies a relationship between the law's curse and Abraham's blessing: 'He redeemed us in order that the blessing given to Abraham might come to the Gentiles' (Gal. 3:14). The curse of the law had to be removed in order for the blessing of Abraham to be given to the nations. The law was, to use Wright's vivid image, a roadblock or traffic jam to the blessing. But why was it a roadblock? Wright finds the answer in Israel's role as a conduit of blessing to the nations that had been hindered by the exile and in the Deuteronomic prophecy that says exile must be completed before the covenant can be renewed (see Deut. 30:1–10).[49] Both of these answers are found in the OT, but they do not get to the heart of Paul's reasoning in Galatians 3:10–14. Paul presents the law as a roadblock to the blessing precisely because it brought about the opposite of the blessing – a curse. God's curse against sin had to be removed in order for God's blessing to come. Paul hears in Israel's history a dissonant chord with notes of blessing (Abraham) and cursing (the law). And he argues that the cross of Christ has now resolved this dissonance by removing the curse of the law in order to establish the blessing of Abraham.

---

46 McLean observes that *exagorazō* means 'to buy' and in the context of slavery means 'buying to set free' (1996: 130).

47 Ibid. 135. This point is missed by Streett, who fails to observe Paul's linking of the curse of the law in 3:10 with Christ's becoming a curse in 3:13 and wrongly concludes that 3:13 does not speak of the divine curse of the law but simply of Christ's public humiliation (2015).

48 Paul omits the explicit reference to God's agency found in the MT and LXX, leading some scholars to suggest that Paul did not view the cross as God's but only the law's curse (e.g. Martyn 1997: 320–321). But we should not make too much of this omission since Paul is not shy in describing elsewhere the cross as God's judgment (e.g. 2 Cor. 5:21; Rom. 8:3). Perhaps Paul omitted a direct statement of divine agency in Gal. 3:13 to emphasize the *law's* role in bringing the curse rather than the blessing.

49 There seem to be two answers in Wright's work: Israel's hindered role (1991: 154; 2013: 864) and the need to fulfil the covenantal promises in Deut. 30 (1991: 140, 146, 151–152; 2013: 867). But Wright himself does not make a clear distinction between the two.

One question that divides interpreters is how Paul relates Gentiles to the curse of the law. Some argue that Paul sees only Israel under this curse, because he uses the first-person plural 'us' in Galatians 3:13. In this view when Paul says Christ redeemed 'us' from the curse of the law, he refers to himself and fellow Jews to the exclusion of his Gentile readers in Galatia, similar to the distinction between '[w]e who are Jews' and 'Gentiles' in 2:15. This line of interpretation often finds two sequential purposes of Christ's death, one for Gentiles and one for Jews: 'He redeemed us [1] in order that the blessing given to Abraham might come to the Gentiles through Christ Jesus, [2] so that by faith we [Jews] might receive the promise of the Spirit' (Gal. 3:14).[50] But several factors lead us to believe that Paul includes Gentiles as part of the 'us' who were redeemed from the curse of the law, even though the law was given specifically to Israel.

First, the indefinite pronoun 'all who' in Galatians 3:10 communicates that the curse comes upon *anyone* who uses the law as a means of justification (including Gentiles).[51] Second, the present tense *are* under a curse' in the same verse shows that Paul's concern is not simply with Israel's past but with the present situation of the Galatians. Third, Paul simply does not use the first-person plural with a consistent reference to Jews in Galatians; in fact, his first use of 'we' includes Paul and the Gentiles (Gal. 2:4). Fourth, a consistent distinction between 'us' Jews and 'you' Gentiles in Galatians 3 – 4 undermines Paul's logic in two passages we will discuss below (3:24–25 and 4:5–6). And finally, since Paul has already emphasized that the Gentiles have received the Spirit by faith in 3:1–6, it seems more likely that 'we' who receive the Spirit in the second purpose clause of 3:14 includes Gentiles, and thus the two purpose clauses are coordinate ways of speaking about the Abrahamic blessing.[52] For Paul, both Abraham's blessing and the law's curse have implications for the Gentiles. This is why he warns the Galatians that those who rely on the works of the law are under its curse.

Paul concludes that the Abrahamic blessing comes by means of union with and faith in Christ Jesus. If we are correct that the two purpose clauses in Galatians 3:14 are coordinate, then the phrases 'through Christ Jesus'

---

[50] E.g. Wright 1991: 154, and esp. Taylor 2012: 298–303. Donaldson sees an inclusive 'we' referring to both Jews and Gentiles in the second purpose clause (1986: 98), and Wright is more open to this reading in his recent work (2013b: 867).

[51] With regard to this pronoun Moo says, 'In effect, Paul is warning the Galatians against joining this group' (2013: 201).

[52] Moo observes that this is the majority view (ibid. 214).

and 'by faith' are parallel statements of the means by which Gentiles receive the Abrahamic blessing. The first phrase echoes the good news of Genesis 12:3 that all the nations will be blessed through Abraham (*en soi*; Gal. 3:8). Paul now says that the blessing comes by participation not only with Abraham (Gal. 3:9) but with or in his descendant Christ Jesus (*en Christō Iēsou*; Gal. 3:14; cf. the echo of Gen. 12:3 in the messianic Ps. 72:17). The second phrase echoes Paul's citation of Habakkuk 2:4 in Galatians 3:11: 'the righteous will live by faith' (*ek pisteōs*). Paul now spells out the object of Christian faith. The Abrahamic blessing comes through *this* faith (*dia tēs pisteōs*); namely, faith in the Christ who was crucified to redeem us from the law's curse.[53]

In this striking final statement Paul speaks of the Abrahamic blessing as 'the promise of the Spirit' (Gal. 3:14). The Spirit is not mentioned in the Abraham narratives, so what is Paul referring to? He is apparently reading God's initial blessing to Abraham in the light of its later flowering in the prophetic promises that God will pour out his Spirit in the new covenant (e.g. Isa. 32:15; Ezek. 36:27–28; Joel 2:28–29). Perhaps he is particularly reading Abraham's blessing in the light of Isaiah 44:3:

> For I will pour water on the thirsty land,
>   and streams on the dry ground;
> I will pour out my Spirit on your offspring,
>   and my blessing on your descendants.[54]
> (Cf. Isa. 59:21)

Paul's statement would surely resonate with Gentile believers in Galatia who had already experienced this 'promise of the Spirit' (cf. 3:1–5). And the idea that God has made this 'promise' to Abraham and his descendants becomes central in Paul's second telling of Israel's story.

In sum, Paul's first telling of Israel's story in Galatians 3 – 4 begins with God's promise to Abraham in Genesis 12 that all the nations/Gentiles will be blessed in Abraham. This blessing of justification was hindered by the

---

[53] The article in *dia tēs pisteōs* is likely anaphoric, referring back to the faith mentioned in 3:11. There is a close relationship between faith in Christ and union with Christ throughout Galatians (e.g. 3:26, where it is difficult to discern a difference between the two).

[54] Harmon sees an allusion to Isa. 44:3 in Gal. 3:14 and 16: 'it would appear that Paul has followed the lead of Isa 44:3–5 in linking the gift of the Spirit to the promise made to Abraham and his seed, a promise that within the context of Isa 44:1–5 even includes Gentiles within its scope' (see Isa. 44:5) (2010: 149).

law's curse against sinners, but the crucified Christ has now redeemed us from this curse and brought about the Abrahamic blessing of justification and the Spirit. Therefore, it is those of faith who are blessed with Abraham; specifically, those who have faith in the crucified Christ.

Argument from history (Gal. 3:15 – 4:7)

Paul's long argument for justification by faith in Galatians 3:15 – 4:7 contains only one OT quotation. And yet it rests heavily on the history of Israel, telling the story from Abraham to the law to Christ and repeating the law-to-Christ sequence three times (see Table 4.1 on p. 89). In this argument the apostle explains the priority of God's promises to Abraham over the law and the temporary role of the law during the time before the coming of Christ. The law was not added as a means by which the Abrahamic inheritance might be attained, in contradiction to the promise. Rather, the law played a temporary, imprisoning role in Israel's history that led to the bestowal of the Abrahamic promise on those who believe in Jesus Christ.

Paul begins his second telling of Israel's story with God's covenant (Gal. 3:15, 17a). He is likely referring both to the covenant ceremony recorded in Genesis 15 and the sign of the covenant recorded in Genesis 17. Paul uses the language of 'inheritance' (Gal. 3:18, 29), which is prominent in Genesis 15:1–8. The very reason God establishes the covenant in Genesis 15:9–21 is to assure Abraham that he and his own son will receive the inheritance.[55] However, the language of 'covenant' is more prominent in Genesis 17, a passage that was likely employed by the troublemakers. Moreover, Genesis 17 is likely the source of Paul's one quotation in Galatians 3:15 – 4:7, 'and to your seed' (Gal. 3:16). This phrase occurs only three times in the Hebrew of the Abraham narratives, and two of the occurrences are in Genesis 17:[56]

---

[55] Watson observes that Paul's use of the terms 'covenant' (*diathēkē*) and 'inheritance' (*klēronomia*) in Gal. 3:17–18 'makes it certain that Paul has Genesis 15.7–21 specifically in mind' (2016: 181).

[56] The three occurrences are Gen. 13:15; 17:7, 8, although the LXX has only the exact phrase 'and to your seed' in Gen. 13:15 and 17:8. Paul may be quoting from the land promise in both Gen. 13:15 and 17:8 (Schreiner 2010: 228), but his language of 'covenant' makes it more likely that he is thinking of Gen. 17 (so Martyn, who sees Paul focusing his attention on Gen. 17:8 [1997: 339–340]). Moo suggests that he may be referring to Gen. 15:18 because it contains the word 'covenant' and the phrase 'to your seed' (2013: 228), but this verse does not contain the word 'and' before the phrase 'to your seed'. Collins suggests Gen. 22:18, which could refer to a singular seed in its context, but, as he acknowledges, the wording is not exact (2003: 83).

I will establish my covenant as an everlasting covenant between me
and you and your descendants after you for the generations to come,
to be your God *and the God of your descendants* after you. The whole
land of Canaan, where you now reside as a foreigner, I will give as an
everlasting possession to you *and your descendants* after you; and
I will be their God.
(Gen. 17:7–8)

Here we see the theological nature of Abraham's family writ large. God
covenants to be the God of Abraham's descendants, a point made twice
in these verses, and to give them the land of Canaan as an everlasting
possession. Thus, the children of Abraham are both the children of God
and the heirs of God (cf. 'since you are his child, God has made you also
an heir', Gal. 4:7). This is because they are children of the covenant God
made with Abraham.[57] Paul himself prefers to speak of this covenant as
God's 'promise' (3:17b) or 'promises' (3:16) to Abraham.[58] This language
of 'promise' allows him to point forward to its future recipients, the
offspring of Abraham, and to illuminate the gracious nature of God's
covenant (3:18).[59]

Paul's main point is that God's gracious promise to Abraham has
temporal priority over the law as the means by which one receives
the inheritance. He emphasizes the priority of Abraham by placing 'to
Abraham' first in the sentence in both Galatians 3:16 and 3:18. It was
to Abraham that the promises were spoken, hundreds of years before the
giving of the law. The law was not added to invalidate God's earlier promises
to Abraham. 'What I mean is this: the law, introduced 430 years later, does
not set aside the covenant previously established by God and thus do away
with the promise' (Gal. 3:17). The law would change the terms and invalidate
the earlier promise if it was added as a means of inheritance. But why?

Paul grounds his point about the temporal priority of the promise in
the fundamental incompatibility of law and promise as the means of

---

57 On Gen. 17:8 as the first occurrence of the covenant formula 'I will be their God', see
Gentry and Wellum 2012: 270–271.

58 The Abrahamic covenant is not identified as a 'promise' in the OT narratives (*TDNT*, 2:
579). But there was a Jewish exegetical tradition contemporary with Paul that identified it as
the 'promise' (e.g. Philo, *On the Change of Names* 201; see Wolter 2015: 388, n. 143).

59 Barclay also notes that '[t]he term "covenant" was perhaps employed too loosely in contemporary Judaism with reference to *both* the patriarchal promises *and* the Sinai Torah to serve
Paul's purposes in distinguishing between them' (2015: 402).

receiving the inheritance: 'For if the inheritance depends on the law, then it no longer depends on the promise' (Gal. 3:18a). It is instructive to compare this statement with what Paul says in Romans 11:6: 'if by grace, then it cannot be based on works; if it were, grace would no longer be grace'. In both statements the apostle's point is that law/works is a fundamentally different means of obtaining salvation than promise/grace.[60] This is why the law would invalidate the promise if it were the means of receiving the inheritance. But Paul's whole point is that it is not. The promise was prior: 'God in his grace gave it to Abraham through a promise' (Gal. 3:18b).

So if the law was not added as the means of inheritance, then what role was it intended to play in Israel's history? 'Why, then, was the law given at all?' (Gal. 3:19); 'Is the law, therefore, opposed to the promises of God?' (3:21). These questions, and their application to the Galatians' situation, dominate 3:19 – 4:11. Paul answers that the law was not given to Israel as a means of life or righteousness (Gal. 3:21), and therefore does not oppose the promise as a means of justification. Rather, *the law was given to play an imprisoning role*: 'But Scripture has locked up everything under the control of sin' (Gal. 3:22).

Paul uses the word 'under' to show the authority of the law 'over' people throughout this argument (3:23, 25; 4:2–5; cf. 3:10 and 4:21).[61] He also uses the metaphor of a legal guardian over an under-age child (3:24–25; 4:1–3) and even the metaphor of a slave under a master as he continues to explain the temporary and negative position of being 'under the law' (4:1–3). But his use of 'under' in Galatians 3:22 stands out because he says the law's role was to imprison 'under *sin*'. Here we see the strikingly negative role of the law in Israel's history. God's purpose for giving the law was not to bring life but to lock people up under the power of their own sin.[62] We should probably interpret Paul's cryptic statement in Galatians 3:19 in the light of this verse as well: The law 'was added because

---

[60] Moo observes that Paul's logic in Gal. 3:18 is also similar to his antithesis of grace and works in Rom. 4:4–5 (2013: 232).

[61] This straightforward reading seems more likely than Wilson's suggestion that 'under law' in 3:23, 4:4–5, 21 and 5:18 is a rhetorical shorthand meaning 'under the curse of the law' (2007: 30–44). Paul could have used the shorthand 'under a curse' as he does in 3:10. Further, 'under the law' in Rom. 6:14–15 and 1 Cor. 9:20–21 clearly means under the authority of the law, not 'under the curse of the law'.

[62] 'Scripture' (*graphē*) in Gal. 3:22 personifies God's intention in giving the law (Schreiner 2010: 244). Cf. Rom. 11:32, which says 'God has bound everyone over to disobedience', using the same verb as Gal. 3:22 (*synkleiō*).

of transgressions' means that the law was added in order to lead to transgressions, specific violations of God's law, imprisoning Israel in their own sin (cf. Rom. 5:20).[63]

This imprisoning role of the law, however, was only a temporary role according to Paul. 'It was added because of transgressions *until* the Seed to whom the promise referred had come' (Gal. 3:19); 'we were held in custody under the law, locked up *until* the faith that was to come would be revealed' (Gal. 3:23). The imprisoning role of the law was temporary because God's ultimate purpose was to make good on his promise to Abraham. 'Scripture has locked up everything under the control of sin, *so that* what was promised, being given through faith in Jesus Christ, might be given to those who believe' (Gal. 3:22).[64] Paul's point seems to be that God gave the law to imprison people temporarily in their sin in order to make it obvious that the Abrahamic promise could not come by means of the law but only by faith in Jesus Christ. That is, it could come only by *God's grace* in Christ ('being given', *dothē*). Thus, in the history of Israel the law was not against God's promise but prepared for the promise's fulfilment in Christ.

Paul's first mention of Jesus Christ in the story, nestled within his argument about the priority of the Abrahamic covenant, presents Christ as the recipient of the Abrahamic promises. 'The promises were spoken to Abraham and to his seed. Scripture does not say "and to seeds", meaning many people, but "and to your seed", meaning one person, who is Christ' (Gal. 3:16). Scholars have puzzled over Paul's argument that Christ is the singular seed of Abraham, since 'seed' is clearly collective in Genesis 17. But Paul's argument does not seem as strange when compared with similar Jewish exegetical arguments.[65] And the key to understanding Paul's point is found in his use of the word 'Christ' (cf. 1 Sam. 2:10; Ps. 2:2).

The word 'Christ' indicates that Paul is reading God's promises to Abraham in the light of their later flowering in the covenant with David,

---

[63] See Schreiner for a discussion of various interpretations and the studied conclusion that Gal. 3:19 means the law was given in order to increase transgression (ibid. 239–240).

[64] Paul may also speak of this purpose in Gal. 3:24 when he says 'the law was our guardian until [*eis*] Christ'. The NIVUK rightly translates *eis* in a temporal sense in context ('until Christ'), but the word may also refer to its goal or purpose ('leading to Christ'; so Moo, who sees a 'combined temporal/telic sense' [2013: 243]).

[65] For rabbinic examples, see Silva 2007: 807. Silva suggests that Paul's readers, including his opponents, would likely have agreed with his argument in Gal. 3:16 (ibid.). Note also the promise to David's 'seed' in 2 Sam. 7:12, which is clearly collective in context but interpreted at Qumran as a reference to the singular Messiah (4QFlor. 10–13).

a covenant that also highlights God's promises to 'seed' (*sperma*; 2 Sam. 7:12; 22:51).[66] Paul is arguing that the Christ, the seed of David, is the seed par excellence of Abraham. He is the 'one person' to whom the promises were ultimately made (Gal. 3:16; cf. 3:19). The reason Paul can make this argument is that he does not view the 'seed of Abraham' as merely a physical category but as a theological category referring to the inheritor of God's promise to Abraham. Ultimately, in the light of God's covenant with David, this is one 'seed', Christ. And yet Paul still understands the 'seed of Abraham' in a collective way: 'If you belong to Christ, then you are Abraham's seed, and heirs according to the promise' (Gal. 3:29). God's promises to Abraham are given to Christ and all who belong to him by faith.[67]

The coming of Christ now signals the end of the law's temporary, imprisoning era. The guardian-like authority of the law is finished now that 'faith' has come, the era in which we are justified by faith (Gal. 3:23–25).[68] The era of the law was like the time an heir is under age and really no different from a slave (4:1–3). But now that era of slavery is finished, for the set time has fully come in which God has sent his Son and his Spirit (4:4–6). Christ's death has not only redeemed us from the curse of the law (3:13) but from the very authority of the law in the old era (4:4–5). '[W]e are no longer under a guardian' (3:25). We are no longer imprisoned by the law.

Paul includes his Gentile Christian audience among those who were formerly under the law but in Christ have been released from it. God intended the law in its imprisoning role to have a universal effect. He says that 'Scripture has locked up *everything* under the control of sin, so that what was promised, being given through faith in Jesus Christ, might be

---

[66] Hays sees Paul using the catchword 'seed' to interpret the promise made to Abraham's seed in the light of 2 Sam. 7:12–14 (1989: 85; so, tentatively, Moo [2013: 230] and Barclay [2015: 412, n. 51]). It may also be significant that the servant of Isaiah is identified as the 'seed of Abraham' (Isa. 41:8).

[67] Our understanding of Gal. 3:16 is similar to Longenecker's: 'Paul is here invoking a corporate solidarity understanding of the promise to Abraham wherein the Messiah, as the true descendant of Abraham and the true representative of the nation is seen as the true "seed" of Abraham – as are, of course, also the Messiah's own, as v 29 insists' (1990: 132).

[68] Hays rightly observes that the coming of *pistis* in Gal. 3:23, 25 'is virtually identified with the coming of Christ himself' (2002: 203). But this should not lead to the conclusion that *pistis* refers to Christ's 'faithfulness', since Paul's use of the verb 'believe' (*pisteuō*) in Gal. 3:22 shows that *pistis* in his argument is a reference to our faith (cf. the argument of McFadden 2015: 260–266).

given to those who believe' (Gal. 3:22).[69] His statement 'we are no longer under a guardian' (Gal. 3:25) must include his Gentile audience, for it is grounded in the fact that 'in Christ Jesus you are all children of God through faith' (Gal. 3:26).[70] Similarly, in the logic of Galatians 4:3–5 both 'we' and 'you' must refer to the same group, including Paul's Gentile audience as 'those under the law', whom God has now redeemed through his Son.

Strangely, the street seems to run both ways in Paul's argument, because he also describes 'our' former enslavement under the law in terms of pagan idolatry.[71] 'So also, when we were under age, we were in slavery under the physical elements of the world' (4:3).[72] Paul seems to be referring to the pagan worship of the physical elements such as fire, or the heavenly bodies as gods (cf. Wis. 13.1–2), gods that ruled over the nations (cf. *Jub.* 16.31–32). The law, with its calendar rules aligned as they were with the physical cosmos, in a sense placed Israel in the same position as pagans who worshipped the sun, moon and stars (cf. 4:9–10).[73] This is why Paul asks the Galatians, who have gone from enslavement in pagan worship to knowing the true God, how they can turn back again to that slavery by keeping the law (4:8–11)! Christ has brought the old era of slavery under the law, sin and idolatry to an end.[74]

Moreover, he has brought about the fulfilment of the Abrahamic promise. This was God's ultimate purpose in sending his Son. 'God sent his Son, born of a woman, born under the law, to redeem those under the law, that we might receive adoption to sonship' (Gal. 4:4–5). Paul uses several different terms in this argument to describe the fulfilment of the

---

[69] The neuter 'everything' (*ta panta*) most likely refers to people in the context of this argument about people (BDF §138.1; cf. 1 Cor. 1:27: 'God chose the foolish things' [*ta mora*], which clearly refers to people). But perhaps Paul has used the neuter to indicate how the effects of sin have spilled over into everything in the world, the 'present evil age' (Gal. 1:4).

[70] The NIVUK's translation 'so' takes *gar* as introducing an inference, but it is much more common for this conjunction to mean 'for', introducing a ground (so Schreiner 2010: 255).

[71] His use of the first-person plural includes himself, a Jew, along with the Gentiles as under the 'elements of the world'.

[72] I have changed the NIVUK's 'elemental spiritual forces' to 'physical elements', the more likely meaning of the word *stoicheia* (following Barclay 2015: 409–410).

[73] Perhaps Paul makes this statement because Israel was caught up in idolatry throughout much of their history.

[74] Interpreters agree that Paul associates the law and the physical elements, but they disagree about how exactly the two ideas are related. Some see an analogy but not a direct relationship (Moo 2013: 263). Others suggest that being under the law is a subset of being under the elements (Donaldson 1986: 96–97, 104). But it seems to us that Paul in effect equates the law and the physical elements as part of the old era (Reicke 1951: 259).

Abrahamic promise to those who believe: 'inheritance' (3:18), 'life' (3:21a), 'righteousness' (3:21b), 'what was promised' (3:22), 'adoption to sonship' (4:5) and 'the Spirit of his Son' (4:6). Although we may prefer a more precise explanation of how these terms relate, Paul does not articulate their relationship but rather uses them almost interchangeably to speak of the Abrahamic blessing of justification.[75] His point is to convince the Galatian believers that in Christ and through faith they are the children of God who have received this promised blessing: '[I]n Christ Jesus you are all children of God through faith' (Gal. 3:26).

The conclusion of Paul's argument from history focuses on the twin themes of family and inheritance, which are so bound up with God's covenant with Abraham: 'If you belong to Christ, then you are Abraham's seed, and heirs according to the promise' (Gal. 3:29). He then rephrases this conclusion in the second-person singular, landing on a strikingly personal note to Gentile believers to whom God has given the Spirit of his Son: 'So you are no longer a slave, but God's child; and since you are his child, God has made you also an heir' (Gal. 4:7).[76] But although his argument is so rooted in God's covenant with Abraham, it clearly reaches beyond it with its focus on Christ, the descendant of David, and the Spirit, the promise of the new covenant. Perhaps we also see in Paul's argument a suggestion that Christ has brought about the hoped-for new creation. He says that because of our union with Christ in baptism '[t]here is neither Jew nor Gentile, neither slave nor free, nor is there male and female, for you are all one in Christ Jesus' (Gal. 3:28). Partaking in Abraham's family and inheritance has nothing to do with the distinctions of the old era, whether rooted in the law, human society or even the old creation. Paul's final pair, 'male and female', is an allusion to the creation narrative (Gen. 1:27).[77] By

---

[75] The closest Paul comes is in saying that the inheritance is the fulfilment of the promise (3:18; cf. 3:29), but he also uses the word 'promise' itself to refer to the fulfilment of the promise (translated 'what is promised' in the NIVUK, 3:22). One might also argue that 'sonship' precedes reception of the Spirit in 4:6, but Paul's point is to associate the two closely rather than give a chronological order (so Longenecker 1990: 173; Schreiner 2010: 272), for in the same verse he says the Spirit makes us cry out as sons to our Father (cf. Rom. 8:15).

[76] The Galatians' own experience of the Spirit supports this conclusion, confirming their mutual sonship with Jesus Christ in crying out as Jesus did in the garden, 'Abba, Father' (Gal. 4:6; cf. Mark 14:36). The bilingual use of 'father' in both Aramaic (abba) and Greek (ho patēr) is perhaps meant to reinforce that both Jews and Gentiles are sons and heirs together (Betz 1979: 211, following Augustine and Luther).

[77] It is likely that this is a purposeful allusion because Paul changes from the conjunction 'nor' (oude) to the conjunction 'and' (kai), and because he uses the adjectives 'male' (arsēn) and 'female' (thēlys), which are found in only one other place in his letters (Rom. 1:26–27).

negating this creation difference Paul is probably implying that belonging to the family of Abraham is partaking in Isaiah's prophesied new creation, just as he invokes the reality of the new creation at the end of the letter to relativize the old-covenant distinction between Jew and Gentile (Gal. 6:15).[78] Paul's argument about the new era of Christ and faith should not be underestimated. Gentile believers are children of Abraham by virtue of the new-creation work of God, something Paul will explore further in his third telling of Israel's story.

To summarize, Paul begins his long argument from Israel's history with the covenant God made with Abraham in Genesis 15 and 17. He observes that these promises were temporally *prior* to the giving of the law, which means that the law was not added as a means of inheritance, for that would be changing the terms of the covenant. Rather, the law was added to imprison Israel (and the world) under the power of sin. This negative role was a temporary one that the law was meant to play as it prepared the way for the coming of Christ. But now that Christ has come we are no longer under the law but are children and heirs of Abraham and God.

Argument from allegory (Gal. 4:21–31)

Paul's final argument about justification appeals to just one episode in the story of Israel – the story of Abraham's two sons, Ishmael and Isaac (Gen. 16–21).[79] He urges the Galatians to listen to what the law itself says about Abrahamic sonship. 'Tell me, you who want to be under the law, are you not aware of what the law says?' (Gal. 4:21). According to Paul, it says that the Abrahamic blessing of justification does not come by means of fleshly requirements but by the promise of God. The story of Ishmael and Isaac, then, is a figurative preview of the law covenant's children of flesh/slavery and the new covenant's children of promise/freedom.

The first thing Paul highlights in this episode is that Abraham had *two* sons (Gal. 4:22). Paul sees a distinction between these two sons in that Ishmael was born 'by the slave woman' but Isaac 'by the free woman' (Gal. 4:22). Hagar, the mother of Ishmael, is repeatedly identified as a 'slave

---

[78] Cf. Martyn 1997: 376–377.

[79] It is probably no coincidence that Paul appeals to the narratives that surround the OT's principal chapter on circumcision (Gen. 17). But it is not clear to us that the troublemakers were appealing to the Hagar–Sarah narratives, as many suggest (e.g. Barrett 1982: 167; Hansen 1989: 213).

woman' in the Abraham narratives (Gen. 16:1–3, 5–6, 8; 21:10 [2×], 12–13, 16).[80] And this is one of the reasons her son did not share in Abraham's inheritance, for Sarah said to Abraham that 'the slave woman's son will never share in the inheritance with the free woman's son' (Gal. 4:30, quoting Gen. 21:10).[81] Further, Paul observes a distinction between the means by which Abraham's two sons were born: 'His son by the slave woman was born according to the flesh, but his son by the free woman was born as the result of a divine promise' (*di' eppangelias*; Gal. 4:23).[82] 'Flesh' here indicates the normal human means of birth, the means by which Ishmael was born when Abraham slept with Hagar because of Sarah's inability to have children (Gen. 16:1–4). 'Promise' indicates the extraordinary and miraculous way in which Isaac was born in the midst of Sarah's barrenness and old age. Isaac was not born by the normal human means of procreation but by the miraculous fulfilment of God's promise (cf. Gen. 17:19; 18:10, 14). In contrast with 'flesh', the word 'promise' in this argument emphasizes the *theological* origin of Isaac's birth. Isaac is distinguished from Ishmael because he was not born by human effort but by God's power.[83]

Paul builds upon this distinction between Ishmael and Isaac an allegorical interpretation of the story that elucidates the enslaving nature of the law covenant and the freedom of the new covenant (Gal. 4:24a). Most scholars observe that Paul's allegory is 'tempered' by typology.[84] Ishmael and Isaac are OT figures who correspond to and foreshadow what God is now doing in Christ and the church. And yet Paul's reading of the story goes beyond typology, inasmuch as Hagar and Sarah are identified as the

---

[80] Note that 'slave woman' in the LXX (*paidiskē*) translates two Hebrew words – *šipḥâ* in Gen. 16:1–3, 5–6, 8, and *'āmâ* in Gen. 21:10 [2×], 12–13, 16.

[81] Paul has modified the ending of Sarah's words from 'with my son Isaac' to 'with the son of the free woman', emphasizing his contrast between slavery and freedom. Moo rightly calls this contrast between slavery and freedom the *leitmotif* of Gal. 4:21–31 (2013: 293).

[82] Cf. 'God in his grace gave [the inheritance] to Abraham through a promise' (*di' eppangelias*; Gal. 3:18).

[83] We can contrast Paul's argument that Isaac was distinguished because he was *not* born according to the flesh with the view of *Jubilees*, a second century BC retelling of Genesis and Exodus. In this telling of Israel's story Isaac is distinguished from Abraham's other sons simply because God chose his physical line to be the people belonging to the Lord (16.17–29). *Jubilees* also seems to highlight the importance of Isaac's being the first person who was circumcised on the eighth day (16.14), something the book emphasizes more than the Genesis account (15.26; cf. Gen. 17:12–14).

[84] Martyn 1997: 436. Thus, it is different from Philo's allegorizing of the law, which transfers 'textual figures from historical particularity into universal truth' (Barclay 2015: 415–416).

law covenant that bears children into slavery and the new covenant that bears children into freedom.[85]

Paul explicitly identifies Hagar with the law covenant given to Israel at Sinai: 'One covenant is from Mount Sinai and bears children who are to be slaves: this is Hagar' (Gal. 4:24). Since he has already argued that God gave the law to imprison people in sin, his identification between the slave woman and the law covenant is not surprising. He solidifies this identity further in the next verse by observing that both are associated with the geographical location of Arabia: '[T]he Hagar-Sinai mountain is in Arabia' (Gal. 4:25a; our tr.).[86] And yet the mountain also corresponds geographically 'to the present city of Jerusalem, because she is in slavery with her children' (Gal. 4:25b).[87] In context, the slavery of Jerusalem and her children must refer to those who were currently labouring under the authority of the law. Jerusalem was the centre of Judaism and probably the home-base of the Jewish Christians who were trying to convince the Galatians to be circumcised (cf. Acts 15:1).[88] Ishmael's mother is the law covenant and corresponds to the present city of Jerusalem in that she is enslaved to the law and bears children who join her in that slavery.

In contrast, Paul implicitly identifies Sarah with the new covenant (Gal. 4:24) and with 'the Jerusalem that is above' (4:26). Commentators are divided over whether the second covenant mentioned in Galatians 4:24 refers to the Abrahamic covenant or the new covenant. The broader

---

[85] Schreiner helpfully observes that 'The fundamental reason for seeing the text as having an allegorical component is the identification of Hagar with the Sinai covenant. Such a move does not comport with typology, where there is a historical connection between the type and its fulfillment. It is difficult to see how Hagar functions as a historical type of the Sinai covenant' (2010: 300).

[86] Most English versions translate 'Hagar' as the subject and 'Mount Sinai' as the predicate: 'Hagar stands for Mount Sinai' (Gal. 4:25, NIVUK). But Paul has already identified Hagar as Mount Sinai and the grammar indicates that *to Hagar Sina horos* should be taken together as the subject. The neuter article *to* agrees with *oros* (mountain), sandwiching *Hagar Sina* as modifiers of *oros*. Some explain the neuter article *to* as introducing a quotation, as in 'the word "Hagar"' (e.g. Betz 1979: 244, n. 65; BDF §267 [1]). But it seems more likely in this context that the article goes with the neuter noun *oros* (so, tentatively, Moo 2013: 302). This translation is often associated with the shorter text of the verse that omits *Hagar* (see Moo, ibid. 303), but it seems more likely that *Hagar* is original to the text and was omitted by a scribe due to its difficulty.

[87] If our translation of Gal. 4:25a is correct, then *de* in 4:25b should be translated in an adversative sense ('and yet' or 'but') rather than a conjunctive sense ('and'; so Moo 2013: 303).

[88] The enslavement of 'the present city of Jerusalem' is likely both a reference to Judaism in general (ibid. 304) and a specific polemic against the opponents (Schreiner 2010: 302), since Paul refers to their troubling of the Galatians in Gal. 4:29. Less likely is the view that Paul refers to the Jerusalem church (Martyn 1997: 439), since both Gal. 2:1–10 and Acts 15 indicate that Paul agreed with the Jerusalem apostles about the circumcision question.

context of the letter up to this point has focused on the Abrahamic covenant (Gal. 3:15–18).[89] But Paul's appeal in the immediate context to the restored Jerusalem of Isaiah leads us to see a reference to the new covenant. He quotes from Isaiah 54:1, a prophecy comforting the barren city in exile with the hope that she will be repopulated again. This comfort is rooted in the surety of the Lord's 'covenant of peace' or new covenant with his people, which is as sure as the covenant God made with Noah after the devastation of the flood (Isa. 54:9–10; 55:3; 59:21; 61:8). The restored and repopulated Jerusalem will be newly created in the new heavens and the new earth (Isa. 65:17). Thus, Paul's appeal to the restored Jerusalem indicates that he is linking Sarah with the new covenant, although perhaps he does not identify it as such directly in order to show the continuity between the Abrahamic covenant and the new covenant.[90]

Unlike Paul's identification of Hagar as the law-covenant, there was already biblical precedence linking Sarah with the new covenant. The only place in the OT where Sarah is mentioned outside the Genesis narratives is Isaiah 51:1–3. This text appeals to Sarah's motherhood as an encouragement that just as God once brought many descendants out of the one man, Abraham, so he will comfort Jerusalem and give her joy. Isaiah then picks up on the barrenness theme associated with Sarah (cf. Gen. 11:30) and applies it to the future restoration of Jerusalem in Isaiah 54:1:

> Be glad, barren woman,
>> you who never bore a child;
> break forth and cry aloud,
>> you who were never in labour;
> because more are the children of the desolate woman
>> than of her who has a husband.
> (Gal. 4:27, quoting Isa. 54:1)

---

[89] This is the main argument that convinces Moo of a reference to the Abrahamic covenant, although he clarifies that 'we must also follow Paul's lead and speak of the Abrahamic covenant as christologically defined' (2013: 301; so Hays 1989: 114–115, followed by Jobes 1993: 317).

[90] Willitts suggests that Isa. 54:1 and its restoration theology should lead interpreters to see a reference to the new covenant (see his extensive discussion in 2005: 199–200, n. 30). Schreiner gives the qualification that 'the new covenant fulfills the covenant made with Abraham, so we should not exaggerate the difference between these two options' (2010: 301).

The barren woman, patterned after Sarah, is the newly created Jerusalem repopulated by her miraculously conceived children of promise.[91]

Isaiah also links the barren woman's children with justification. His encouragement to rejoice follows Isaiah 52:13 - 53:12, the passage that explains why the servant must suffer death: for the transgressions and iniquities of Israel (53:4-6). It also says that the servant will 'justify many' (53:11), probably the source of the Christian doctrine of justification even before Paul's writings.[92] Further, in the consolation of Isaiah 54, the restored Jerusalem is told that the Lord will vindicate or justify her against the accusation of her enemies (54:17). Thus, in the context of Isaiah's prophecy the miraculous children of the new covenant are those who are righteous through the vicarious suffering of the servant; that is, they are justified in Christ.

Paul's contribution to Isaiah's linkage of Sarah with the new covenant and justification is to see *freedom* as the point of correspondence between Isaac and the children of the new covenant: 'But the Jerusalem that is above is free, and she is our mother' (Gal. 4:26). In the context of his argument about the enslaving role of the law (3:23 - 4:7; 4:24) Paul must be speaking about freedom from the law.[93] Sarah and her son Isaac were free just as the newly created Jerusalem and her children are free from the law.

It is interesting that Paul identifies the restored Jerusalem as the 'above Jerusalem' (*anō Ierousalēm*). In contrast with the 'now Jerusalem', one would expect him to identify the city as the 'future Jerusalem' or the 'then Jerusalem'. But Paul does not see her as fundamentally future because the new covenant has already been established by the death of Christ and is bearing children in Galatia who are justified by faith and have the Spirit.[94]

---

[91] On Isaiah's prophetic transformation of Sarah's barrenness theme, see Jobes 1993: 306-309. The married woman who is taunting is also part of the barrenness theme in the OT (1 Sam. 1:3-8; cf. 2:1-10).

[92] Stettler follows Stuhlmacher in arguing that Rom. 4:25 represents a traditional formula based upon Isa. 53 and concludes that 'even before Paul, justification was linked to Christology on the basis of Isaiah 53:10-12' (2015: 172).

[93] *Pace* Coppins, whose careful work notes the force of Jones's observation that Paul never explicitly speaks of 'freedom from the law' in Galatians (2009: 90; although cf. Rom. 7:1-4). Coppins argues that the slavery/freedom spoken of in Gal. 4:21-31 is simply a metaphor for an absolutely negative and absolutely positive situation (ibid. 107-108). But in our view Paul's 'under the law' language (e.g. 4:21) and broader argument gives warrant to the idea that this freedom includes freedom from enslavement to the law and the physical elements of the world.

[94] De Boer observes that 'Paul sees Isa. 54:1 as "already" fulfilled or at least in the process of being fulfilled' (2004: 374-375; cf. 384). And Wolter contrasts Paul's emphasis on the already fulfilled promise of Isa. 54:1 with the Hebrew Bible, Targums, LXX, Philo and the rabbis, who see it as a future hope (Wolter 2013).

And yet it is not quite correct to identify her as the present city of Jerusalem, because the current inhabitants of the city are still enslaved under the authority of the law. So Paul mixes temporal with spatial categories, speaking of the Jerusalem above that will one day come down to earth.[95] *This* Jerusalem, he argues, is free from the enslavement of the law.

The final verses in Galatians 4:28–31 continue Paul's figurative reading of Abraham's two sons but also draw a conclusion from it.[96] The Gentile believers in Galatia are, like Isaac, children of the promise (4:28) and children of the free woman (4:31). Paul draws this conclusion because their mother is Sarah – the repopulated Jerusalem of the new covenant who bears the miraculously conceived children promised by God in Isaiah. Thus, we see again that Paul's use of 'promise' in this argument is a way of referring to the theological character of God's children: they are not produced by human means, but in a miraculous, divine way, just like Isaac's birth. In fact, Paul speaks of Isaac as 'the son born by the power of the Spirit', just as the Gentile believers had received God's Spirit, the promise of the new covenant (3:2–5, 14; 4:6). In contrast, Paul identifies the Jewish-Christian troublemakers with Ishmael, 'the son born according to the flesh' (4:29).[97] As Ishmael mocked Isaac (Gen. 21:9), so they were causing trouble among the Gentiles who have the Spirit. And Paul cites Sarah's words to Abraham as God's word ('Scripture') to the Galatians: 'But what does Scripture say? "Get rid of the slave woman and her son, for the slave woman's son will never share in the inheritance with the free woman's son"' (Gal. 4:30, quoting Gen. 21:10).[98]

Thus, Paul's allegorical argument from Genesis 16 – 21 both reinforces and advances his arguments from Scripture and history. Gentile believers

---

[95] Hebrews and Revelation also refer with spatial categories to the restored Jerusalem of Isaiah: the 'city' in the heavenly homeland (Heb. 11:10, 14–16), the 'heavenly Jerusalem' (Heb. 12:22) and the new Jerusalem coming down from heaven (Rev. 3:10; 21:2, 10).

[96] Cosgrove says that the phrase '[n]ow you, brothers and sisters' (*hymeis de adelphoi*) is transitional and does not indicate a conclusion (1987: 223). But even though it is not formally marked, the flow of the argument indicates that Gal. 4:28 is an *implicit* conclusion, which is then repeated and formally marked as a conclusion in 4:31: 'Therefore, brothers and sisters, we are not children of the slave woman, but of the free woman.'

[97] Moyise observes that Paul has 'overturned the traditional interpretation (Jews are descended from Sarah and Gentiles from Hagar)' (2010: 42). Cf. again *Jub.* 16.17–19.

[98] If Paul's point was simply that the slave woman's son would not share the inheritance, then he would not need to cite the first half of Gen. 21:10. Thus, it seems likely that Paul intends this quotation as a command to the Galatians to expel the troublemakers (so Martyn 1997: 446). The fact that the command is in the singular does not tell against this, since Paul also addresses his audience in the singular in Gal. 4:7 (*pace* Schreiner 2010: 306, n. 69).

are the children of Abraham, who inherit God's blessing. Moreover, they are the children miraculously conceived by the Spirit in fulfilment of God's promise. The law was given by God in a temporary, imprisoning role, and it enslaves those who place themselves under its authority. This is the very slavery from which Christ in the new covenant has set us free. 'It is for freedom that Christ has set us free. Stand firm, then, and do not let yourselves be burdened again by a yoke of slavery' (Gal. 5:1).

Summary

In Galatians 3 – 4 Paul has left us with three apostolic versions of the story of Israel. The first reaches back to the initial blessing of Abraham in Genesis 12, arguing that Christ took upon himself the curse of the law in order to bring this blessing to believers in Christ. The second emphasizes the priority of God's promises to Abraham and his offspring (Christ) in Genesis 15 and 17 over the late-coming law. The law was not intended to be a means of obtaining these promises but only a temporary measure, imprisoning the world in sin until the coming of Christ and faith. The final version focuses on the episode of Ishmael and Isaac in Genesis 16 – 21, seeing in Abraham's two sons harbingers of those enslaved by the law and those freed from it by the Spirit in the new covenant. In each version of the story Paul is labouring to prove from the OT that Jews and Gentiles are righteous before God by faith in Jesus Christ and not by works of the law. Thus, Gentile believers in Christ are the offspring of Abraham, the miraculously conceived children of God, justified by faith. They should not put this grace in jeopardy by trying to be justified by the law.

The contribution of Paul's summary

Paul's biblical theology in Galatians 3 – 4 overlaps with what we have seen in Matthew and Luke: it finds the story's climax in the person and work of Christ; it focuses on the covenants; and it makes use of figurative readings. One distinctive contribution Paul makes in this passage is his use of three different approaches of telling the story (Scripture, history, allegory), in one letter! But his most important contribution to biblical theology in Galatians 3 – 4 is his explanation of the role of one of the most central institutions in Israel's story: the law. Paul argues that the law was never intended to be the climax of the story but rather was meant to play a secondary, negative, temporary and preparatory role.

First, Paul argues that the law is *secondary* to the Abrahamic covenant in Israel's story. It is secondary in the sense that it comes after the Abrahamic covenant. In fact, Paul is specific – it was 'introduced 430 years later' (Gal. 3:17). He highlights the chronological distance between Abraham and the law in contrast with a tendency among some Jews of his period to conflate Abraham and the law.[99] Why? Because he wants to show that the Abrahamic inheritance rests upon the prior promise and not upon the law. Thus, the law is also secondary to the Abrahamic covenant in the sense that it was never intended to bring about the Abrahamic blessing. The blessing was intended to be brought about by means of the promise (Gal. 3:18), by means of faith (Gal. 3:9) and by means of Christ (Gal. 3:14). It was never meant to be brought about by means of the law. What then was the intended role of the law?

Second, Paul argues that the law was intended to play a *negative* role in Israel's story. This is perhaps the most surprising element of his argument. The law does not bring about the blessing of Abraham but rather a curse upon sinners who break it (Gal. 3:10). It was not added to the prior promise in order to bring about the fulfilment of that promise but rather to increase transgressions (3:19) and imprison the world under the power of sin (3:22). This is why life under the law was (and is) like slavery (4:1, 3, 24–25). And this is why Christ came to redeem us from the curse of the law (3:13), from the era of the law's authority (4:5) and from the enslavement to the law (4:26, 31; cf. 5:1). We should observe here that Paul is not arguing that the law itself is negative or bad (cf. Rom. 7:12). Rather, he is arguing that the law was intended to play a negative role in the history of Israel (and the world). That is to say, the law was meant to point out and aggravate Israel's real problem: their sin.

Third, Paul argues that this negative role of the law was only a *temporary* role. It played this role only until the coming of Christ, the seed of Abraham (3:19). Now that the era of Christ and faith has come, the temporary, imprisoning role of the law is over (3:23–25). This leads to our final point.

---

[99] E.g. *Jubilees* says that Abraham kept the festival laws before they were even given (*Jub.* 6.17–19). Sirach says that Abraham 'kept the law of the Most High' (Sir. 44.20a). Philo sees Abraham as the living or unwritten law before it was given (*On Abraham*). And Josephus finds the moral of the whole history of Israel to be that God blesses those who keep the law (*Jewish Antiquities* 1.14). The OT itself gives some warrant for this trajectory when the Lord tells Isaac that Abraham 'obeyed me and did everything I required of him, keeping my commands, my decrees and my instructions' (Gen. 26:5). But Paul argues that one should not press this trajectory, for the Mosaic law came centuries after God's promise to Abraham (Gal. 3:17).

Fourth, Paul argues that the law was intended to play a *preparatory* role in Israel's story. Its negative role in the story has a positive purpose at the end of the day: to lead to God's gracious gift in Christ. God's gracious promise came to Abraham before the giving of the law, and his gracious fulfilment of the promise came to believers in Jesus Christ after the giving of the law. Moreover, God gave what was promised *to those who were imprisoned under sin by the law*:[100] 'Scripture has locked up everything under the control of sin, so that what was promised, being given through faith in Jesus Christ, might be given to those who believe' (Gal. 3:22).[101] Paul's point is that the reason God imprisoned everyone under the control of sin was so that he might graciously *give* the promised inheritance to sinners who believe in Christ. In other words, the negative, imprisoning role of the law is the dark backdrop against which we see God's grace in Christ. The blessing is given to those who were cursed (3:13–14); life and righteousness is given to those under the control of sin (Gal. 3:21–22); and adoption to sonship is given to those enslaved under the law (4:3–5). The law in its preparatory role teaches us that Abrahamic sonship and inheritance really are a matter of God's grace in Christ, a point upon which we will reflect at length when we look at Romans 9 – 11.

Conclusion

Galatians 3 – 4 repeats the story of Israel three times and puts the law in its rightful place in biblical theology. Against those who were pressuring Gentile believers to be circumcised Paul argues that God did not give the law to justify but in order to highlight his grace! The law was given to imprison the world under the authority of sin until Christ came to redeem us from its curse and free us from its slavery. Why then would Gentile believers set aside the grace of God in Christ by trying to go back under the law and be justified (5:4)? Paul concludes again and again in these chapters that Gentile believers in Christ are the children of Abraham and heirs of God's promise of justification. The children of Abraham are those

---

100 Wolter rightly observes that 'the law occupies a lesser position . . . because the arc of promise and fulfillment from Abraham to Christ goes over it' (Gal. 3:16–19; 2015: 348). Though perhaps it is better to say that the arc does not go over the law but *through* it and yet *still* God fulfils his promise.

101 The wording here is remarkably similar to Paul's concluding statement in Rom. 9 – 11: 'For God has bound everyone over to disobedience so that he may have mercy on them all' (Rom. 11:32).

who believe as Abraham did (3:8). The 'offspring of Abraham' par excellence is the Christ and therefore anyone who belongs to him by faith (3:16, 29). Those who inherit the blessing are not the children of flesh but the miraculous children of promise who have the Spirit (4:28–29). But if this is true, how then should Gentile believers think of Jews who have not believed in Christ? This is the question driving one of the most important examples of biblical theology in the NT, Romans 9 – 11.

5

Romans and Israel's identity

The goal of this book has been to observe the exposed iceberg of apostolic biblical theology, and in this chapter we come to one of its highest peaks, Romans 9 – 11. This complex argument is the longest SIS in the NT,[1] and contains the most concentrated series of OT quotations in all of Paul's letters and perhaps the entire NT.[2] So far in the book we have seen that the apostles view Israel's story continuing in the life, death and resurrection of Jesus Christ (Matt. 1). It is a story built upon God's covenantal promises now fulfilled in Christ and full of pre-figurations of his rejection and vindication (Jesus' parable of the tenants, Acts 7 and 13). Even the great institution of the law was meant to lead to faith in Jesus Christ, imprisoning Israel under the power of their sin in order to highlight the radiance of God's grace to believers in Christ (Gal. 3 – 4). In this chapter we will see how the apostle Paul wrestles with the very identity of Israel, obviously one of the main characters of the story, in the light of their unbelief in the gospel.

As we have done in the previous chapters, we will begin by examining the context of the SIS. We will see that the context of Romans 9 – 11 leads Paul to tell the story in a different way than he did in Galatians, for Galatians 3 – 4 addresses believing Gentiles, whereas Romans 9 – 11 addresses unbelieving Jews. This context enlightens how Paul tells the story, for he focuses on Israel's past, present and future in order to support a long and complex argument that shows God has been faithful both to his Word and to his people. Paul's argument about Israel's future is the most

---

[1] Hood and Emerson include Rom. 9 – 11 in their list (2013: 324). And Wright observes that 'Romans 9 belongs smack in the middle of that second-temple genre which consists of retellings of Israel's story,' a story Paul continues telling in Rom. 10 – 11 (Wright 2013: 1158–1161).

[2] Seifrid observes the 'flood of citations in chapters 9–11', in which Paul makes 'the most extensive and concentrated use of Scripture in all his letters' (2007: 638). Only sections of Hebrews rival Rom. 9 – 11 in direct citations of the OT.

controversial aspect of this story, especially the *crux interpretum* of Romans 11:26, where Paul says that 'all Israel will be saved'. While we will address this passage below, we must not allow it to distract from our purpose of explaining how Paul tells the content of Israel's story, which gives more attention to the present state of Israel. Having examined the content of the story, we will then, in the final section of the chapter, address the major contribution that Romans 9 – 11 makes to apostolic biblical theology.

Wrestling with the present state of unbelieving Israel in the light of the climax of the story, the coming of the Messiah, Romans 9 – 11 contributes to biblical theology in its deep reflection upon the very identity of 'Israel'. Paul argues that Israel have never had a fundamentally ethnic identity but have always had (and always will have) a *theological* identity – Israel are the people who have mercifully been called by God.

The context of Paul's summary

Romans 9 – 11 did not arise from the heat of conflict like Galatians 3 – 4 but from a slow-burning 'great sorrow and unceasing anguish' in Paul's heart over Israel's unbelief (Rom. 9:2). Paul is eager to prove the genuineness of his grief: 'I speak the truth in Christ – I am not lying, my conscience confirms it through the Holy Spirit' (9:1). His claim likely anticipates the accusation that he has abandoned his own people in his mission to the Gentiles.[3] But the truth is quite the opposite. Paul never directly states the source of his grief in 9:1–5, but makes it clear in the course of the larger argument that the reason for his anguish is Israel's failure to believe in Jesus Christ and be saved (9:32–33; 10:1–13, 16; 11:20, 23). He is thinking primarily of their rejection of the gospel as it was being preached throughout the Roman world, since he speaks of belief as a confession that Jesus is the resurrected Lord (10:9). Paul grieves over their rejection of the gospel and could even wish himself to be 'cursed and cut off from Christ' so that his 'brothers' can be saved (9:3; cf. 10:1).[4] Thus, recent attempts to argue that Paul called only Gentiles, and not Jews, to believe in Christ have radically misunderstood the apostle in these chapters.[5] Romans 9 – 11

---

[3] So Longenecker, who observes that '[t]his claim of truthfulness is the strongest of all such attestation statements in Paul's NT letters' (2016: 782).

[4] The NIVUK translates 'my brothers' (*tōn adelphōn mou*) in Rom. 9:3 as 'my people'.

[5] Wright observes that 'Those who have tried to advocate a new approach to Paul at this point have done their best to play this down, but it is inescapable. The basic category to which

arises from Paul's wrestling with the tragic situation of Israel's failure to believe in good news about their own Messiah/Christ (cf. 9:5).[6]

It is interesting to observe that Paul actually begins the story in Romans 9 – 11 where he ended it in Galatians 3 – 4: with Abraham's two sons.[7] However, this different historical context leads Paul to tell the story in a different way in Romans. In Galatians, where Paul was trying to convince believing Gentiles that they did not need to be circumcised, the story of Ishmael and Isaac reinforces his larger point that Gentile believers in Christ are, like Isaac, the miraculous children of Abraham who will inherit God's blessing.[8] But in Romans, where Paul is wrestling with the problem of unbelieving Jews who have not obeyed the gospel, the story of Ishmael and Isaac functions to address the opposite side of the coin: if Gentiles who have come to believe in Christ are the miraculous children of Abraham, then what about the vast majority of Israelites who have rejected this gospel? Are they the children of God? This different context explains why the content of the story in Romans 9 – 11 seems so different from that in Galatians 3 – 4.[9] Paul's focus is not on the role of the law and the Gentiles but rather on the identity of 'Israel' in the past, the present and even the future.

The fundamental argument that forms the literary context of the story in Romans 9 – 11 is that God has been faithful in the midst of Israel's unbelief.[10] At the foundation of Paul's argument is the familiar OT idea that Israel have priority in the possession of God's saving benefits: 'Theirs

---

Paul returns several times is that of *unbelief*' (2013: 1161; emphasis original). For an early response to this position see Hafemann 1988.

[6] Paul repeatedly uses the verb *legō* (I say) in these chapters (9:1; 10:18–19; 11:1, 11, 13), similar to 1 Cor. 7, which offers his conclusions from wrestling with this difficult issue (see *legō* in 1 Cor. 7:6, 8, 12, 35). Cf. also Gal. 5:2. Of course, Paul can use the verb *legō* in other situations as well; e.g. to clarify something he has said (Gal. 4:1).

[7] Paul's first citation in Rom. 9 – 11 is Gen. 21:12, and his last citation in Gal. 3 – 4 is Gen. 21:10.

[8] And thus they should reject those who, like Ishmael, were harassing the children of promise by trying to force them to be circumcised.

[9] Thus, there is no reason to posit a change in thinking from Galatians to Romans as Longenecker does. He suggests that Paul writes differently in Romans under the pressure of his upcoming trip to Jerusalem, where he will need to explain his gospel to the Jerusalem apostles, but that Galatians represents Paul's *true* convictions (2002: 80–82).

[10] It is remarkable that with all of the renewed interest in the place of Rom. 9 – 11 over the past few decades there is a rough consensus that Paul tells the story of Israel in these chapters to uphold God's faithfulness (e.g. Hafemann 1988: 43; Wright 1991: 234; Kim 2000: 6). An exception is Gaventa, who doubts that Paul's audience would question God's faithfulness. She argues that the primary issue is what Paul has been saying about Israel so far in the letter (2010: 257).

is the adoption to sonship; theirs the divine glory, the covenants, the receiving of the law, the temple worship and the promises. Theirs are the patriarchs, and from them is traced the human ancestry of the Messiah' (Rom. 9:4–5). Paul has described many of these privileges as the possession of all believers: 'adoption to sonship' (8:15), 'glory' (e.g. 5:2), the Spirit of the new covenant (e.g. 2:28–29), the ability to fulfil the law (8:4), the Abrahamic promise (4:16) and Christ himself (e.g. Rom. 5:8). But he clarifies here that these saving benefits belong squarely to Israelites, even though most Jewish people are not partaking in them because of their rejection of their Messiah. Herein lies the problem, a problem Paul anticipates in Romans 3:3–4: 'Will their [Israel's] unfaithfulness nullify God's faithfulness? Not at all! Let God be true, and every human being a liar' (cf. 2 Tim. 2:13). In Romans 9 – 11 Paul develops this argument, claiming specifically that God has been faithful both to his Word and to his people.

First, Paul argues that God has been faithful to his Word, anticipating and countering someone who would conclude from the present tragedy that God has not upheld his word to Israel.[11] To this Paul responds, 'but I am surely not saying that the word of God has fallen!' (Rom. 9:6a; our tr.).[12] Many interpreters view this verse as a guiding statement for all of 9:6 – 11:32.[13] Goodrich has articulated the most recent argument for this view, observing that 9:6a certainly introduces 9:6b–29, that it introduces 9:30 – 10:21 because these verses explain how Israel's stumbling was prophesied in God's Word and that it is a close conceptual parallel with the opening statement of 11:1–32 ('God did not reject his people', 11:2).[14] Thus, we should view Romans 9:6a as a kind of thesis statement for all of Romans 9 – 11. The Word of God has not fallen, a point Paul proves by

---

[11] We view Rom. 9:6 – 11:32 as the logical alternative to the implication of 9:1–5. So Cranfield: 'Paul wishes to exclude what might seem to be the implication of what he has just said in vv. 1–5' (1979: 472).

[12] Our rendering of *ouch hoion de hoti ekpeptōken ho logos tou theou* differs slightly from the NIVUK in four ways: we have translated the conjunction *de* (but); we have brought out the emphasis indicated by *ouch hoion* (a Hellenistic idiom that equals *ouch dēpou* [BDAG, s.v. 'hoios'; BDF §304]); we have brought out the implied *legō* ('I say'; see BDF §480 [5]); and have translated *ekpeptōken* with a present perfect rather than a past perfect in order to show in English that Paul is talking about the current state of God's Word (so ESV).

[13] Kim calls Rom. 9:6a the 'main thesis' of Rom. 9 – 11 (2000: 146–147). Gaventa observes that many commentators hold this position, with which she agrees (2010: 258, n. 14). And Haacker observes that German scholars often view 9:6a as the *Schlüsselaussage* (key statement) of the passage (2010: 63).

[14] Goodrich 2016: 61–62.

appealing to Scripture at a level seen nowhere else in his letters. Israel's present situation corresponds to their past as recorded in Scripture and fulfils the prophecies of Scripture. Israel's story itself is the evidence God has been faithful to his Word.

Second, the story of Israel in Romans 9 – 11 is also evidence that God has been faithful to his people. Romans 9:6a is thematically a guiding statement, but formally it is only one step in a chain of reasoning in which Paul upholds not only God's faithfulness to his Word but to his people. For the apostle, God's faithfulness to his Word *entails* his faithfulness to his people. This entailment becomes especially prominent in Romans 11, where he argues that 'God did not reject his people, whom he foreknew' (11:2). One difficulty in understanding this argument is that Paul uses the designation 'God's people' in Romans 9 – 11 both for ethnic Jews (11:2) and for Gentile believers (9:24–26). Similarly, he uses 'Israel' as both an ethnic category of those descended from Jacob (9:6a) and as a theological category of those who inherit Abraham's blessing (9:6b). This is one reason why interpreters disagree about whether 'all Israel' in 11:26 refers to ethnic Jews or includes the Gentiles. God's faithfulness to his Word entails his faithfulness to all of 'his people', including Gentiles.[15] But the apostle's focus in Romans 9 – 11 is on God's faithfulness to the ethnic nation of Israel, especially in Romans 11.

Many interpreters have suggested that Paul in a sense reverses the priority of Israel in Romans 11. The prophets expected that the restoration of Israel would lead to the eschatological pilgrimage of the Gentiles (e.g. Isa. 2:1–4), but Paul says that the salvation of the Gentiles will come *before* the restoration of Israel.[16] However, Donaldson has now cautioned against reading Romans 11 with this background, since Paul never clearly cites the texts associated with the eschatological pilgrimage.[17] Moreover, in

---

[15] Many scholars have noted that the saving benefits given to all believers in Rom. 1 – 8 are jeopardized if God is not faithful to his original word to ethnic Israel: 'If God has not fulfilled his promises made to Israel, then what basis has the Jewish-Gentile church for believing that the promises will be fulfilled for them?' (Munck 1967: 35).

[16] E.g. Sanders 1983: 195. Commentators include Dunn (1988: 655) and Moo (2018: 702, n. 625). Some suggest that this eschatological pilgrimage theme is what motivated Paul's collection of an offering from the Gentiles for the Jerusalem church (cf. Isa. 60:1–7).

[17] Donaldson 1993: 91–92. He also suggests that an inversion of the order would actually be an abandonment of the tradition, in which 'the salvation of the Gentiles follows the redemption of Israel as a matter not simply of sequence but of *consequence*' (ibid.; emphasis original). Seifrid also pushes back against those who see a reversal of the pilgrimage theme and suggests instead that Paul sees Israel's restoration in the risen Christ to whom the Gentiles are now coming (2007: 673).

our view, *interpreters should not confuse the current hardening of Israel in God's plan with a reversal of their priority in salvation.*[18] The salvation of the remnant demonstrates that the Jews are still prior. And Paul further reiterates the priority of the Jews in salvation when he warns Gentile believers of pride in 11:17–24. One point of his famous olive tree analogy is to show the Gentiles that their salvation is unnatural, whereas the salvation of the Jews is natural.[19] Paul concludes this passage with a lesser to greater argument, based on the priority of the Jews in salvation:

> After all, if you were cut out of an olive tree that is wild by nature, and contrary to nature were grafted into a cultivated olive tree, how much more readily will these, the natural branches, be grafted into their own olive tree!'
> (Rom. 11:24)

Romans 11 continues to affirm the priority of the Jews in God's saving plan.

We now begin to see how these chapters fit into the overall argument of Romans. Part of the thesis of this long and complex letter is that the gospel is 'the power of God that brings salvation to everyone who believes: *first to the Jew*, then to the Gentile' (Rom. 1:16). But outside his brief mention of Jewish advantage in 3:3, Romans 9 – 11 is the only place in the letter where Paul explains at length the priority of the Jews in salvation. Thus, Romans 9 – 11 is not an appendix to Romans 1 – 8 but an integral part of Paul's theological argument.[20] The story of Israel is a story of God's

---

[18] E.g. Beale and Gladd (2014) suggest that Paul affirms a 'Jew first, then Greek' pattern in the beginning of the spread of the gospel, which follows the typical OT pattern (e.g. Isa. 49:5–6); but then he discloses the mystery (from Deut. 27 – 31) that there will be a 'Gentile first, then Jew' pattern for the majority of the church age (88–91, 97–98). But their discussion seems to assume that 'first' in Rom. 1:16 means only 'prior in time', whereas we think it refers to Israel's priority as the original possessors of God's saving promises in Scripture (Rom. 3:1–2; 9:4–5). So Cranfield, who says that Rom. 9 – 11 demonstrates we cannot explain 'first' in Rom. 1:16 as merely 'the historical fact that the gospel was preached to the Gentiles' (1975: 91). Paul consistently argues for a 'Jew first' pattern in Romans.

[19] Some argue that the temptation for Gentile believers in Rome to boast over unbelieving Jews is one of the driving factors in this section if not the entire letter (e.g. Wright 1991: 234). This boasting was a significant problem addressed in Rom. 11, but it has a limited role in explaining all of Rom. 9 – 11, which is concerned more with the faithfulness of God.

[20] Most scholars today would agree with this statement, against the older view in both English and German scholarship (on English scholarship, see Reasoner 2010: 76–78; on German scholarship, see Stenschke 2010: 224–225). Dodd is probably the most colourful example, who says that these chapters 'can be read and understood independently, and equally

faithfulness to his Word, which entails his faithfulness to his people, 'to the Jew first, and also to the Greek' (Rom. 1:16; our tr.).

The content of Paul's summary (Rom. 9 – 11)

Most commentators see three steps in Paul's argument (9:6–29; 9:30 – 10:21; 11:1–32), framed by an introductory lament (9:1–5) and a concluding doxology (11:33–36).[21] These three steps roughly correspond to Israel's past, present and future. The focus of the story is actually on the present state of Israel, for this part of the story spans all three steps in Paul's argument (9:24–11:10; see Table 5.1). Paul shows that even Israel's present state of unbelief in the gospel corresponds to what God has done in the past. God's Word has not failed, because Israel's identity has never fundamentally rested upon ethnic descent but upon the merciful call of God. In the present God is mercifully calling Gentiles to believe but only a remnant of Jews. The irony of this present situation fulfils the prophecy that God would place Christ as a stumbling stone and harden ethnic Israel. However, God has not rejected his people! Rather, their stumbling is the means by which God is saving the Gentiles and will eventually save

Table 5.1 The story of Israel in Romans 9 – 11

Paul's arguments	God's Word has not failed (9:6–29)	God has placed Christ as a stumbling stone (9:30 – 10:21)	God has not rejected his people (11:1–32)
Plotline of Israel's story	Israel's past → (9:6–23)	Israel's present → (9:24 – 11:10)	Israel's future (11:11–32)

without them the epistle could be read through without any sense of a gap in the sequence of thought' (!) (Dodd 1932. Still, we must be wary of overcorrection. There is truth in Käsemann's observation that 'Apart from ch. 16, no part of the epistle is so self-contained as this' (1980: 253). While every paragraph before Rom. 9:1 has a conjunction or inferential particle continuing the argument of the letter, Rom. 9:1 begins a fresh argument.

[21] E.g. Dunn 1988 and Longenecker 2016. The ancient chapter divisions (*kephalaia*) also divide the text in this way. Fitzmyer's outline is similar, except that he includes the doxology as a part of 11:1–32 (1993). Moo and Schreiner see 11:1–10 as either a transitional summary of the previous argument (Moo 2018) or as a part of the previous argument (Schreiner 2018). But even though 11:1–10 summarizes points made in 9:24–32 and 9:30 – 10:21 we think that Paul's question in 11:1 ('I ask then: did God reject his people?') opens a new stage in his argument.

the Jews as well. It is the means by which he will eventually show mercy to all.

Israel's past (Rom. 9:6–23)

Paul begins his argument for God's faithfulness by demonstrating that, according to Scripture itself, 'Israel' was never strictly a category of ethnicity but refers to the people who have been called into existence by the will of God.[22] Israel's current rejection of Jesus Christ does not mean that the Word of God has fallen, precisely because 'not all who are descended from Israel are Israel' (Rom. 9:6).

It is important to observe that in the very beginning of his argument in Romans 9 – 11 Paul uses the word 'Israel' with two different meanings. His first use – those 'from Israel' (*hoi ex Israēl*) – refers to the physical nation or what he elsewhere calls 'Israel according to the flesh' (1 Cor. 10:18; our tr.).[23] And his second use refers to 'God's children' (Rom. 9:8), those who inherit God's blessing to Abraham, or what we will call 'theological Israel'.[24] Paul's point here is not that ethnic Israel and theological Israel are mutually exclusive but rather that they are not coterminous (see Figure 5.1 on p. 126). Israel's story as recorded in the Bible demonstrates that from its very beginning 'Israel' was never simply identified by ethnic descent but rather by God's call.

The apostle proves his distinction between ethnic Israel and theological Israel with a straightforward reading of the Pentateuch narratives, beginning with Abraham. Not all of Abraham's children were the 'offspring' to whom the promises were made.[25] Rather, 'It is through Isaac that your offspring will be reckoned' (Rom. 9:7, quoting Gen. 21:12). He

---

[22] Cf. Gaventa: 'Paul is about to demonstrate, the entity known as "Israel" is not and never has been defined by birth but only by God's creation; it is not a biological but a theological category' (2010: 259).

[23] Jewett observes that in the LXX the word *Israēl* in the phrase *ex Israēl* always refers to the 'commonwealth of Israel' and not to the patriarch Jacob (2007: 574, n. 41).

[24] Many commentaries use the term 'true Israel'. It is notable that the church fathers tended to connect Romans 9 – 11 with Paul's internal/external Jew dichotomy in 2:17–29 (Reasoner 2010: 79).

[25] In the argument of Rom. 9:7–8, *sperma* ('offspring' or 'descendants') refers to theological Israel in 9:7b and 9:8, the narrower category. Thus, we think it likely that *sperma* indicates the narrower category of theological Israel in 9:7a as well, making it the predicate of the sentence ('not all of Abraham's children are his true descendants', NRSVA; so Moo 2018: 595, n. 133). Most commentaries however take *sperma* in 9:7a as the subject or broader category of physical Israel (noted by Jewett [2007: 575]; so NIVUK). This would not change the argument, but would mean that Paul uses *sperma* in two different senses in 9:7–8 (so Piper 1993: 68, n. 47).

is thinking specifically of Ishmael here, since this divine word came to Abraham while he was upset about his son Ishmael's being sent away. God tells Abraham that his offspring will come through Isaac, not Ishmael. Both were Abraham's ethnic descendants but God chose only the family of Isaac to be his 'offspring' (theological Israel). Paul explains, 'In other words, it is not the children by physical descent who are God's children, but it is the children of the promise who are regarded as Abraham's offspring' (Rom. 9:8). Again he distinguishes between ethnic Israel, 'the children by physical descent', and theological Israel, 'God's children'. Being the 'offspring' of Abraham was never simply a matter of physical descent.

Paul argues next that the same distinction is seen in the birth of Jacob and Esau, perhaps anticipating someone who would think that Ishmael was distinguished from Isaac because his mother was the slave Hagar.[26] But Paul points out that God made such a distinction even among those born of the same mother and father, Rebecca and Isaac, in one act of conception (Rom. 9:10). The prophetic promise to Rebecca was that 'The older will serve the younger' (Rom. 9:12, quoting Gen. 25:23), a promise confirmed by the sharp distinction between Jacob's and Esau's descendants, as it was written in Malachi: 'Jacob I loved, but Esau I hated' (Rom. 9:13).[27] Paul observes that this distinction between Jacob and Esau did not follow from their physical descent or their moral actions. The divine word was spoken 'before the twins were born or had done anything good or bad' (Rom. 9:11). It is interesting that he brings moral action into what has so far been an argument about ethnicity. Paul views the two as bound together, originating from humanity or 'flesh'.[28] Fleshly considerations such as ethnicity and moral actions are not the means by which 'God's purpose in election' stands (Rom. 9:11). It is 'not by works' (Rom. 9:12)! What, then, is the basis upon which God chooses his children, theological Israel?

Paul's answer is that it is 'by him who calls' (Rom. 9:12). In other words, *'Israel' is fundamentally defined as those who have been called into existence*

---

[26] So Moo 2018: 599.

[27] Paul's citation has different word order from the LXX and MT ('Jacob I loved' instead of 'I loved Jacob'). Perhaps he purposely changed the order in order to sharpen the antithesis between Jacob and Esau (Steyn 2015: 52). Alternatively, Thielman argues that it is to add force to his argument, stressing 'the surprising nature of God's selection of Jacob when according to cultural expectation and even legal right (see Deut. 21:15–17) Esau deserved God's blessing' (1994: 174, n. 13).

[28] Note that the NIVUK's 'children by physical descent' in Rom. 9:8 is literally 'children of flesh' (*tekna tou theou*).

by God. The verb 'to call' (*kaleō*) is important in the argument of Romans 9:6–29 and means 'to choose for receipt of a special benefit or experience'.[29] It occurs first in Paul's opening quotation of Gen. 21:12: 'It is through Isaac that your offspring will be reckoned [literally, "called", *klēthēsetai*]' (Rom. 9:7). This opening quotation gives Paul's argument a vocabulary, which he then applies to God's choice of Isaac as standing 'not by works but by him he calls' (9:12) and later to God's calling of people from both the Jews and the Gentiles (9:24).[30]

In Pauline theology 'calling' is a way of describing God's elective work in conversion.[31] He is 'the one who called' believers (Gal. 1:6, 15; cf. Rom. 8:30); believers are those 'called to be his holy people' (Rom. 1:7) or 'called . . . into fellowship with his Son' (1 Cor. 1:9). This work of calling is the fulfilment of 'God's purpose in election' (Rom. 9:11) and of the divine promise. Isaac was called as the offspring of Abraham not simply because he was Abraham's fleshly descendant but because *God* had promised that he would be born: 'At the appointed time I will return, and Sarah will have a son' (Rom. 9:9, quoting Gen. 18:14). Further, God's work of calling is a kind of birth or new creation. Paul speaks of the God of Abraham as 'the God who gives life to the dead and *calls* into being things that were not' (Rom. 4:17).[32] God *calls* those designated 'not my people' to become 'my people' (Rom. 9:25). Thus, when Paul identifies 'Israel' as the people *called* by God, he means the people *called into existence* by the will and promise of God.[33] The basis upon which 'Israel' stands is neither ethnic descent nor moral effort, but God himself.

Paul appeals to the exodus narratives to buttress this theological basis for 'Israel'. He anticipates a false conclusion from his argument that God calls his people apart from ethnic or moral consideration. 'What then

---

[29] BDAG, s.v. '*kaleō*', meaning 4. The verb is used in this way by Paul, Peter, the author of Hebrews and in Jesus' teaching; e.g. 'I have not come to call [*kalesai*] the righteous, but sinners to repentance' (Luke 5:32).

[30] Cf. *kaleō* in Paul's quotations of Hos. 1:10 and 2:23, which are discussed below.

[31] Ridderbos speaks of 'calling' in Pauline theology as the 'effectual calling by the gospel through which God's electing grace is realized, not on the ground of human works or merit, but of his antecedent saving purpose (2 Thess. 2:13ff.; 2 Tim. 1:9; Rom. 8:29ff.; 9:12)' (1975: 235–237).

[32] We should observe that Paul is referring to the birth of *Isaac*, the offspring of Abraham, in Rom. 4:17.

[33] Ridderbos observes that although Paul derives the term 'calling' from the OT, 'He gives this word a pregnant significance . . . by understanding it of the word of divine power by which God calls into being the things that do not exist and by which he works what he commands (Rom. 4:17; 9:11, 25; 1 Thess. 5:24)' (1975: 235).

shall we say? Is God unjust? Not at all!' (Rom. 9:14). The objection likely comes from the perspective of a Jewish person who has not believed in Christ since it is so similar to the Jewish objection mentioned in Romans 3:5.[34] Is it unjust for God to call people apart from ethnic or moral consideration? Paul observes in response that this is exactly what God said to Moses:

I will have mercy on whom I have mercy,
   and I will have compassion on whom I have compassion.
(Rom. 9:15)

Further, God was even behind the raising up and hardening of Pharaoh, the enemy of God's people (9:17).[35] Paul concludes from the story of the exodus that 'God has mercy on whom he wants to have mercy, and he hardens whom he wants to harden' (Rom. 9:18).

In sum, the story of Israel's past according to Paul demonstrates that God himself has chosen his people. Here Paul demonstrates the theological basis of Abraham's 'offspring'. Israel were never designated the children of God because of ethnic descent or moral prowess but because of God's merciful call.

Paul's point not only clarifies the theological grounds of Israel's existence in the past but also makes a distinction between ethnic Israel and the children of God in the present.[36] We say this because the present situation of Israel's unbelief is the context which generates Paul's argument that God's Word has not failed. Why has it not failed? 'For not all who are descended from Israel are Israel' (Rom. 9:6). In other words, the distinction between ethnic progeny of Abraham and the children of God typifies what God is doing in the present. Just as God made a distinction among the sons of Abraham and the sons of Isaac, so he is now making a distinction among the descendants of Jacob/Israel. Not all of those who belong to the ethnic nation of Israel belong to theological Israel.

---

34 Contra Wright's recent argument that this conclusion would come from a Gentile shocked to hear of the doctrine of election in Israel's story (2013: 1186), although he is correct to observe that much of Rom. 9:6–23 is standard Jewish theology (ibid. 1184–1187).

35 The apostle clearly draws the hardening theme in Rom. 9:18 from the exodus narratives even though it is not in his quotation of Exod. 9:16 (so Wagner 2002: 54).

36 So Wright 2013: 1184, n. 525; contra several prominent NT scholars who have recently argued that Paul does not make a division between ethnic Israel and true Israel in this passage (Barclay 2015: 528; Gaventa 2010: 259–261; Eastman 2010: 382–383).

Paul also views the exodus narratives as a type of the present situation: just as God had mercy on Israel and hardened Pharaoh, so in the present time he is having mercy on believers in Christ and hardening unbelieving Israel. This may sound outrageous to an unbelieving Jew, but the exodus teaches that 'God has mercy on whom he wants to have mercy, and he hardens whom he wants to harden' (Rom. 9:18).[37]

We can picture Paul's opening argument as a Venn diagram that pulls apart the strict correspondence between ethnic and theological Israel (see Figure 5.1). Such a strict correspondence, Paul argues, was never Israel's story in the past, just as it is not their story in the present. Thus, the present situation in which many Jews have rejected the proclamation of the gospel does not mean that God has been unfaithful to his Word or his people.

Figure 5.1 **'Israel' in the past**

Israel's present (Rom. 9:24 – 11:10)

Paul outlines the present stage of Israel's story as a tragic irony anticipated by Moses and the prophets: the Gentiles have been called into existence by the will of God, whereas ethnic Israel, apart from a remnant, have been hardened. Or, to use his later image of the olive tree, the Gentiles have been grafted into theological Israel, but the majority of ethnic Israel have been cut off the tree. Romans 9:24 takes the first step in this direction when Paul says God has 'called' us 'not only from the Jews but also from the Gentiles'. Up to this point Paul's distinction between ethnic and

---

[37] Barclay is formally correct that Paul never *explicitly* compares unbelieving Israel to Ishmael, Esau or Pharaoh (2015: 528). But such a comparison is implied in the fact that Paul grounds his distinction between physical Israel and theological Israel in the distinctions found within the patriarchal and exodus narratives. It is also confirmed by his later explicit discussion about the hardening of Israel (Rom. 11:7–10).

theological Israel has simply made the point that not all of ethnic Israel will necessarily be saved. But in Romans 9:24 he clarifies that God has 'called' not only some of the Jews but also some of the Gentiles to be part of theological Israel (see Figure 5.2 on p. 137).

Those who interpret Paul's statement 'all Israel will be saved' (Rom. 11:26) as speaking about a future salvation of ethnic Israel will often argue that the word 'Israel' always refers to ethnic Israel in Romans 9 - 11.[38] Even in Romans 9:6, where Paul uses the word 'Israel' in two ways, first to refer to the ethnic nation and second to refer to true Israel, or what we have called 'theological Israel', it is argued that this second use refers only to *Jewish* Christians.[39] However, while it is true that the immediate referent of theological 'Israel' in 9:6b is those who have been 'called' from the Jews, there are weighty reasons to understand this category of theological Israel, which Paul introduces in 9:6b, as a category that also includes believing Gentiles. First, and most important, in Romans 9:24–26 Paul uses the verb 'call' three times to describe the salvation of the Gentiles. This is the same verb he has used to speak of what fundamentally identifies theological 'Israel' (Rom. 9:6b): they are the people 'called' by God (cf. Rom. 9:7, 12). It seems unlikely that if we were to ask Paul 'Does this theological Israel you are talking about include believing Gentiles?' he would answer 'no' in the light of what he says in 9:24–26. Second, in the immediate context of 'Israel' in Romans 9:6b, Paul identifies this theological Israel as 'Abraham's offspring' (9:7–8), 'God's children' (9:8) and the 'children of promise' (9:8), supporting his argument by appealing to the Isaac and Ishmael narratives in Genesis 16 - 21. This is the same argument he makes

---

[38] E.g. Fitzmyer says that to understand 'all Israel' in Rom. 11:26 as spiritual Israel 'goes against the meaning of *Israël* in the rest of Romans' (1993: 624). The first edition of Moo's commentary says that 'Paul has used the term "Israel" ten times so far in Rom. 9-11, and each refers to ethnic Israel' (1996: 721). This sentence also occurs in the second edition, but interestingly he has added a caveat in parentheses: '(with the possible exception of one occurrence in 9:6)' (2018: 736).

[39] E.g. Fitzmyer considers whether 'Israel' in Rom. 9:6b could include Gentiles in 'the Israel of God' as Gal. 6:16 does; but concludes instead that it 'refers to Jewish Christians, to those of ethnic Israel who have put faith in Christ' (1993: 560). Schreiner argues that, although seeing 'Israel' in 9:6b as a reference to Jews and Gentiles harmonizes with Paul's theology, here the term 'Israel' is 'restricted to ethnic Jews who believe in Jesus as Messiah' (2018: 482–483). Moo argues this position in the first edition of his commentary: 'Israel' in Rom. 9:6b 'denotes a smaller, spiritual body *within* ethnic Israel' that does not include Gentiles in this context (1996: 547; emphasis original). But in his second edition he has changed to a view that seems similar to our own: '[Paul's] point here is simply to claim that spiritual Israel is not the same as biological Israel. Just who "populates" that spiritual Israel is not yet revealed and will become evident as Paul's argument unfolds' (2018: 595).

in Galatians with reference to believing Gentiles: they are Abraham's offspring (Gal. 3:29), God's children (Gal. 3:26) and the children of promise (Gal. 4:28), points that he supports by appealing to the Isaac and Ishmael narratives in Genesis 16 – 21 (Gal. 4:21–31). Third, as is often acknowledged, it is common for Paul to identify believing Gentiles as true or theological Israel both inside and outside his letter to the Romans: believing Gentiles are inward Jews who have been circumcised by the Spirit (Rom. 2:26–29; Phil. 3:3), called to be God's people (Rom. 9:24–26) and are 'fellow citizens with God's people and also members of his household' (Eph. 2:19).[40] Fourth, although this point is debated, it is likely that Paul explicitly includes believing Gentiles as part of the 'Israel of God' in Galatians 6:16.[41] Finally, we suggest that to say that 'Israel' in Romans 9:6b includes only ethnic Jews, albeit believing ethnic Jews, undermines the very point the apostle is trying to make in this verse – that 'Israel' is *not* defined by physical descent but by God's own promise and call (see 9:8). Therefore, his second use of 'Israel' in Romans 9:6 is by its definition not a reference to 'ethnic Israel' but to 'theological Israel', those whom *God has called* 'not only from the Jews but also from the Gentiles' (Rom. 9:24).[42]

Paul sees an anticipation of this call of the Gentiles in Hosea's prophecies that the northern kingdom of Israel that has been cast off in divorce will one day again be his people:

'I will call them "my people" who are not my people;
and I will call her "my loved one" who is not my loved one,'

and,

'In the very place where it was said to them,
"You are not my people,"
there they will be called "children of the living God."'
(Rom. 9:25–26)

---

[40] Filtvedt also adds the interesting point that Paul's phrase 'Israel according to the flesh' in 1 Cor. 10:18 implies an existence of an 'Israel according to the Spirit' (2016: 128).

[41] For a recent argument in favour of this view, see Filtvedt 2016. He concludes that '[t]he strongest argument for the view that non-Jews are included in God's Israel seems to be the observation that the recipients of the letter have not been sufficiently prepared for the introduction of an exclusively Jewish Israel in 6.16. The location of 6.16 within the flow of Paul's argument suggests that Paul is reiterating a point already made' (ibid. 138).

[42] One of the authors of this book disagrees with this paragraph and sees the second 'Israel' in Rom. 9:6b as a reference only to believing, ethnic Jews. He is, of course, in the esteemed company of Fitzmyer and Schreiner.

Hosea describes a divorce in which the covenant people become a people not in covenant with God.[43] Then he envisions another reversal in the future in which the people not in covenant with God will be his people.[44] This idea that God will call a people not in covenant with him (i.e. Gentiles) is what Paul sees as a prophecy of God's current work among the Gentiles.

The verb 'call' is important for Paul in his appeal to Hosea. His quotation of Hosea 1:10 follows the Greek translation ('they will be called') rather than the Hebrew ('it will be said to him'). And his quotation of Hosea 2:23 also uses the verb 'I will call', which is not found in either the MT or LXX (both have 'I will say'). His use of this verb was surely purposeful, linked to his initial citation of Genesis 21:12, and describing God's creative work of calling his people into being. If theological 'Israel' is defined as the people who have been called by God (9:7, 11), then we must conclude that Gentiles are now a part of this theological people, the 'children of the living God'.

Conversely (de),[45] Isaiah 'cries out' in prophecy that only a remnant of ethnic Israel, only a small remaining portion of Abraham's numerous descendants, will be saved:

Though the number of the Israelites be like the sand by the sea,
only the remnant will be saved.
(Rom. 9:27, quoting Isa. 10:22)

Unless the Lord Almighty
    had left us descendants,
we would have become like Sodom,
    we would have been like Gomorrah.
(Rom. 9:29, quoting Isa. 1:9)

Isaiah's prophecy refers to the small number of survivors after the exile who will trust in the Lord and return to their God (cf. Isa. 10:20–21). The

---

[43] The covenant formula 'my people' is reversed to 'not my people' (observed by Wagner 2002: 86–87).

[44] The importance for Paul of Hosea's use of the covenant formula may be seen in his reversal of the two halves of the verse so that his citation emphasizes 'my people' (Käsemann 1980: 274; so Steyn 2015: 55; although Seifrid sees an omission rather than reversal [2007: 647]).

[45] We are taking de in Rom. 9:27 as an adversative particle drawing a contrast between the Gentiles and Israel in Rom. 9:24–29 (so Cranfield 1979: 501). Cf. the contrast between Gentiles and Israel in 10:20–21.

survival of the remnant contains an element of hope inasmuch as it demonstrates that God has not totally rejected his people, an element Paul will highlight in Romans 11:1–10.[46] But Isaiah's remnant theme is also a prophecy of God's judgment of Israel in that the remnant is contrasted with Israel's numerous descendants. Israel of old was almost like Sodom and Gomorrah in being annihilated by God. And Paul sees in Israel's past a foreshadowing of the current situation. While it is true that God is calling some from the Jews, it is only a remnant. The majority of physical Israel have not been saved.

Thus, the present state of Israel's history is a tragic irony. Some of the Gentiles have been called to be God's people, but the majority of Israel have not. This situation was anticipated in Scripture, and thus the Word of God has not fallen. But Paul still finds it to be deeply ironic, and captures this irony with the image of a race or pursuit: '[T]he Gentiles, who did not pursue righteousness, have obtained it, a righteousness that is by faith; but the people of Israel, who pursued the law as the way of righteousness, have not attained their goal' (Rom. 9:30–31). The Gentiles have obtained what they were not pursuing but Israel have failed to obtain what they were pursuing (cf. 11:7). How could this have happened? Paul's answer is that Israel have pursued the law and God himself in the wrong way.

He spells out this misguided pursuit in the parallel arguments of Romans 9:30–33 and 10:1–4.[47] Israel pursued the law and its righteous-ness,[48] but they pursued it in the wrong way, 'not by faith but as if it were by works' (Rom. 9:32). Similarly, Paul testifies that 'they are zealous for God, but their zeal is not based on knowledge' (Rom. 10:2). In both cases he describes a misguided, misinformed pursuit. Israel were running hard after the law and God but running in the wrong direction. Paul explains more specifically in both arguments that Israel were running in the

---

[46] This theme of hope is particularly highlighted by Wagner, but to the exclusion of judgment (2002: 106–110). In our view he imports too much of Rom. 11 into Rom. 9.

[47] We are dependent on Ortlund's observation of the parallel nature of these two arguments: 'both passages explain that despite the presence of a truly laudable element (9.31a; 10.2a), Israel have failed to attain their goal (9.31b; 10.2b–3) due to undertaking it in the wrong way (9.32a; 10.2b–3) and being blind to Christ (9.32b–33; 10.4)' (2012: 125).

[48] Paul literally says that Israel pursued 'the law of righteousness' and did not obtain the 'law' (Rom. 9:31). Some will argue that Paul does not mean Israel was pursuing righteousness by the law, because they were pursuing the law, not righteousness (e.g. Sanders 2015: 678). But 'law of righteousness' likely means something like 'the law that leads to righteousness', so that to pursue the law is to pursue its righteousness (cf. Fitzmyer: 'By this phrase Paul undoubtedly means a law that would lead Israel to uprightness' [1993: 578]).

direction of their works rather than in the direction of Christ. They pursued the law 'as if it were by works' (Rom. 9:32). And their zeal for God was misinformed because 'they did not know the righteousness of God and sought to establish their own' (Rom. 10:3). Although advocates of the new perspective on Paul have argued that Second Temple Judaism was not legalistic in any sense, Paul himself characterizes Israel's misguided pursuit as works-righteousness ('as if it were by works') or self-righteousness ('sought to establish their own [righteousness]').[49] He draws a contrast between 'the righteousness that is by the law', which calls for doing (Rom. 10:5), and 'the righteousness that is by faith', which calls for believing in Christ (10:6–9).[50] Israel's pursuit of the law and zeal for God in the wrong direction ironically led them away from righteousness and salvation because it led them away from Christ.[51]

Christ, then, is at the heart of the irony of the present stage of Israel's history. Paul argues that Israel have 'stumbled over the "stumbling stone"' (Rom. 9:32), drawing the language of his argument from Isaiah:

See, I lay in Zion a stone that causes people to stumble
    and a rock that makes them fall,
    and the one who believes in him will never be put to shame.
(Rom. 9:33, quoting Isa. 28:16 and 8:14)

Paul combines two texts from Isaiah, identifying Christ as both the stone who is the Lord himself (8:14) and the stone whom the Lord will lay in Zion (28:16). These texts, written during the crisis of the Assyrian invasion, called upon Israel to trust in the stone for salvation (28:16; cf. 8:12–13, 17) but also warned that the stone would be a cause of stumbling (8:14). Paul argues that God has now done what he said he would do by laying Christ

---

[49] Most new-perspective scholars would respond that Paul is not referring to moral striving to keep the law but rather views the law primarily in terms of works such as circumcision that establish a national righteousness for Jews only (e.g. Dunn 1988: 593, 596). Sanders though argues that Paul is simply using arguments that he did not really believe in order to establish a conclusion he had come to on other grounds (2015: 677–680).

[50] This contrast is clearly anticipated in the two kinds of righteousness described in Rom. 10:3. Thus, it is most unlikely that Paul quotes from Lev. 18:5 to refer to the righteousness of faith and sees no contrast between two different conceptions of righteousness (contra Hays 1989: 76).

[51] Cf. Ortlund's careful study and conclusion that 'Paul's articulation of Israel's fault in 9.30–10.3 is concerned not with their failure to discharge the law but with their success . . . Israel's fault is bound up with their pursuit of (not disdain for) the law and their zeal for (not contempt of) God' (2012: 135; emphasis original).

as a cornerstone of stumbling and salvation.[52] Israel, misguided in their pursuit of the law, have now stumbled over this stone. Misinformed in their zeal for God, 'they did not submit to God's righteousness' in Christ, 'the culmination of the law so that there may be righteousness for everyone who believes' (Rom. 10:3–4).

We can see one aspect of what Paul means in describing Christ as the 'culmination of the law' in his use of the language of Deuteronomy 30:12 and verse 14 to describe the message concerning faith that he proclaims (Rom. 10:6–8).[53] This is one of the oddest citations in his letters, because on its surface it appears to support a pursuit of the law by works, exactly what he has just said was Israel's misstep:

> Now what I am commanding you today is not too difficult for you or beyond your reach. It is not up in heaven, so that you have to ask, 'Who will ascend into heaven to get it and proclaim it to us so that we may obey it?' Nor is it beyond the sea, so that you have to ask, 'Who will cross the sea to get it and proclaim it to us so that we may obey it?' No, the word is very near you; it is in your mouth and in your heart so that you may obey it.
> (Deut. 30:11–14)

Hays justly observes that 'It would not be easy to find another text in the Old Testament that looks less promising for Paul's purposes.'[54] But Paul is probably not aiming to give a straightforward interpretation of these verses, for he omits the verb 'to obey', which occurs three times in the MT and four times in the LXX of this passage. He also introduces the quotation with 'the righteousness that is by faith says' rather than 'as it is written', and begins it with the words of Deuteronomy 9:4 ('do not say in your heart'), a passage that warns Israel of trusting in their own righteousness:

---

[52] Paul makes it clear in Rom. 10:11 that he interprets the 'stone' in Isa. 8:14 or 28:16 as a reference to Christ. It is unlikely that he intends the stone to be a reference to both the law and Christ (*pace* Wright 2013: 1178–1179), although Wright is correct that conceptually in Paul's argument a rejection of Christ is also a rejection of the law that pointed to him (ibid. 1179). The origin of Paul's messianic-stone exegesis most likely goes back to Jesus' own exegesis of 'the stone the builders rejected' in Ps. 118:22.

[53] '[H]ere Paul makes clear what he means by describing Christ as the goal of the law' (Seifrid 2007: 654). Seifrid sees Paul's emphasizing his accessibility (ibid. 658).

[54] Hays 1989: 79. Watson observes that 'The key terms in the Leviticus text [Lev. 18:5] – "doing" and "life" – are both present in Deut. 30. The nearness of the word means that "you can do it"' (2016: 338).

Do not say in your heart, 'Who will ascend into heaven?' (that is, to bring Christ down) or 'Who will descend into the deep?' (that is, to bring Christ up from the dead). But what does it say? 'The word is near you; it is in your mouth and in your heart,' that is, the message concerning faith that we proclaim: if you declare with your mouth, 'Jesus is Lord,' and believe in your heart that God raised him from the dead, you will be saved.
(Rom. 10:6–9)

What is Paul doing here? It seems he is borrowing Moses' language about the law's accessibility and applying it to the accessibility of Christ himself, the culmination of the law.[55] In other words, he views the nearness of Israel's law in the old covenant as a foreshadowing of the nearness of Christ and the gospel in the new covenant.[56] Just as the law came down the mountain from God, so Christ has already come down from God.[57] And just as God delivered his people through the sea, so Christ has been delivered from death in his resurrection. Paul's point is that Christ has come near in the gospel he is now proclaiming about faith – that God will save anyone who believes he has raised Jesus from the dead and confesses that Jesus is Lord (cf. Rom. 10:13). And once again the language of Scripture has given Paul's argument a vocabulary, shaping the apostle's language about nearness of the 'word about Christ' (10:17; cf. 10:8) and the role of the 'mouth' and 'heart' in offering the proper response of faith in the risen Christ (Rom. 10:9–10). This is the response the Gentiles have offered, but that Israel have failed to give (10:16).

As ironic and surprising as the present situation may seem, Paul insists that it was made known to Israel in the law and prophets:

First, Moses says,

> 'I will make you envious by those who are not a nation;
> I will make you angry by a nation that has no understanding.'

---

[55] Baruch similarly borrows the language of Deut. 30:12–13 to speak of wisdom (*Bar.* 3.29–30).

[56] Deut. 30:10–12 comes on the heels of the promise of the new covenant that after exile God will circumcise the hearts of his people who turn to him.

[57] Most commentators see a reference to the incarnation (e.g. Schreiner 2018: 545), although Dunn suggests a reference to the exaltation (1988: 605).

And Isaiah boldly says,

> 'I was found by those who did not seek me;
>   I revealed myself to those who did not ask for me.'

But concerning Israel he says,

> 'All day long I have held out my hands
>   to a disobedient and obstinate people.'
> (Rom. 10:19–21, quoting Deut. 32:21 and Isa. 65:1–2)

Paul quotes from the Song of Moses at the end of Deuteronomy and from the end of Isaiah.[58] Scholars have rightly puzzled at the division Paul makes between Gentiles and Jews in two consecutive verses of Isaiah 65. In the first verse he follows the same hermeneutic we saw in his quotations of Hosea (Rom. 9:25–26) by seeing in God's promise to save disobedient Israel of old (Isa. 65:1) an anticipation of the current salvation of dis- obedient Gentiles.[59] And yet in the next verse he sees in ancient Israel's persistent disobedience a foreshadowing of *the Jews'* current rejection of the gospel. How can Isaiah 65:1–2 typify both believing Gentiles and unbelieving Jews? Because Paul views both Gentiles and Jews in the same situation – confined to disobedience in order that they may be shown mercy (cf. Rom. 3:23; 11:30–32). The Gentiles are being shown mercy now ('I was found by those who did not seek me'), but God is also holding out his hands to 'a disobedient and obstinate people', Israel. This means that even in his negative depiction of the disobedient nation of Israel Paul has hope for their salvation.

In fact, in Romans 11 Paul emphatically refuses to conclude from the current situation that God has rejected Israel: '[D]id God reject his people? By no means!' (Rom. 11:1). *It is crucial to see that Paul's distinction between ethnic Israel and theological Israel in Romans 9:6 does not mean that God has rejected ethnic Israel.* It is striking that he continues to refer to the ethnic nation as 'God's people': 'God did not reject his people, whom he

---

[58] Wagner finds a number of verbal and conceptual links between these two passages, not least Israel's idolatry (Deut. 32:16–17; Isa. 65:3; 2002: 202–203). We will discuss Paul's quotation from the Song of Moses below since the jealousy motif becomes important in Rom. 11:11–16.

[59] Wagner observes that Paul typically finds Gentiles in prophecies about Israel by locating them in negative descriptions of disobedient Israel (ibid. 212).

foreknew' (Rom. 11:1).[60] Paul continues to affirm that the nation as a whole is God's covenant people whom he has corporately foreknown or chosen.[61] This does not mean that he views all of ethnic Israel in the present time as saved, because he prays for their salvation (10:1) and views them as disobedient to the gospel (10:16). But it does mean that God has certainly not rejected ethnic Israel corporately as his people. Paul argues this point emphatically in Romans 11, holding forth himself and the rest of the Jewish remnant as his primary piece of evidence.

Paul's remnant theology in Romans 9 – 11 highlights both God's judgment upon ethnic Israel (9:27–29) and his commitment to their future salvation (11:1–6).[62] His first discussion of the Jewish remnant appeals to Isaiah 1:9 and 10:22, but in Romans 11:1–6 he leans on Elijah's despair that he was the only one left when Israel had rejected the Lord for the worship of Baal:

> Don't you know what Scripture says in the passage about Elijah – how he appealed to God against Israel: 'Lord, they have killed your prophets and torn down your altars; I am the only one left [*hypeleiphthēn*], and they are trying to kill me'? And what was God's answer to him? 'I have reserved [*katelipon*] for myself seven thousand who have not bowed the knee to Baal.'
> (Rom. 11:2–4, quoting 1 Kgs 19:10, 18)

Paul concludes with the language of Scripture: 'So too, at the present time there is a remnant [*leimma*] chosen by grace' (Rom. 11:5). His reasoning is typological, finding in Elijah's situation a foreshadowing of the current situation.[63] Israel, in their rejection of Christ, have once again rejected

---

[60] Similarly, Paul uses the term 'offspring of Abraham' (*sperma Abraam*) with reference to theological Israel or those whom God calls to be his children in Rom. 9:7–8 (cf. Gal. 3:29), but continues to use the term to refer to himself as a physical 'descendant of Abraham' (*ek spermatos Abraam*) 'from the tribe of Benjamin' (Rom. 11:1).

[61] Thus, Paul has a concept of corporate foreknowledge or election of the nation that is distinguished from his understanding of individual foreknowledge or election for salvation (Moo 2018: 692–693; cf. Rom. 8:29).

[62] So Hafemann 1988: 49. This dual function of remnant theology is characteristic of the theme in the OT prophets (for a survey, see Longenecker 2016: 805–810).

[63] Such typological reasoning is also implied in his initial statement 'God did not reject his people, whom he foreknew' (Rom. 11:2), for it alludes to Israel's rejection of God in asking for a king (1 Sam. 12:22). When they realize what they have done and fear God's judgment, Samuel reassures the nation that God will not reject them for the sake of his own name. This same statement is also found in Ps. 94:14, which speaks of the Lord's discipline but not rejection of his people.

their God. But God has never rejected his people, for he has always kept for himself a remnant.

The remnant theme also reinforces the theological basis of God's people. The remnant consists of God's elect who have been 'chosen by grace' (Rom. 11:6).[64] They are those who have been called into existence by God, but not by their own moral worth: 'if by grace, then it cannot be based on works; if it were, grace would no longer be grace' (Rom. 11:5). Alternatively, the rest of the nation were 'hardened' (Rom. 11:7). Readers should feel the full weight of this passive verb 'hardened' and its implied divine agent:

[A]s it is written:

> 'God gave them a spirit of stupor,
>   eyes that could not see
>   and ears that could not hear,
> to this very day.'

And David says:

> 'May their table become a snare and a trap,
>   a stumbling-block and a retribution for them.
> May their eyes be darkened so they cannot see,
>   and their backs be bent for ever.'
> (Rom. 11:8–10)

Paul argues that both God and Christ are behind Israel's hardening. His first citation conflates Deuteronomy 29:4 with Isaiah 29:10, texts that speak of Israel's hard heart and God's judgment. His second citation appeals to Psalm 69:22–23, a psalm of David that the apostles often interpreted messianically.[65] Paul cites the verses in which David calls for retribution on his enemies. The tragic irony of Israel's hardening and the

---

[64] Note the connection in Greek between 'chosen' in Rom. 11:5 (*kat' eklogēn*) and 'elect' in 11:7 (*eklogē*).

[65] Cf. John 2:17 (quoting Ps. 69:9a), John 15:25 (quoting Ps. 69:4) and Rom. 15:3 (quoting Ps. 69:9b). The most relevant example relating to Rom. 11:9–10 is Acts 1:20, because the latter quotes from the same section about David's enemies (Ps. 69:25) and applies it to Judas, Jesus' betrayer. Dodd concludes that the apostles 'were aware of the psalm in its entirety as a source of *testimonia*' to the gospel (1953: 96).

Gentiles' salvation was neither unforeseen by God (Rom. 9:33) nor unintended by him (11:8). The hardening is God's doing, and yet hardening is not his final purpose for ethnic Israel.

In sum, Paul sees Christ and the message about faith at the heart of Israel's present situation. The irony is part of the identity of the stone himself, for he is both a cause of salvation and of stumbling. The Gentiles have obtained salvation because they have believed in him, and Israel have not because they have stumbled on him. Believing Gentiles have been included as part of theological Israel, along with the believing Jewish remnant, whereas the rest of Israel have been hardened (see Figure 5.2). The tragic irony of the present situation, however, was not unanticipated by God. In fact, he is the one behind it. He has been faithful to his Word in establishing a stone of salvation and stumbling in Zion, and even in hardening his people. One should not conclude from this that he has rejected the ethnic nation of Israel. The remnant points to the hope of salvation in the future, which Paul will explain as he delves into the 'mystery' of Israel's hardening in Romans 11:11–32.

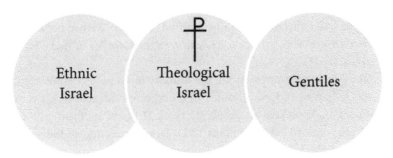

Figure 5.2 **'Israel' in the present**

Israel's future (Rom. 11:11–32)

God's final purpose for all of 'his people' according to Paul is to show them mercy. 'For God has bound everyone over to disobedience so that he may have mercy on them all' (Rom. 11:32). The apostle emphatically rejects the conclusion that God's hardening of Israel reflects his final purpose for the ethnic nation. '[D]id they stumble so as to fall beyond recovery? Not at all!' (11:11). Thus, however we interpret the meaning of the *crux interpretum* in 11:26 ('and in this way all Israel will be saved'), it seems certain that Paul upholds God's merciful purpose for both Gentiles and for ethnic Israel beyond the current remnant in some way. God's purpose is not the destruction of the nation, even though it may appear so at the present time.

Paul's explanation of Israel's future is an exercise in biblical theology. There is a sense in which the current situation of Israel's hardening and the salvation of the Gentiles is a 'mystery' that was not clearly revealed until Christ came (Rom. 11:25). But Paul also bases his hope for Israel's future squarely on the testimony of Scripture.[66] His first argument builds on the jealousy motif in the Song of Moses, the great prophecy about the future of Israel that would function as a witness against them after the exile. In Deuteronomy 32:21 Moses warns Israel that God will respond with a fitting recompense to their idolatry, their stirring him to jealousy with 'what is no god'. He will stir them to jealousy 'by those who are not a people', favouring a foreign nation and sending Israel into exile. Paul sees in this judgment a foreshadowing of Israel's current judgment and quotes Deuteronomy 32:21 to the effect that Israel should have known God would turn his favour to 'those who are not a nation' in order to make them envious (Rom. 10:19). Now he uses this logic of jealousy to argue that Israel have not fallen beyond recovery: 'Rather, because of their transgression, salvation has come to the Gentiles to make Israel envious' (11:11).

Thus, like the remnant motif, the jealousy motif both communicates God's judgment of Israel (Rom. 10:19) and reminds them of his commitment finally to save his people (11:11; cf. 11:14).[67] Paul focuses on the final purpose of God in Romans 11:11. Israel's rejection of the gospel has led to the salvation of the Gentiles with the ultimate purpose of stirring Israel to jealousy through the Gentiles who have been called to be God's people. Paul, under the influence of Deuteronomy 32:21, makes God's purpose his own as he preaches the gospel. He magnifies his preaching to the Gentiles in order to make his own people jealous and

---

[66] *Pace* Wright, who sees Paul 'out on his own' in Rom. 11 because 'There are no Jewish texts, in scripture or in the second-temple period, that address the question of what happens when the Messiah turns up and most of Israel rejects him' (2013: 1159–1160).

[67] Bell argues that the verb 'make envious' (*parazēloō*) means 'provoke to anger' in Rom. 10:19 but 'provoke to emulation' in 11:11 because the first passage uses it to speak of God's current judgment and the second passage of future salvation (1994: 39–41). But perhaps it is better to locate this difference in the function of the motif rather than the meaning of the verb 'provoke to envy'. Bell is certainly correct to observe that Paul speaks of God's stirring his people to jealousy both as judgment and as ultimate salvation.

save some of them (Rom. 11:13–14). In these verses Paul makes explicit
what was left implicit in his initial statement of the jealousy motif in
verse 11: God's final purpose of making Israel envious is that they might
be saved. So Paul labours in his ministry to the Gentiles 'in the hope that
I may somehow arouse my own people to envy and save some of them'
(Rom. 11:14).[68]

Moses' jealousy motif not only informs Paul's mission but has made
a deep imprint on his theological reasoning in this chapter. Paul sees a
causal relationship between the hardening of Israel, the salvation of the
Gentiles and the salvation of the Jews. Israel's transgression against God
'means [salvific] riches for the world' (Rom. 11:12; cf. 10:11–12). Israel's
natural branches were broken off the olive tree so that the Gentiles could
be grafted into theological Israel (11:17, 19). It is 'as a result of their [Israel's]
disobedience' that the formerly disobedient Gentiles 'have now received
mercy' (11:30). But the salvation of the Gentiles is not the end of God's
hardening of ethnic Israel. Rather, 'because of their transgression,
salvation has come to the Gentiles *to make Israel envious*' (Rom. 11:11).
Paul glorifies his ministry to the Gentiles *in order to stir them to envy and
salvation* (Rom. 11:14). Israel too has 'now become disobedient *in order
that they too may now receive mercy*' (Rom. 11:31).[69] Thus, Paul sees in
Israel's hardening not only God's hand of judgment but also his purpose
of mercy. Israel's rejection of the gospel has begun a chain of causation
that will eventually lead to their own salvation.[70]

Observe, then, that even though Paul has made a distinction between
ethnic Israel and theological Israel (Rom. 9:6), he has not made an absolute
distinction. There is an organic connection between ethnic Israel and
theological Israel that cannot be severed, which can be seen in his famous

---

[68] Baker has argued that these are two separate purposes: making his people jealous is
speaking of Israel's judgment, while saving some of them is speaking of their salvation (Baker
2005: 471, 483–484). But the two outcomes are stated consecutively in one purpose clause and
seem to have a logical connection: Paul wants to stir his people to jealousy *so that* some of them
will be saved.

[69] The syntax of Rom. 11:31 is difficult and commentators disagree on whether the phrase
'God's mercy to you' is the result of Israel's disobedience (Dunn 1988: 687–688) or the means
by which Israel will finally receive mercy (Cranfield 1975: 583–585).

[70] Perhaps the apostle even sees this chain of causality ending in the resurrection. He reasons
that if the rejection of Israel has brought about the reconciliation of the world, what could their
acceptance bring except 'life from the dead' (11:15; cf. v. 12)? Some interpreters, however, take
the phrase 'life from the dead' as a metaphor: 'when a Gentile comes into the family of Christ,
it is as it were a *creation ex nihilo*, but when a Jew comes in it is like a resurrection' (Wright
1991: 248).

analogy of the olive tree (Rom. 11:17–24).[71] Paul compares the ethnic origins of his people to the 'root' of an olive tree that has put out branches in individual Jewish people.[72] Some of these natural branches have been broken off the tree, meaning that not all of physical Israel is part of theological Israel. And wild olive branches, or Gentiles, have been grafted into the olive tree to share in the nourishment of the root, meaning that some Gentiles are now a part of theological Israel. Why have ethnic Jews been cut off and Gentiles grafted in? '[T]hey were broken off because of unbelief, and you stand by faith' (11:20). Coming on the heels of 9:30 – 10:21, 'unbelief' and 'faith' surely designate how ethnic Israel and Gentiles have responded to the gospel of Jesus Christ. And so Paul's olive tree analogy up to this point makes the same argument we have observed since 9:6 and represented in our Venn diagrams. Ethnic Israel have pulled away from theological Israel and the Gentiles have been called into Israel because God has established Christ as a rock of stumbling and salvation. But Paul's olive tree analogy adds one more step – the idea that God will graft Israel in again if they turn in faith:

> And if they do not persist in unbelief, they will be grafted in, for God is able to graft them in again. After all, if you were cut out of an olive tree that is wild by nature, and contrary to nature were grafted into a cultivated olive tree, how much more readily will these, the natural branches, be grafted into their own olive tree!
> (Rom. 11:23)

Here Paul's argument goes beyond the free offer of the gospel to every Jew and Gentile (cf. Rom. 10:13) and proposes that *there is something in the ethnicity of Jewish people that makes it more natural for them to be saved.*

---

[71] Paul uses this analogy to warn Gentile believers against boasting over Jewish unbelievers, dialoguing with one such imaginary Gentile who might be tempted towards such arrogance. Our focus will be on how the analogy tells the story of Israel.

[72] Interpreters disagree on the identity of the 'root'. Most view it as the fathers, for Paul later says that Israel is loved by God because of the patriarchs (Moo 2018: 717). Cf. Paul's contemporary Philo on Abraham: 'Surely he is indeed the founder of the nation and the race, since from him as root sprang the young plant called Israel' (*Who Is the Heir?*, 279). Others suggest that the root is Jesus Christ, the offspring of Abraham and David, noting that Paul later quotes Isa. 11:10: 'The Root of Jesse will spring up, / one who will arise to rule over the nations; / in him the Gentiles will hope' (Rom. 15:12; Khobnya 2013: 265). Some see a reference to the Jewish remnant (Hafemann 1988: 51). In any event, the point of the analogy is that God made promises to an ethnic people: Abraham and his offspring.

What divides interpreters of Romans 9 – 11 is what Paul says about *how* and *when* this salvation will take place. We come at last to the *crux interpretum*, 'all Israel will be saved' (Rom. 11:26). In order to keep Gentile believers in Rome from pride over unbelieving Israel Paul states clearly a 'mystery' that has now been revealed in the gospel:

> Israel has experienced a hardening in part until the full number of the Gentiles has come in, and in this way all Israel will be saved. As it is written:
>
> > 'The deliverer will come from Zion;
> > he will turn godlessness away from Jacob.
> > And this is my covenant with them
> > when I take away their sins.'
>
> (Rom. 11:25–27)

Israel's hardening was anticipated by the prophets, but it was still hidden in the mysterious plan of God and not clearly revealed until Christ came. God intended to harden a part of ethnic Israel to the gospel during the time that the Gentiles enter into the people of God (cf. 11:7). Indeed, we can say from the broader argument that God has now hardened ethnic Israel *in order that* the full number of the Gentiles might believe the gospel and experience the riches of salvation and God's mercy (cf. Rom. 11:12, 15, 28, 30). But what does Paul mean when he states the final part of the mystery, 'and in this way all Israel will be saved'? There are three basic positions among Paul's interpreters.

First, many Reformed theologians have argued that 'all Israel' refers to the elect remnant of Jews who will come to faith in Christ throughout church history.[73] Paul has already argued that God is saving a remnant of Jewish Christians (Rom. 11:5), and as more Jews are stirred to jealousy more will be added to this remnant. Second, many throughout church history have interpreted this statement as a reference to the whole church, Jews and Gentiles together, who will be saved.[74] These first two views are

---

[73] E.g. Bavinck, Berkhof, Ridderbos and Hoekema (Merkle 2000: 711, n. 11). For a contemporary defence of this view, see Merkle 2000.

[74] E.g. Irenaeus, Clement of Alexandria and John Calvin (Fitzmyer 1993: 623–624). N. T. Wright has made the most compelling modern case for this view (see Wright 1991: 236–251; 2013: 1156–1256).

similar to each other in a number of ways. They both see Paul's statement in Romans 11:26 as something that will take place in the present time of church history as Gentiles stir the Jews to jealousy and salvation (cf. Rom. 11:13–14, 30–31).[75] They both take the adverb 'in this way' as a reference to the manner in which God will save 'all Israel'; namely, through the salvation of the Gentiles, which will then stir the Jews to jealousy.[76] And they both view Paul's supporting quotation about the deliverer coming from Zion (Isa. 59:20–21) as fulfilled in Christ's first coming.[77] However, the majority of commentators today argue for a third view – that Paul refers to the salvation of the ethnic nation of Israel after the Gentiles have come in and God removes the present hardening, turning them to faith in Christ. In this position Paul is referring to something that will take place in the future. Many argue that the adverb 'in this way' should be translated 'and then', indicating that 'all Israel will be saved' *after* the full number of the Gentiles are saved.[78] And many view Paul's citation about the deliverer coming from Zion as a reference to the second coming of Christ when he comes from the heavenly Jerusalem to redeem his people.[79]

The authors of this book unfortunately do not agree about this *crux interpretum* in Romans 9 – 11, so we have decided to leave this question open. These positions certainly differ from one another in emphasis, but we want to observe they all agree that God has not rejected ethnic Israel. Paul sees a divine intention to save ethnic Israel, whether that be through the stirring up of the Jews to jealousy in the present or the salvation of the nation in the future (or both). Even though ethnic Israel and theological Israel are not coterminous, Paul argues there is a deep connection between them. The Jewish people are 'holy' because the root of their ethnic origin is holy (Rom. 11:16).[80] This means they can be viewed from two perspectives. 'As far as the gospel is concerned, they are enemies [of God] for your

---

[75] Merkle observes the emphasis on the present situation in Rom. 11:1, 5, 13–14, 30–31 and the threefold 'now' in 11:30–31 (2000: 713–714). Wright also observes that '[t]his process takes place "now"' (1991: 249). Unfortunately, the most important 'now' in Rom. 11:31, the one that refers to Israel's salvation, is textually uncertain.

[76] Merkle 2000: 716–717 and Wright 1991: 249–250.

[77] On this quotation as a reference to the first advent see Bruno 2008.

[78] Van der Horst has now proven that this temporal meaning of the adverb *houtōs* is possible (2000).

[79] E.g. Schreiner 2018: 603–604. Although Wolter now suggests that Paul simply quotes Isaiah to prove that this deliverance will eventually come 'from Zion', that is from God himself, without giving details about how it will happen (2018: 130–136).

[80] See n. 72.

sake'; that is, for the sake of the Gentiles so that they might be saved.
'[B]ut as far as election is concerned, they are loved [by God] on account
of the patriarchs, for God's gifts and his call are irrevocable' (Rom. 11:29).
Here Paul speaks of their corporate election, just as he spoke of their
corporate foreknowledge in 11:2. Ethnic Israel is hardened to the gospel,
but are also loved. There is a sense in which God has chosen them to be
his people. This clearly does not mean that Paul thought every Jewish
person is or will be saved. But it does mean that even in the mystery of
their hardening God has not rejected his people Israel. The gospel is still
'first to the Jew'. But it is also 'to the Gentile'. For Paul's conclusion is not
simply about God's faithfulness to his people Israel but to all of his people:
'God has bound everyone over to disobedience so that he may have mercy
on them all' (Rom. 11:32).

These concluding words give a final example of how the OT has
influenced the very language of Paul's argument. In Romans 9:15 he
appeals to the revelation of God's name to Moses:

> I will have mercy [eleēsō] on whom I have mercy [eleō],
>   and I will have compassion [oiktirēsō] on whom I have
>   compassion [oiktirō].
> (Rom. 9:15, quoting Exod. 33:19)

He then uses this language to speak of the 'objects of his mercy [eleous],
whom God prepared in advance for glory' (Rom. 9:23). Now in conclusion
he picks up this language again to demonstrate God's faithfulness both
to his Word and to his people:

> Just as you who were at one time disobedient to God have now
> received mercy [eleēthēte] as a result of their disobedience, so they
> too have now become disobedient in order that they too may now
> receive mercy [eleēthōsin] as a result of God's mercy [eleei] to you.
> For God has bound everyone over to disobedience so that he may
> have mercy [eleēsē] on them all.
> (Rom. 11:30–32)

Perhaps even the well-known opening of the next section in Romans has
been influenced by Exodus 33:19: 'Therefore, I urge you, brothers and
sisters, in view of God's mercy [oiktirmōn] . . .' (Rom. 12:1). Using the

language of the Bible, Paul concludes that the people of God are fundamentally defined not as those who have obeyed God, but as the disobedient who have been shown the mercy of God.

Summary

In Romans 9 – 11 Paul argues that the story of Israel demonstrates that God has been faithful to his Word and his people. He first reaches into Israel's past to demonstrate that there never was a strict correspondence between ethnic Israel and the children of God. 'Israel' in the true sense has always been defined by God's own merciful call. Paul then focuses his attention on the present state of Israel in which many of the Gentiles have experienced God's merciful call, but only a remnant of the Jews are being saved. It is a tragic irony that the Gentiles have believed in the gospel of Jesus Christ while the Jews have not. This hardening of Israel fulfils Isaiah's prophecy that God would establish the Messiah as a stone of stumbling, and yet it was also hidden as part of the 'mystery' of God's merciful plan to bring the Gentiles into the people of God and eventually show mercy to ethnic Israel as well. Thus, when Paul says that not all of ethnic Israel is a part of theological Israel, he certainly does not mean that God has rejected or replaced his people. Rather, Israel's disobedience has brought God's mercy to the Gentiles, which will also lead to God's mercy to the Jews as they turn to faith in Jesus Christ. Thus, the story of Israel is a story of the glory of God displayed in his mercy towards disobedient Jews and Gentiles: 'To him be the glory for ever! Amen' (Rom. 11:36b).

The contribution of Paul's summary

The point at which the story of Israel in Romans 9 – 11 most overlaps with what we have seen in our previous chapters is that at its centre or climax is Christ, the stone of salvation and stumbling (Rom. 9:33). Further, like Matthew and Luke, Paul appeals throughout this story to the patterns of Scripture that foreshadow what God is now doing in Christ and the church (typology).[81] God's dealings with patriarchs, Pharaoh, Elijah and Israel in the exile have all shaped how Paul explains the current situation. The

---

[81] Cf. Hays: 'The purpose of Romans 9–11 . . . is to show that God's dealing with Israel and the nations in the present age is fully consistent with God's modus operandi in the past and with his declared purposes' (1989:64).

remnant theme may be the clearest example of typological reasoning in these chapters, since Paul explicitly compares the present time with Elijah's day: 'So too, at the present time there is a remnant chosen by grace' (Rom. 11:5). Although the most interesting example is the way in which Paul sees the accessibility of the law as a foreshadowing of the accessibility of Christ himself in the preaching of the gospel (Rom. 10:6–9). But once again Paul's main contribution is in his explanation of a specific part of the story – his deep and nuanced reflection about one of the most important characters in Israel's story: 'Israel' itself.

On the one hand, Paul argues that 'Israel' has always been a theological category, a people defined not by ethnic descent or moral effort but by God's own call or choice of individuals (Rom. 9:6–23). The distinction God made among Abraham's and Isaac's children foreshadows the distinctions he is currently making among the children of Jacob/Israel. Theological 'Israel' is actually narrower than the twelve tribes. But it is also broader, for God has also called some of the Gentiles to be his people (9:24–25). We should observe that, because it is rooted in OT history, this is not technically a 'redefinition' of Israel. Paul's entire point is that this is the way it has always been.

On the other hand, Paul continues to maintain that the physical people of Israel are still God's people, corporately foreknown, chosen, beloved and called by God (Rom. 11:1–2, 28–29). In other words, we should not push the typology of Abraham's and Isaac's children too far. There is still truth in the idea that the twelve tribes of Jacob/Israel are the chosen, corporate people of God. And God will not reject his people. Salvation is 'first to the Jew' (1:16). It is more 'natural' for the Jew (11:24). This does not mean that every single Israelite is or will be saved. But it does mean that God's final purpose for Israel is mercy.

Interpreters often struggle to reconcile these two viewpoints. How can Paul say 'Israel' was never a matter of ethnic descent but then maintain that God will not abandon Israel because of their ethnic descent? Many have concluded that the two viewpoints cannot be reconciled.[82] Wright attempts to eliminate the contradiction with his argument that 'all Israel' refers to both Jews and Gentiles in Christ; thus, Paul maintains the same position

---

[82] The latest example of such an argument is the careful exegetical study of Rom. 11:25–32 by Wolter, who concludes that Paul here is inconsistent in solving the problem of Israel ('Paul nicht in der Lage ist, das Israel-Problem widerspruchsfrei zu lösen'; 2018: 138).

throughout, that it is not a matter of physical descent.[83] But even if Wright's position is correct, we are not convinced that this eliminates the tension in Romans 9 – 11, for Paul still calls ethnic Israel the chosen people of God whom he will not abandon (11:1–2, 28–29). In other words, Paul still has room in his theology for the corporate election of the ethnic nation of Israel.

We suggest that Paul's two viewpoints of Israel as both a 'theological' and 'ethnic' category are two biblical viewpoints the apostle holds in paradoxical tension and resolves in the mercy of God.[84] Paul demonstrates clearly that from the beginning of Israel's story in the OT God's children have been determined by his call and unconditional choice. In other words, his children are determined by his unconditioned mercy:

> I will have mercy on whom I have mercy,
>> and I will have compassion on whom I have compassion.
> (Rom. 9:15, quoting Exod. 33:19)

And yet the apostle continues to affirm the priority of the nation of Israel as those to whom God's promises of salvation belong (Rom. 1:16; 9:4–5). However, this priority and privilege does not rest upon their physical lineage but upon God's own gracious gifts and calling (11:29).[85] In other words, both 'theological' and 'ethnic' Israel at the end of the day are really 'theological Israel', because God is the one who determines who his people are by his own mercy. He is currently showing this mercy to the Gentiles but will also show his mercy to the Jews. 'For God has bound everyone over to disobedience so that he may have mercy on them all' (Rom. 11:32).[86] Israel's story does not end with Israel but goes to the rest of the world; on the other hand, it does not leave ethnic Israel behind.

Thus, the story of Israel reinforces Paul's larger argument about the gospel in Romans; in particular the idea that justification before God is

---

[83] See Wright 1991: 236, 251.

[84] Cf. Cranfield's studied observation on Rom. 1:16 that '[t]he paradoxical insistence both on the fact that there is no [difference] (3.22; 10.12) and also at the same time on the continuing validity of the [Jews . . . first] (in spite of the actual order of salvation disclosed in 11.25f) belongs to the substance of this epistle' (1975: 91).

[85] So Haacker, who says that God's reliability is the fundamental reason that Paul sees a future for Israel (2010: 64). Moo observes that Rom. 9 does not eliminate any ethnic privilege and that Rom. 11 does not base Israel's salvation on ethnicity or merit but that both passages root salvation in God's own will (2002: 255–258).

[86] Schreiner observes that 'Romans 11:32 is the crucial text' for explaining the seeming contradiction in Rom. 9 and 11 (2018: 465).

'not by works'.[87] In Romans 9:11–12 Paul says that God's purpose in choosing Jacob rather than Esau was 'not by works but by him who calls' (Rom. 9:12). Here Paul's earlier antithesis between works of the law and faith in Romans 3 – 4 becomes a contrast between works and the call of God.[88] Another variation on this theme is found in Romans 11:5–6, in which Paul contrasts works with the gracious election of the remnant of Jews who have believed in Jesus Christ. And one of the clearest explanations of the difference between righteousness by works and righteousness by faith in the entire letter is found in Romans 9:30 – 10:13. Paul has not moved past his main point of the letter in Romans 9 – 11, but, like a good novelist, has prepared readers for this discussion since the beginning of the letter.[89] Israel's own experience is a parable of the gospel. God will be faithful to his Word and people despite their current rejection of Christ. For salvation is ultimately rooted in his mercy.

Finally, we have observed throughout this chapter that Paul's language in Romans 9 – 11 is often generated by the very language of Scripture.[90] The words of his OT citations become the warp and woof of many of his own arguments; in particular, 'calling' (Rom. 9:24; cf. Gen. 21:12; Hos. 1:10), 'stumbling stone' (Rom. 9:32; cf. Isa. 8:14), 'with your mouth'/'in your heart' (Rom. 10:9–10; cf. Deut. 30:14), 'remnant' (Rom. 11:5; cf. Isa. 1:9; 10:22; 1 Kgs 19:10, 18), 'envy' (Rom. 11:11, 14; cf. Deut. 32:21) and, of course, 'mercy' (Rom. 11:30–32; cf. Exod. 33:19). Paul had not only deeply thought about the problem of Israel's unbelief; he had deeply searched the words of Scripture for a solution.

Conclusion

The story of Israel in Romans 9 – 11 is itself a parable of the gospel of Christ. The tragedy of Israel's unbelief does not invalidate the gospel but

---

[87] Barclay argues that the theme that holds Rom. 9 – 11 together 'is the incongruity of divine election – the lack of correspondence between the mercy of God and the worth of its recipients' (2015: 556).

[88] Rom. 9:11–12 should have a bearing on the claim of the new perspective that 'works of the law' do not refer to 'good works' in Paul, for in this passage the apostle defines these works in terms of moral action: 'before the twins were born or had done anything good or bad' (Rom. 9:11).

[89] Fitzmyer 1993: 539, 541.

[90] Our observations about this phenomenon have been stimulated by Aageson's work. E.g., 'As we have seen in 9:7,15,24–28,30–33, and 10:8–14, it is frequently the scriptural text which generates the words and ideas which Paul then develops and weaves into his discussion' (1986: 277).

rather proves it to be true, because it shows that God's people have always been fundamentally identified by his merciful call. This is true for 'Israel' in the past, for the Gentiles who have been called to be 'God's people' in the present, and for both Gentiles and Jews in the future. God has been faithful both to his Word and to his people, and the history of Israel's past, present and future demonstrates his faithfulness to be true. God has not rejected his people, and neither has Paul, even though he is an apostle to the Gentiles. He affirms that Gentiles are God's children, just as he argues in Galatians, but he also says God has not rejected ethnic Israel. In fact, it is more natural for the Jews than the Gentiles to be saved. Paul's long argument in support of God's faithfulness has left Christians with a rich example of how the story of the OT can explain our current moment and lead us to praise the wisdom of God. In the next chapter, on Hebrews 11, we will see how biblical theology can not only be used to explain our present moment but to exhort us pastorally to persevere in the faith.

6
Hebrews and Israel's inheritance

With Hebrews 11 we come to our final and, arguably, most complete SIS in the NT.[1] Given the attention Hebrews pays to the relationship between Judaism and Christianity, the latter fact is, perhaps, not all that surprising.[2] Hebrews's summary, however, is distinct for other reasons. As we shall see, it tells the story of Israel in a slightly different way from what we have seen thus far. For starters, Israel is viewed only positively.[3] Our previous summaries included unfaithful characters from Israel's story. In Hebrews, however, every character included is held out as an example for the audience to emulate. Beyond this, Hebrews's summary tells us how the earliest Christians understood one of the fundamental 'institutions' in Israel's story – the land inheritance. Hebrews, in fact, tells us more clearly than anywhere else in the NT whether or not the earliest Christians thought Canaan played any continuing role in God's purposes for his people.

To see what Hebrews's summary contributes to our investigation of early Christian biblical theology, we will, as elsewhere in this book, begin by exploring the summary's context and content. The context will tell us what Hebrews is trying to do with the summary. It will tell us, in other words, why the author tells the story of Israel in the first place. Identifying the function of the story will begin to show us how the author himself understands the story he tells. The content, moreover, will then tell us how the specific contours of the summary – the characters and events the author includes – serve the summary's function. Here we will explore what the author 'operationalizes' from Israel's story to serve his rhetorical agenda and, therefore, how he understands the specific elements from

---

[1] E. Stauffer described Heb. 11 as 'the only summary that has come down to us *intact* from the primitive church' (1955: 40–41; emphasis added).

[2] Guthrie 2007: 919.

[3] Cf. however Heb. 3:7 – 4:13.

Israel's story that he selects. Only once this preliminary groundwork is complete – only after we see why the author tells Israel's story and how – will we be ready to take a step back and reflect on the author's biblical-theological contribution.

Before we jump in, however, we first want to preview what we will see in this chapter. What we will see is that Hebrews's summary, as indeed is the case for Hebrews generally, functions to encourage its audience to hold fast to their Christian confession. The author was well aware of the pressures facing his friends, tempting them to abandon their faith, not least in a crucified Messiah. And his summary, found in Hebrews 11, is one means he uses to forestall that sort of behaviour, behaviour he characterizes as apostasy (Heb. 6:6).[4]

Specifically, Hebrews's summary encourages persevering faith by showing a beleaguered audience that such faith is actually possible. There was, the author insists, a 'great cloud of witnesses' from Israel's past surrounding them, testifying to this very fact (see Heb. 12:1). What is more, the specific witnesses selected for the summary prove that persevering faith is possible even in the face of social alienation and death, which were the very pressures causing the audience so much trouble. It was, in fact, God's promises that had sustained the witnesses' faith in the midst of their suffering, and it was those same promises that could (should) sustain the audience as well. The 'ancients' (elders; *hoi presbyteroi*), as the author calls these first-covenant witnesses (Heb. 11:2; see his description of the 'outdated' – *elder* – covenant in 8:13), had been able to persevere precisely

---

[4] We will assume a few things in our reading of Hebrews, which we simply wanted to list here. Justification for these assumptions can be found in lots of places, including e.g. Compton 2015: 13–18 and the literature cited there. (1) We assume the author is male (probably *not* Paul; cf. Heb. 2:1–4 with Gal. 1:11–12) and refer to him throughout with masculine pronouns, simply because this aligns with what we find the author doing in the summary. 'I do not have time to tell' (*diēgoumenon*) the author says in 11:32, referring to himself with a masculine participle. It is of course possible this is only a literary convention. But one wonders why an author so well known by the audience and, in fact, depending on that mutual knowledge for the letter's effect (see e.g. 13:22–25) would resort to pseudonymity. (2) We will assume Hebrews is a letter largely based on its epistolary ending (13:22–25). This, of course, does not rule out the possibility that Hebrews began its life as a sermon or series of sermons. (3) We will assume, moreover, that the audience was mixed – both Jew and Gentile – and Christian, in some danger of abandoning Christianity as a result of persecution, both past, present and anticipated (see e.g. 2:1; 3:1, 6, 12, 14; 4:1, 11; also vv. 14, 16; 6:1, 11–12; 10:22–23 in the light of e.g. 6:10; 10:32–34; 12:4 and 13:13–14), and that it treasured the OT. What else are we to make of all the attention the author gives to the OT and to providing persuasive warrants (i.e. contextually sensitive warrants) for his arguments from the OT? (On the equation of 'persuasive' and 'contextually sensitive', see Compton 2015: 17, n. 43.)

because they knew that their hope, the referent of God's promises, was not in this world, nor in this life. The ancients knew, as Hebrews's audience must, that the believer's – Abraham's – inheritance has always been heavenly and is accessed only by those possessing enduring life (i.e. *resurrected* life). In other words, it is the author's understanding of Israel's story, of Abraham's inheritance, that is operationalized to sustain his audience in its fight for faith. Or, to say it another way, the summary's biblical-theological contribution is, at the same time, the summary's rhetorical point.

The context of Hebrews's summary

We will begin by answering the question 'What is the author trying to do with his summary?' Why or to what end does he tell Israel's story? We will answer this question by putting the author's summary in its context, and we will begin with the widest lens, the argument of Hebrews itself.

The argument of Hebrews

As any cursory reading of Hebrews reveals, the letter moves back and forth between exposition and exhortation. Its argument, however, is fundamentally carried forward by its expositions, which can be divided into two main groups or sets: Hebrews 1 – 2 and Hebrews 5 – 10.[5] As we will see, both sets make the same argument. Both tell the same story, only from different perspectives. One tells the story from the perspective of creation, and the other from the perspective of Israel. The story each tells is intended to address – to help – an audience suffering persecution and, as a result, doubting its Christian confession, specifically the scriptural plausibility of the Christian Messiah, which is to say, of a *suffering* Messiah.

To address this urgent need the author shows that the suffering and death of the Messiah did not contradict but were anticipated in the Hebrew scriptures, not least in a text right at the centre of the audience's faltering Christian confession, Psalm 110:1. If the audience was willing to accept the fact of Jesus' resurrection and to interpret that fact as Jesus' messianic enthronement, which is precisely what the early Christian application of Psalm 110:1 was intended to do, then the alleviation of their doubts was

---

[5] Heb. 1 – 2 contains three expositional units: 1:5–14; 2:5–9; and 2:10–18. Heb. 5 – 10 contains seven: 5:1–10; 7:1–10; 7:11–28; 8:1–13; 9:1–10; 9:11–28; 10:1–18.

close at hand, literally, only a few lines away in Psalm 110:4, with its description of a priestly Messiah. Hebrews's argument shows that Psalm 110:1 and 4 contain not only the audience's confession but also the resolution to their doubts.

As we said, the author makes this argument in two steps. First, in his first set of expositions (Heb. 1 – 2), he uses Psalm 110:1 to interpret Jesus' resurrection as his messianic enthronement (Heb. 1:5–14), then to connect Jesus' enthronement with his fulfilment of – securing – Psalm 8 and its vision for humanity generally (Heb. 2:5–9), and, finally, to begin to explain why Jesus was enthroned through suffering (Heb. 2:10–18). The author, in other words, begins to explain why the vision of Psalm 8, put at risk by humanity's sin, could be secured and, therefore, regained, only by a suffering Messiah. Second, in his second set of expositions (Heb. 5 – 10) the author corroborates this initial sketch of the Christian confession, this time through the lens of Israel's story. Thus, in Hebrews 5 – 7 he uses Psalm 110:1 and now Psalm 110:4 to show that the Messiah was all along expected to be a (superior) priest. In Hebrews 8 – 10 he then argues, once more on the basis of Psalm 110:1 and 4, that this anticipated messianic priest was all along expected to solve the human problem, first identified in 2:5–9, through his own self-sacrifice.

Again, in both sets of expositions, Hebrews 1 – 2 and 5 – 10, the story is the same, though it is told from different perspectives. Before the author introduces the Levitical cult or Melchizedek, before he looks squarely at Psalm 110:4 in Hebrews 5 – 10, he first establishes the larger story in which these things find their place. Priest, sacrifices and sacred spaces, the stuff of Hebrews 5 – 10, were established with a larger story in mind. They were introduced to solve or, at the very least, to prepare to solve the human problem described in Hebrews 1 – 2. These institutions in Hebrews 5 – 10 were introduced for the purpose of enabling humans to regain the 'glory and honour' (2:7) lost in the fall. In short, before Jesus is the better priest, the author insists he is first the better or true Adam.[6]

The exhortations of Hebrews

Hebrews's summary is part of Hebrews's exhortatory programme (see Table 6.1). While there is vigorous debate about the letter's structure,[7]

---

[6] For this reading of Hebrews, see Compton 2015: 38–53.
[7] See e.g. Joslin 2007; Guthrie 1998.

Table 6.1 The location of Hebrews's summary

1:1–4	Introduction
1:5–14	Exposition
2:1–4	Exhortation
2:5–18	Exposition
3:1 – 4:16	Exhortation
5:1–10	Exposition
5:11 – 6:20	Exhortation
7:1 – 10:18	Exposition
10:19 – 13:19	Exhortation
13:20–25	Benediction and postscript

here all that is necessary to see is that Hebrews's summary falls within a larger exhortatory unit, Hebrews's last, which comes after the author's second telling of the human story (Heb. 5 – 10) and just before his closing benediction and postscript (Heb. 13:20–21 and 22–25).

If, as we noted, Hebrews's expositions fundamentally carry forward the author's argument, what then is the function of Hebrews's exhortations? Or, to put it another way, if the author's expositions argue for the validity of the Christian confession, then what is the utility of the letter's several exhortations? As the figure above shows, Hebrews's exhortations follow its expositions. The order is not only sequential, however, but is also logical in that the exhortations urge the appropriate response to the argument they follow, something signalled by the inferential conjunction found at the beginning of nearly each one (see 'therefore'; e.g. in 2:1 and 3:1).[8]

We see this sort of connection, in fact, in the exhortatory unit in which the author's summary is found (10:19 – 13:19). The author connects this exhortation to the preceding argument (see 'therefore' in 10:19) and, in this case, also briefly summarizes that argument before proceeding. As we would expect, the summary in 10:19–21 recalls those elements of the Christian confession just enunciated in the previous exposition of Hebrews 5 – 10:[9]

---

[8] 'Therefore' in each instance translates various Greek particles (e.g. *dia touto, hothen, oun*, etc.).

[9] The summary here in 10:19–21 looks all the way back to 5:1–10, which is left-bracketed by an almost identical summary. On this inclusio, see e.g. Nauck 1960: 199–206.

Therefore, brothers and sisters, since we have confidence to enter
the Most Holy Place by the blood of Jesus, by a new and living way
opened for us through the curtain, that is, his body, and since we
have a great priest over the house of God . . .

The author characterizes the essence of the confession here as confident
access to God ('enter the Most Holy Place') through Jesus' self-sacrifice
('by the blood of Jesus'; 'his body') and present priestly service ('a great
priest').

This recalls the second way the author describes the Christian
confession, the second way he tells the human story. In the earlier part of
his letter, in the exposition of Hebrews 1 – 2, the author described this
access to God as entry into 'the world to come' (2:5). There, as well, it was
'death' and 'sins' (2:14–15, 17), owing to Adam's sin (implicit in 2:7), that
prevented humans from God's original intention, namely, a kingly rule
over creation, characterized by 'glory' and 'honour' (2:5–9, citing Ps.
8:6–8). It was only through the representative death of a human, a second
Adam, that this original intention could be fulfilled, that humans could
regain their lost glory and honour and be given access into and rule over
'the world to come', this place where Jesus had already, according to Psalm
110:1, triumphantly entered (2:9–10).[10]

The summary in 10:19–21 reflects the second way the author tells the
same story in Hebrews 5 – 10. In this set of expositions the lens is no
longer creation but Israel. But the plot is the same: How is it that humans
will gain not 'the world to come' but, now, 'the Most Holy Place' (10:19;
see also 9:8), not 'glory and honour' but, now, 'eternal salvation' (5:9; 7:25;
cf. 1:14), 'eternal redemption' (9:12), the ability to 'serve the living God'
(9:14), an 'eternal inheritance' (9:15; cf. 1:14; 11:8–9), 'perfection' (10:14)
and complete 'forgiveness' (10:18; cf. 9:22)? While Israel's cult (its priests,
sacrifices and sacred space) and covenant could not (admittedly)[11] solve
the problem, they did show how it would be solved (see e.g. 8:1–5, 7–13;
10:5–10). They pointed to the necessity of a representative, this time not a
new Adam but a new priest, who would offer a better sacrifice and, in so
doing, open a way to God himself (10:20), a way into the holiest place
behind the curtain, where God dwells (10:19).

[10] For this reading of 2:5–18, see esp. Compton 2015: 19–65.
[11] Caird 1959.

What is important to see for our purposes is that in both ways of telling the Christian story, through both the wide and narrower lens, the goal is the same: access to 'the Most Holy Place' where God is, which is to say, as Hebrews puts it elsewhere, access to 'heaven', 'the world to come' and, as we find in Hebrews's summary in chapter 11, Abraham's better and heavenly inheritance (vv. 13–16). What is more, the only way to reach this goal, the only way to gain access, to receive the inheritance, to rule over the world to come, is through Jesus' atoning sacrifice, which is precisely where the audience's doubts are concentrated. Jesus' death for human sin, the author everywhere insists, is the only way of enabling humans to dwell with God. This is the Christian confession the author here summarizes in Hebrews 10:19–21 and in which Hebrews's summary in chapter 11 urges persevering faith.

Having summarized the Christian confession of Hebrews 5 – 10, the author then turns in 10:22 and beyond to urge his audience to hold fast to this confession through a series of concluding exhortations (see Table 6.2). Hebrews's summary, therefore, is one means the author employs in this final exhortatory unit to urge his audience to persevere in their hold on and hope in the access to God that Jesus' priestly service provides (10:19–20).

What we see when we look at the summary's immediate context is that the summary plays the role of showing that the kind of faith the author calls for – persevering faith – is possible.[12] The summary reminds the audience that so many in Israel's history have already done precisely what the author and, in fact, God is calling them to do. So many, too many to list, have run and finished the same race the audience is running, and the author's summary implies that if this great company has persevered, so too can they.

The exhortation that immediately follows Hebrews 11 justifies our reading of the summary's function. In Hebrews 12:1–4, before issuing a fresh exhortation, the author draws an inference from the story of Israel he has just told. 'Therefore,' he says, 'since we are surrounded by such a great cloud of witnesses . . . let us run with perseverance' (12:1). Here the author draws his readers' attention to the fact of this great cloud of faithful in order to encourage their own faith. The 'cloud', described in the author's summary, shows that what the author is calling for in his

---

[12] Cosby puts it this way, '[T]he faith *exhorted* in 10:19–39 is the faith *defined* in 11:1 and the faith *illustrated* in 11:3–38' (1988: 260; emphases original).

Table 6.2 Locating the function of Hebrews's summary

10:22–25   Since the audience has guaranteed access to God, it must, therefore, persevere in its 'faith' and 'hope', and, as an expression of 'love', must help others do the same.

10:26–31   If the audience lets go of its faith, if it tramples 'the Son of God underfoot' (v. 29), it will face God's judgment.

10:32–39   But the audience can take heart. Its track record suggests it will not let go of its faith. It has weathered persecution with grace in the past; surely it can do it a while longer (cf. 9:28).

11:1–40   *The author's SIS.*[13]

12:1–4   The summary should encourage them, as will keeping an eye on Jesus. He also endured great hardship. And, more than that, his hardship secured faith's hope, the access to God described in 10:19–20.

12:5–11   All this should remind the audience that hardships serve God's purposes. Hardships are not evidence of God's displeasure or, worse still, his absence. Instead, they show his love by preparing his sons and daughters – the audience – for future reward – 'li[fe]', God's 'holiness' and a 'harvest of righteousness and peace'.

12:12–17   All this, moreover, is what they need to use to encourage one another (cf. 10:24–25), not least those among them running with a limp or those like Esau ready to forsake their inheritance for temporary relief.

12:18–24   After all, the goodness of the inheritance, here once more described as a destination (cf. 10:19–20), more than compensates for the difficulty of the journey.

12:25–29   If it, in fact, shrinks back from its Christian confession now, this will be considered nothing less than abandonment *of God*. The audience, therefore, must hold fast to God's good promise of an unshakable kingdom, letting that promise fuel its faith and the present ministry (*latreuōmen*) that such faith invariably produces (if, of course, God so wills it; cf. 6:3).

13:1–19   The author describes this present ministry as well-pleasing sacrifices and concludes his exhortation by listing in summary form several examples.

---

[13] The cohesion of 11:1–40 is suggested e.g. by (1) 10:39/11:1: change from imperative to indicative mood in 11:1; (2) vv. 1–40: repetition of *pist-* (vv. 1, 3 . . . 39); *emartyrēthēsan*, v. 2// *martyrēthentes*, v. 39; and (3) v. 40/12:1: change from indicative to subjunctive/imperative mood.

exhortation (see *hypomonēs*, 10:36//*hypomonēs*, 12:1) is possible. The '*great cloud*' attests – witnesses – to the possibility of persevering faith.

This observation about the summary's function is corroborated by several features in the summary itself. First, the summary is bracketed by parallel assertions. In Hebrews 11:2 the author begins by noting that the 'ancients' were commended for their faith. He then concludes in verse 39, noting that 'all' were 'commended for their faith'. The summary, in other words, begins and ends by drawing our attention to others who persevered in faith, which, in the light of 12:1–4, suggests that the summary begins and ends by drawing the audience's attention to the possibility of persevering in faith. The proximity of 'these all' in 11:39 to the 'great cloud' of 12:1 grounds the plausibility of this observation.

Second, in an extended editorial comment, inserted into the summary in verses 13–16, the author says, 'All these people were still living by faith when they died.' In the light of what we have seen in 12:1–4 and in 11:2 and 39, the emphasis in this comment falls squarely on 'all' in verse 13: '*All* these people were still living by faith . . .'

Third, another of the author's editorial comments points in the same direction. In the comment of verse 32, which prefaces the author's second list of ancients (vv. 33–38), the author writes, 'And what more shall I say? I do not have time to tell about Gideon, Barak, Samson and Jephthah, about David and Samuel and the prophets' (v. 32). The emphasis is, once more, on the size of the company of witnesses. Here, specifically, it is on the fact that the author could easily come up with further additions to the 'great cloud', if only he had the time. This emphasis, then, likely explains why the author departs here in verse 32 (and, in fact, in the list that follows) from his normal ordering of ancients. He does not, as elsewhere, follow a canonical order. Rather, every other example in this verse is out of canonical sequence (see Table 6.3).

Table 6.3 'Out-of-order' ancients in 11:32

Gideon	Judges 6 – 8
Barak	Judges 4
Samson	Judges 13 – 16
Jephthah	Judges 10 – 12
David	1 Samuel 16 – 1 Kings 2
Samuel and the prophets	1 Samuel 1 – 28

The author appears to illustrate with this list what he has just said in verse 32a: He 'do[es] not have time to tell' about all the faithful from Israel's history. After all, he could talk about 'Gideon', but, if he did, he would have to skip over 'Barak'. He could talk about 'Samson', but, again, if he did, he would have to skip over someone, in this case, 'Jephthah'. He could talk about 'David', but he would have to skip over 'Samuel and the prophets'. His point, once again, is that the cloud is simply too 'great' to describe fully. There are simply too many faithful to list. The evidence for the possibility of persevering in faith is, in other words, overwhelming.[14]

In fact, the author's pace quickens considerably in the second list of ancients, which verse 32 prefaces.[15] More examples are given in less space than is allotted for the examples in the author's first list (vv. 3–31). This, alongside the author's 'out-of-order' ancients in verse 32, seems further designed to emphasize what the author says in verse 32a. There just is not enough time to describe all the faithful, even if the author speeds up.

Finally, one more detail in the author's summary corroborates the function we have identified of showing the possibility of persevering in faith. In the very first example given, the author, somewhat surprisingly, draws attention to the audience's own faith. 'By faith', he says in 11:3, 'we understand that the universe was formed at God's command'. The focus of this example, in the light of what we have seen thus far, appears once more to be on the fact that the very thing the audience thought might not be possible was the very thing it had already done. This reading of verse 3, in fact, is of a piece with something the author says earlier, just before the summary. 'Remember', he notes in 10:32, 'those earlier days . . . when you endured [*hypemeinate*; cf. 10:36//12:1] . . .' What the author exhorts, in other words, the audience has shown, proving again that his exhortation to persevere in faith is indeed possible.

---

[14] See similarly Attridge 1989: 347.

[15] In the first list of ancients (vv. 3–31) there is an average of fewer than one indicative verb (0.86 to be exact) per verse. In the second list (vv. 32–38) that average increases to three per verse. This increase in pacing is even more obvious in the amount of space given to the ancients described. In vv. 3–31 397 words are used to describe 7 ancients (Noah, Abraham [incl. Sarah], Isaac, Jacob, Moses [incl. Moses' parents], Israel [two generations], Rahab), compared with 85 words used to describe (approx.) 15 ancients in vv. 32–38 (Gideon, Barak, Samson, Jephthah, David, Samuel, prophets, unnamed women, 'others' [v. 35], 'some' [v. 36], 'they' [4×, v. 37], 'they' [v. 38]). Even if we consider Sarah, Moses' parents and the two generations of Israelites separately and combine the ancients of vv. 37–38 into one, the word-to-ancient ratio is still much greater in the first list than in the second (397 words / 11 ancients vs. 85 words / 11 ancients).

Summary of context

Hebrews insists that the Christian story fulfils rather than contradicts the Hebrew scriptures. The author, as we have seen, tells this story in two ways: first through the wide-angle lens of creation's story and second through the narrower lens of Israel's story. In both cases he shows that sin prevents humans from entering God's presence and that a representative death, of a second Adam and a better priest, is the only way to solve this problem. The author's exhortations, therefore, urge the audience to hold fast to this story, to this confession, and the summary, which is part of the author's final exhortation, serves this agenda by showing that such tenacious faith is entirely possible. A 'great cloud', too large to describe fully in the time the author has, testifies to this very fact. In short, the author uses Israel's story to encourage his audience to persevere in their faith.

What remains is to see how, specifically, the author brings Israel's story to bear. After all, if all the author wants to do is to draw the audience's attention to the *size* of the cloud, then a list, such as we find in verse 32, would work well enough. What we need to see, in other words, is the rationale for the shape of the summary, the rationale for the specific exemplars and events selected. To see this, we will take an in-depth look at the summary's content.

The content of Hebrews's summary (Heb. 11)

What we see when we look at the summary's content is that the author tells Israel's story to show that persevering faith is possible, specifically by his showing that the 'great cloud' of ancients persevered in similar circumstances and with similar resources. That is to say, the summary underscores the similarities between the ancients and the audience, showing that the ancients persevered in faith in the face of circumstances just like those the audience itself is experiencing and by fixing their eyes on resources just like those the audience itself has access to in the Christian confession.

These two similarities not only explain the specific content of the author's summary, but also reveal the author's primary contribution to our understanding of early Christian biblical theology. As we will see, the ancients persevered in hardships because they knew, as the audience itself must know, that their object of faith, the inheritance promised to all of

Abraham's descendants, could not be touched by this world's troubles. Neither social alienation nor death could touch the ancients' hope, precisely because that hope was not in this world nor was it in this life. It was a hope in a future resurrection and a heavenly inheritance. It was, in fact, a hope in an enduring body that would give believers access to this heavenly inheritance.

Due to the nature of the author's summary, both emphases must be inferred from the story itself. Nowhere does the author explicitly tell us why he has chosen each exemplar and event beyond the fact that each contributes in one way or another to the summary's function of showing that persevering faith is possible (see 12:1–4). He nowhere tells us in so many words that his curated gallery of ancients is meant to highlight the circumstances and resources the ancients shared with the audience. Rather, he leaves to his readers the responsibility of inferring all this from the way he narrates the story.

Two features in the author's story, however, point us to these emphases: the story's structure and its repeated themes.

Structural and thematic clues

The author's summary should be divided into four parts: (1) an introduction (vv. 1–2),[16] (2) a list of faithful from Israel's pre- and early history (List 1, vv. 3–31), (3) a list of faithful from Israel's later history (List 2, vv. 32–38) and (4) a conclusion (vv. 39–40).

The introduction and conclusion are signalled by the (virtual) repetition of the phrase 'the ancients were commended', found in verses 2 and 39 (cf. v. 39, '*these* were all commended'). The two lists of faithful between the introduction and conclusion, Lists 1 and 2, are delineated by at least four features in the story.[17]

1 The introductory formula 'by faith' (*pistei*) occurs throughout List 1, whereas 'through faith' (*dia pisteōs*) occurs in List 2.[18]

---

[16] The seam between the introduction and first ancient list is contested, considering the occurrences of *blep-* (vv. 1, 7) and *mart-* (vv. 2, 4 [2×], 5; not again until v. 39). The author's programmatic *pistei*, which begins in v. 3 and extends until v. 31 and his clear inclusio in vv. 2//39, however, suggest an intentional seam, even while we recognize the presence of some overlap between his introduction and first list.

[17] Rhee's structural proposal suffers from not taking sufficient account of *both* lists (1998: 327–345).

[18] For *pistei*, see vv. 3, 4, 5, 7, 8, 9, 11, 17, 20, 21, 22, 23, 24, 27, 28, 29, 30, 31 (and nowhere else in the summary). For *dia pisteōs*, see v. 33 (and v. 39).

2   The author inserts a first-person editorial comment in verse 32a, prefacing and, therefore, delineating List 2.
3   List 1 is canonically ordered; List 2 is not (see Table 6.4).
4   The author's narrative pace changes dramatically in List 2.[19]

Beyond signalling this four-part high-level structure, the author gives us a handful of further structural clues. For example, in List 1 (vv. 3–31) there are three parts: List 1A (vv. 3–7), List 1B (vv. 8–22) and List 1C (vv. 23–31). Each of these parts is signalled primarily by its content. List 1A focuses on Israel's prehistory from Genesis 1 to 7. List 1B focuses on Abraham and his descendants from Genesis 12 to 50. And List 1C focuses on Moses and Israel from Exodus 2 to 14 and Joshua 6, understandably skipping over the unfaithful wilderness generation in between (cf. Heb. 3:7 – 4:11).[20] List 1A, moreover, includes four events. Lists 1B and 1C also contain four events, each associated with one main exemplar (Abraham and Moses respectively), and three additional events associated with the main exemplar's descendants/followers.

Further, there are three parts to List 2 (vv. 32–38): List 2A (v. 32), List 2B (vv. 33–35a) and List 2C (vv. 35b–38). List 2 begins with a brief first-person editorial comment and then follows this with two lists, each containing ten events. The first, List 2B, contains ten examples of faith's triumphs, and the second, List 2C, contains ten examples of faith's challenges.

Inserted, moreover, into both Lists 1 and 2 are four of the author's own editorial comments. These are set apart principally by their content. Each reflects on rather than advances the author's summary. In one case the editorial comment is also signalled by a change in voice, from third to first (see v. 32a, 'And what more shall *I* say?'). One of these comments is very brief (v. 38a), two are slightly longer (vv. 6, 32) and one is extended (vv. 13–16).

Alongside these structural clues are thematic clues. These too are designed to reveal the story's emphases. As we noted, List 2 contains two lists; the first gives ten examples of faith's triumphs and the second gives ten examples of faith's challenges or sufferings. We see something similar

---

[19] See n. 15 above.
[20] Cf. Eisenbaum's less likely proposal. She argues that the author 'end[s] the bulk of his summary just before the establishment of the nation . . . just as [Israel] enters what is truly her national phase' (1997: 396).

Table 6.4 The structure of Hebrews's summary

Unit	Subunit	Ancient	Event	Hebrews	Canonical (and non-canonical) ordering
Introduction, verses 1–2					
	A	(Audience)	Creation	v. 3	Gen. 1 – 2
		Abel	Offering	v. 4	Gen. 4
		Enoch	Translation	v. 5	Gen. 5
			Editorial comment, v. 6		
		Noah	Flood	v. 7	Gen. 6 – 7
	B	Abraham	Call	v. 8	Gen. 12
			Sojourn	vv. 9–10	Gen. 12
			Birth of Isaac	vv. 11–12	Gen. 17, 21
			Editorial comment, vv. 13–16		
List 1			Offering of Isaac	vv. 17–19	Gen. 22
		Isaac	Death	v. 20	Gen. 27
		Jacob	Death	v. 21	Gen. 47
		Joseph	Death	v. 22	Gen. 50
	C	Moses	Birth	v. 23	Exod. 2
			Identification with God's people	vv. 24–26	Exod. 2
			To Midian[21]	v. 27	Exod. 2
			Passover	v. 28	Exod. 12
		Israel (1)	Red Sea	v. 29	Exod. 14
		Israel (2)	Conquest (Jericho)	v. 30	Josh. 6
		Rahab	Conquest (Jericho)	v. 31	Josh. 6
	A		Editorial introduction, v. 32		
	B	Faithful (+)	'conquered kingdoms'	v. 33a	e.g. Judg. 4 (Barak)[22]
			'administered justice'	v. 33b	e.g. 2 Sam. 8 (David)
			'gained what was promised'	v. 33c	e.g. Judg. 4 (Barak)
			'shut the mouths of lions'	v. 33d	Dan. 6 (Daniel)
			'quenched the fury of the flames'	v. 34a	Dan. 3 (Daniel's friends)
List 2			'escaped the edge of the sword'	v. 34b	e.g. 1 Sam. 19 (David)
			'whose weakness was turned to strength'	v. 34c	e.g. Judg. 16 (Samson)
			'who became powerful in battle'	v. 34d	e.g. 1 Sam. 17 (David)
			'routed foreign armies'	v. 34e	e.g. Judg. 7 (Gideon)
			'received back their dead'	v. 35a	e.g. 1 Kgs 17 (widow of Zarephath [Elijah])

Table 6.4 The structure of Hebrews's summary (*cont.*)

Unit	Subunit	Ancient	Event	Hebrews	Canonical (and non-canonical) ordering
			'tortured'	v. 35b	e.g. 2 Macc. 7 (Jewish martyrs)
			'faced jeers and flogging … chains and imprisonment'	v. 36a	e.g. 2 Macc. 6 – 7 and 4 Macc. 12 (Jewish martyrs)
			'put to death by stoning'	v. 37a	e.g. 2 Chr. 24 (Zechariah)
			'sawn in two'	v. 37b	e.g. *Mart. Ascen. Isa.* 1, 5 (Isaiah)
List 2 (*cont.*)	C	Faithful (–)	'killed by the sword'	v. 37c	e.g. Jer. 26 (Uriah)
			'went about in sheepskins and goatskins'	v. 37d	e.g. 2 Kgs 1 (Elijah)
			'destitute'	v. 37e	e.g. 1 Kgs 17, 19 (Elijah)
			'persecuted'	v. 37f	*see above*
			'ill-treated'	v. 37g	*see above*
			Editorial comment, v. 38a		
			'wandered'	v. 38b	e.g. 1 Kgs 18 – 19 (prophets)
Conclusion, vv. 39–40					

in List 1. Here we find a total of eighteen events, and these are equally divided between nine examples of faith's triumphs or positive outcomes (vv. 3, 5, 7, 11-12, 17-19, 28-31) and nine examples of faith's challenges or negative outcomes (vv. 4, 8-10, 20-27). In fact, in addition to this thematic symmetry in Lists 1 and 2 there is a certain sequence to the development of these themes. Each part of Lists 1 and 2 gradually multiplies examples of triumph or suffering. Each successive part begins with the same number of examples, again whether positive or negative, that the previous part concludes with (see Table 6.5). Thus, List 1A ends with two positive examples, and List 1B begins with two negative examples. List 1B ends with three negative examples, and List 1C begins with three negative examples. There is a break in the sequence between Lists 1 and 2. List 2B begins with ten, not four, examples. Still, List 2B ends with (contains) ten positive examples, and List 2C begins with (contains) ten negative examples.

What is more, not only do the author's examples focus on the themes of faith's triumphs and sufferings, but each, with the exception of the

---

[21] Bruce 1990: 312-313.
[22] For these and additional options, see e.g. Koester 2001.

Table 6.5 Positive/negative sequence

Examples	+	−	+	−
List 1A	1	1	2	
List 1B		2	2	3
List 1C		3	4	
Lists 2B, 2C			10	10

first (v. 3), focuses on the same types of triumph and suffering. Each has something to do with either death or social alienation (see Table 6.6).[23]

The author, in fact, draws the audience's attention to these same two themes – social alienation and death – in the exhortation that immediately follows the summary of chapter 11. In 12:1–4 the author says that Jesus, just like the ancients, faced death and social alienation. Jesus faced 'the cross' and 'its shame' (v. 2). An almost identical note is sounded near the end of the letter, when the author reminds the audience, 'Jesus also suffered outside the city'; therefore, they must 'go to him outside the camp, bearing the disgrace he bore' (13:12–13).

Again, all this tells us where the story's emphases lie. The story's structure and themes are clues, intended to tell us why the author tells Israel's story the way he does. To see what these clues reveal, however, we will need to take a closer look at each.

Structural and thematic emphases

What we see when we take a closer look at the story's themes is that the 'great cloud' of ancients, along with Jesus himself, is intended to highlight the similarities between the ancients' experiences and the audience's own. The story's themes are designed to show the audience that persevering in faith is possible even in the face of social alienation and death, obstacles overcome by the ancients and presently troubling the audience. In fact, the correspondence between the audience's situation and the ancients' goes a long way towards explaining the author's example-selection strategy.

---

[23] Cf. Eisenbaum (1997), who sees four common elements in each example/event selected, two of which are similar to our own (namely 1 and 4): (1) 'Death or Near-Death Experience', (2) 'Ability to See into the Future (The Meaning of the Heroes' Faith)', (3) 'Alteration of Status' and (4) 'Marginalization'. Eisenbaum's proposal, however, is slightly out of step with Hebrews, not least since she brackets out from consideration vv. 32–38, causing her to understate not only the summary's sufferings but also its triumphs (see e.g. ibid. 385).

Table 6.6 Death and social alienation in the author's summary

Reference	Criterion	Evidence	+/−
v. 4	Death	'Abel still speaks, even though he is *dead*'.	−
v. 5	Death	'Enoch . . . did not experience *death*'.	+
v. 7	Social alienation	'Noah . . . *condemned the world*'.[24]	+
vv. 8–10	Social alienation	'Abraham . . . made his home . . . *like a stranger* in a foreign country'.	−
vv. 11–12	Death	'Sarah . . . was past childbearing age'. Abraham was 'as good as *dead*'.	+
vv. 17–19	Death	'God could . . . raise the *dead*.' Abraham 'receive[d] Isaac back from *death*'.	+
v. 20	Death[25]	'Isaac blessed Jacob and Esau in regard to *their* future.'	−
v. 21	Death	'Jacob . . . *dying*, blessed . . . Joseph's sons . . . and worshipped'.	−
v. 22	Death[26]	'Joseph, when *his end* was near . . . gave instructions concerning . . . his bones'.	−
v. 23	Death[27]	'[T]hey were not afraid of the *king's edict*'.	−
vv. 24–26	Social alienation	'He regarded *disgrace* for . . . Christ as of greater value than the treasures of Egypt'.	−
v. 27	Death	'[Moses] left Egypt, not fearing the *king's anger*'.[28]	−
v. 28	Death	'[H]e kept the Passover . . . and [escaped] the *destroyer*'.	+
v. 29	Death	'[T]he people passed through the *Red Sea* . . . but . . . the Egyptians . . . drowned'.	+
v. 30	Death	'[T]he walls of Jericho fell'.	+
v. 31	Death	'[S]he . . . was *not killed* with those who were disobedient'.	+
v. 33a	Death	'conquered *kingdoms*'	+
v. 33b	Death[29]	'administered *justice*'	+
v. 33c	Death[30]	'*gained* what was promised'	+
v. 33d	Death	'shut the mouths of *lions*'	+
v. 34a	Death	'quenched the fury of the *flames*'	+
v. 34b	Death	'escaped the edge of the *sword*'	+
v. 34c	Death[31]	'whose weakness was turned to strength'	+
v. 34d	Death	'who became powerful in *battle*'	+
v. 34e	Death	'routed foreign *armies*'	+
v. 35a	Death	'received back their *dead*, raised to life again'	+
v. 35b	Death	'*tortured*, refusing to be released so that they might . . . better resurrection'	−
v. 36	Social alienation	'faced *jeers* and *flogging* . . . chains and imprisonment'	−
v. 37a	Death	'put to *death* by stoning'	−
v. 37b	Death	'*sawn* in two'	−
v. 37c	Death	'*killed* by the sword'	−
v. 37d	Social alienation[32]	'went about in sheepskins and goatskins'	−
v. 37e	Social alienation	'destitute'	−
v. 37f	Social alienation	'persecuted'	−
v. 37g	Social alienation	'ill–treated'	−
v. 38b	Social alienation	'wandered'	−

What we see when we take another look at the story's structure is that this 'great cloud' of ancients, again, along with Jesus himself, is intended to highlight the similarity between the hope that sustained the ancients and the hope that can presently sustain the audience. The story's structure shows the audience that they too can persevere in the face of social alienation and death, precisely because of 'the joy . . . set before [them]' (12:2). This joy – their hope and the ancients' – is not in this world nor in this life.

In short, what we see when we look at the emphases revealed by the story's structure and themes is that both serve the summary's larger function of showing that persevering in faith is possible. The story's themes show that such faith is possible even amid the circumstances in which the audience finds itself, and the story's structure shows that such faith is possible precisely because of the nature of the audience's hope.

Structural emphases

As we noted, the story's structure highlights the believer's hope. The two, deliberately structured lists of ancients, Lists 1 and 2 (vv. 3–31 and vv. 32–38), highlight the believer's hope in an enduring, which is to say resurrected, life. Or, to put it another way, the story's two lists of ancients emphasize the reason why believers can persevere in the face of death.

---

[24] Cf. *kosmon*, v. 7//*kosmos*, v. 38, and nowhere else in Heb. 11.

[25] Unlike the account in Gen. 27 (see specifically vv. 1–2, 4, 7, 10, 41 and, perhaps, 45), the author makes no explicit comment about Isaac's death. However, both this source text (Gen. 27) and the present context (Heb. 11:21–22) suggest v. 20 implies Isaac's death.

[26] As we will see below, social alienation is present in the three concluding events in the Abraham list (vv. 8–22). Like Abraham these too died away from home (vv. 13–16).

[27] As Bruce notes, 'Had their [Moses' parents] defiance of the law been discovered, the penalty would have been severe' (1990: 309).

[28] The king's anger in the original account (Exod. 2:15) was directed towards killing Moses. On the apparent discrepancy between Exod. 2:14–15 and Heb. 11:27, see Bruce; e.g. 1990: 312–313.

[29] This designation owes both to the description's context – with its overwhelming emphasis on triumph over death – and to our earlier identification of the event's source in the life of David (2 Sam. 8:15–18), which speaks of David's administering justice via his military victories over God's enemies (see e.g. Bergen 1996: 351, 'Joab [v. 16; cf. 20:23] was charged with the task of bringing divine justice militarily on those who opposed the Lord'; see e.g. 2 Sam. 8:1–14).

[30] For this designation, see the discussion under 'Thematic emphases' below.

[31] Justification for this categorization is based on the surrounding examples, which suggest 'weakness' here refers to physical weakness, likely caused by an external force, and thus 'strength' refers to the ability to overcome that external force.

[32] Justification for this description and the four that follow (vv. 37e, 37f, 37g and 38b) is found in the author's editorial comment in v. 38a, which (surprisingly) summarizes their situation as indicating not that they were not worthy of the world, as their social alienation surely declared to those without eyes of faith, but rather as indicating that 'the world was not worthy *of them*'.

Their hope cannot be cancelled out by death, because it lies beyond death. What is more, the author's editorial comments highlight the believer's hope in a heavenly inheritance. Social alienation is not a threat to the audience because the audience's home, like that of the ancients, is other-worldly and, therefore, cannot be touched by ostracism from this world.

The story's lists: emphasis on hope beyond this life

Both lists emphasize the believer's hope in an enduring life in the same way. Both have chiastic structures, with centres focusing on resurrection.[33]

Thus, in List 1 the highlighted middle of the structure is found in verses 17-19, where the author says, 'Abraham reasoned that God could even raise the dead, and so in a manner of speaking he did receive Isaac back from death.' On either side of List 1's centre in verses 17-19, we find corresponding emphases. Thus, the author's editorial comment in verses 13-16 focuses on the challenges of faith – social alienation and death – experienced by Abraham and his heirs, as do the final examples from the Abraham list in verses 20-22. The correspondence between the first three events in the Abraham list (vv. 8-12) and the first three events in the Moses list (vv. 23-27) is seen, moreover, in their parallel emphases on departing (vv. 8 and 27),[34] alienation (vv. 9-10 and 24-26) and faithful parents and promised/promising children (vv. 11-12 and 23). Finally, the correspondence between the remaining events in List 1, namely between the first four (vv. 3-7) and last four events (vv. 28-31), is seen principally in the deliverance that both Noah (v. 7) and Moses (v. 28) provided. 'Noah . . . built an ark to save his family' from God's judgment, and Moses 'kept the Passover . . . so that [God's][35] destroyer . . . would not touch . . . Israel'.[36]

---

[33] We owe this insight to Cockerill 2000.

[34] NB: Abraham *exēlthen mē epistamenos pou erchetai*//Moses **katelipen** Aigypton *mē phobētheis ton thymon tou basileōs*. Cockerill correctly adds, 'They [vv. 8 and 23] differ, however, in emphasis: the Abrahamic example focuses on the place to which Abraham is going; the Mosaic, on the place that Moses is leaving' (ibid. 228).

[35] Cf. e.g. Exod. 11:4; 12:12, 27, 29 with 12:23.

[36] Cockerill 2000: 231. Granted, dividing v. 28 from vv. 23-27 runs against one of the author's structuring devices, namely the 4 + 3 pattern found in the Abraham and Moses subunits. We would expect any chiastic structure to honour these patterns, and thus divisions. What use are these patterns, in other words, if they do not play a role in revealing the author's emphasis (i.e. chiastic structure)? An explanation for transgressing the structural clue of the 4 + 3 pattern, and therefore for including v. 28 with vv. 29-31, includes (1) the importance (length) and therefore inclusion of the author's editorial comments (vv. 13-16) in the chiasm, (2) the clear parallels between vv. 13-16 and vv. 20-22, (3) the resulting correspondences between the first three events in the Abraham list (vv. 8-12) and the first three events in the Moses list (vv. 23-27), (4) the shifts between vv. 23-27 and vv. 28-31 from suffering to triumph

A: Deliverance of God's people (List 1A; vv. 3–7)
> B: Departure, alienation, parents/children (List 1B; vv. 8–12)
>> C: Alienation and death (editorial comment; vv. 13–16)
>>> D: *Resurrection hope* (List 1B; vv. 17–19)
>> C': Death and alienation (List 1B; vv. 20–22)
> B': Departure, alienation, parents/children (List 1C; vv. 23–27)

A': Deliverance of God's people (List 1C; vv. 28–31)

List 2 is structured in the same way, and its centre has the same focus on resurrection. The middle of List 2 is found in verses 35a and 35b, where the author says, 'Women received back their dead' (v. 35a) // '[O]thers . . . refus[ed . . . release] so that they might gain an even better resurrection'. The centre of List 2 corresponds, in fact, to the seam between its list of ten triumphs and ten sufferings (Lists 2B and 2C; vv. 33–35a and vv. 35b–38), and in these two lists we find corresponding emphases.[37]

A: Sociopolitical triumph (List 2B; v. 33a, b, c)
> B: Escape from death (List 2B; vv. 33d, 34a, b)
>> C: Sociopolitical triumph (List 2B; v. 34c, d, e)
>>> D: *Resurrection* (List 2B; v. 35a)
>>> D': *Better resurrection* (List 2C; v. 35b)
>> C': Sociopolitical censure and imprisonment (List 2C; v. 36)
> B': Experience of death (List 2C; vv. 37a, b, c)

A': Sociopolitical alienation (List 2C; vv. 37d, 38)

The story's editorial comments: emphasis on hope beyond this world
Two of the author's four editorial comments inserted into his lists highlight the believer's hope in a heavenly inheritance, which the author equates with Abraham's inheritance, the object of the ancients' hope.

We see this connection between the believer's hope and Abraham's land inheritance, beginning in Hebrews 11:8, when the author identifies the referent of Abraham's faith (or hope, v. 1, 'what we hope for') as his land

---

(note 36 *cont.*) and from Egypt to Exodus (on these shifts, see ibid. 227; also 231), (5) the resulting correspondence between vv. 7 and 28, and (6) the dual purpose of vv. 3–7 as both part of List 1 (vv. 3–31) and a quasi-introduction (cf. n. 16 above), with its attention to the audience's *own* faith, its introduction of the triumphs and sufferings of faith (vv. 4–5), and its editorial comment in v. 6, which adds to the definition of faith in v. 1, and moreover sets v. 7 off from vv. 3–5.
[37] Ibid. 222.

inheritance. He says, 'By faith Abraham, when called to go to a place he would later receive as his inheritance, obeyed and went, even though he did not know where he was going.' In the original narrative the author draws from here, that place to which Abraham 'went' was the land of Canaan (see Gen. 12:1, 5, 7; 15:7–8, 16, 18–21). It was this place, promised to Abraham, that he and his heirs died without receiving (Heb. 11:13; cf. v. 22, in the light of Gen. 50:24).[38] This is what the author means in 11:13 when he says, 'They [i.e. Abraham and his heirs] did not receive the things promised; they only saw them and welcomed them from a distance, admitting that they were foreigners and strangers on earth' (cf. v. 9, 'he made his home in the promised land like a stranger in a foreign country'). In fact, when the author goes on to describe what exactly it was that the ancients failed to receive, he explicitly refers to it as a place – a 'country' and a 'city' (v. 16; cf. v. 10: '[H]e was looking forward to the city with foundations').

The author restates the conclusion of 11:13 in his story's conclusion, once more asserting, 'These [i.e. the ancients of Lists 1 and 2] were all commended for their faith; yet none of them received what had been promised' (v. 39). In other words, what the ancients hoped for but did not receive was precisely the land, the inheritance, promised to Abraham (see Table 6.7).

In the author's conclusion he also draws a connection between the ancients' hope and the audience's, though the connection here is but a whisper:

These [i.e. the ancients] were all commended for their faith, yet none of them received what had been promised [i.e. Abraham's land inheritance], since God had planned something better for us [i.e. the audience] so that only together with us would they be made perfect. (Hebrews 11:39–40)

What the author says here is that neither the audience nor the ancients could receive what was promised – Abraham's inheritance – without first

---

[38] In 11:22 the author says that it was 'by faith' that Joseph, Abraham's great-grandson, not only 'spoke about the exodus' but also 'gave instructions concerning . . . his bones' (v. 22). These 'instructions', which the author expects his readers will remember, were that Joseph's brothers should take his bones out of Egypt and bury them in 'the land [God] promised on oath to Abraham, Isaac and Jacob' (Gen. 50:24; cf. also Josh. 24:32), which is to say, in the 'promised land' (Heb. 11:9), Abraham's 'inheritance' of Canaan (v. 8).

Table 6.7 Parallels between verses 13 and 39

Verse 13, 'the things promised'	Verse 39, 'what had been promised'
'All these people'	'These . . . all'
'by faith' (cf. '[T]hey were longing . . . Therefore God is not ashamed', v. 16)	'commended for their faith'
'They did not receive the things promised'.	'[N]one of them received what had been promised.'
'[T]hey were foreigners and strangers on earth [gēs]'.	'They wandered in deserts and mountains, living in caves and in holes in the ground [gēs]' (v. 38).

experiencing perfection, and perfection, while not available during the ancients' lifetimes, was now available during the audience's, which is what the author means when he says, 'God had planned something better for us [i.e. the audience and all post-advent believers].' This 'something better', however, probably includes not simply the experience of perfection but also its benefits, which is to say, spiritual access to Abraham's inheritance now (10:19–22) and bodily access later (cf. 13:14).[39]

This inference from the author's conclusion is corroborated by the story's introduction, which draws a clearer line between the audience's and ancients' hope and, therefore, between the audience's hope and Abraham's inheritance. '[F]aith is confidence in what we hope for [cf. 'what had been promised', v. 39] and assurance about what we do not see. *This* is what the ancients were commended for' (vv. 1–2). It is not simply the ancients' faith – the ancients' hope – that the audience must imitate, but the direction of that faith as well. *This* will commend them to God, just as it did the ancients. After all, as the author puts it in v. 16, 'Instead, [the ancients] were longing for a better country – a heavenly one [cf. 'what we hope for', v. 1]. Therefore God is not ashamed to be called their God [i.e. God *commends* them], for he has prepared a city for them.' Faith – hope – *in Abraham's land inheritance* is what commended the ancients and what the author implies will commend the audience as well.[40]

---

[39] See Easter 2014: 94. The same is true presently for the ancients as well. See 'spirits of the righteous made perfect', Heb. 12:23.

[40] See ibid. 87–88. A handful of further observations from Hebrews add to the plausibility of this connection between Abraham's inheritance and the believer's hope: (1) In 10:34 the author reminds the audience that in times past they 'joyfully accepted the confiscation of [their]

It is this hope, therefore, in Abraham's inheritance that the author highlights in his story, principally in two of his editorial comments. But it is also found elsewhere. For example, in the first two events selected from Abraham's life (List 1B, vv. 8–22), the author emphasizes social alienation and the believer's corresponding hope. Abraham, Isaac and Jacob, we are told in vv. 8–10, lived in Canaan like 'stranger[s]' because they were looking for a God-built city (v. 10). The same emphasis concludes the Abraham list (vv. 20–22), where the author notes both the deaths of Abraham's heirs and their non-reception of the inheritance (see esp. v. 22).[41] Alienation, moreover, is front and centre in the longest example given in the Moses list (vv. 24–26). It is also the main and last emphasis in the author's list of faithful sufferers found at the end of List 2, just before the story's conclusion (vv. 36a, 37d–g, 38b).

Here too the author inserts an editorial comment, underscoring this emphasis on social alienation. In verse 38a, the author's final editorial comment, he not only highlights social alienation but also explains it,

---

property [*hyparchontōn*; cf. the use of this participle in Acts 4:32], because [they] knew that [they] had better and lasting [*menousan*] possessions' (cf. *menō* in 12:27; 13:14; Cockerill 2012: 669, n. 38). He goes on to tell them that so long as they '[do] not throw away [their] confidence' – if only they 'persevere[d]' (v. 36) in their 'faith' (v. 38) – they would 'be richly rewarded' (*misthapodosian*; v. 35; see also 'receive what he has promised', v. 36; objects of God's 'pleasure', v. 38; and 'saved', v. 39). This language of reward, in fact, is used in the summary to refer to Abraham's inheritance. Moses, we are told, 'regarded disgrace for the sake of Christ as of greater value than the treasures of Egypt, because he was looking ahead [*apeblepen*; cf. *idontes*, Heb. 11:13] to his reward [*misthapodosian*]' (v. 26; cf. also 11:6). This reward, in the original narrative from which the author draws, is Abraham's land inheritance. In Exod. 3:10 God tells Moses that he is to 'bring [his] people the Israelites out of Egypt' and 'into a good and spacious land, a land flowing with milk and honey – the home of the Canaanites' (v. 8; see similarly Exod. 3:17; 13:5; etc.). (2) In 2:5 the author talks about the 'world to come' (2:5), which, he says, is subjected to God's sons and daughters – believers (v. 10) – whom he refers to as 'Abraham's descendants' (2:16). Hebrews, moreover, associates this 'world to come' with the heavenly place Jesus, the believer's 'forerunner' (6:20) and 'pioneer' (2:10; 12:2), entered at his exaltation (1:6; read in the light of 1:3 and, therefore, Ps. 110:1; see e.g. Moffitt 2011: 73–74; see also 75–80), which then corresponds to the way the author describes Abraham's inheritance in Heb. 11 (esp. v. 16). (3) In the author's first extended exhortation (3:1 – 4:13) he describes the believer's hope as a place of 'rest', towards which all of God's people pilgrimage and, much like the inheritance in Heb. 11, as a place one must persevere in faith (and obedience, 11:8) to enter (3:11, 19; 4:1, 3, 5–6, 10–11; see e.g. Lincoln 1983: 208–209; Easter 2014: 80–81). (4) We see a similar connection in 12:18–29 when the author tells his readers that they 'have come to Mount Zion, to the city of the living God, *the heavenly Jerusalem*'. (5) The author refers to the believer's hope in 9:15 as the 'eternal inheritance', which is accessed only through the forgiveness of sins made available through the new covenant. This echoes the argument in 11:39–40, where the author says that reception of the promised place ('what had been promised', v. 39) is predicated on perfection, which includes forgiveness of sins (see n. 51 below). On the centrality of place in Hebrews and its association with Abraham's inheritance, see esp. Harris 2009: 165–255.

[41] See n. 38 above.

telling his audience that God's people are alienated from this world precisely because the world 'was [and, therefore, is] not worthy of them'.

The chief locus for this emphasis, however, is found in another editorial comment, the author's longest. In verses 13–16 the author inserts an extended comment, nearly dividing his Abraham list in half. Here, as in verse 38a (cf. also v. 10), he reinterprets the audience's alienation and clarifies the nature of their hope, insisting that God's people should expect to be outsiders, 'foreigners and strangers on earth' (v. 13). After all, the object of their hope, the place for which they 'long[ed]' was a 'heavenly' country (v. 16), which is to say their hope and, therefore, their home was not in this world.

This distinction between the present world (i.e. Canaan) and the believer's inheritance helps, in fact, to illuminate two other parts of the author's story. In 11:10 the author describes Abraham's inheritance as a God-built city: he was 'looking forward to the city with foundations, whose architect and builder is God'. One suspects Abraham knew, as the author assumes his audience will as well, that 'God is the builder of every-thing' (Heb. 3:4; cf. 11:3), including all the cities that existed in Canaan during Abraham's sojourn (11:9). Here, however, the author appears to be pointing to something beyond the fact that God is, in some ultimate sense, responsible for everything that is. In fact, in the light of the author's description of this same city in 11:16 (i.e. related to a *heavenly* country), it appears the author wants us to see that the object of Abraham's earnest faith was God-built in another way.

In Hebrews this language is also used to describe heavenly things in contrast with earthly things. The heavenly tabernacle is described as God-built ('set up by the Lord', 8:2), in 'heaven itself' (9:24) and, moreover, 'not a part of this creation' (9:11). The earthly tabernacle, however, is described as just the opposite. It is human-built and, therefore, very much a part of this creation (see 8:2; 9:11, 24). Thus, it appears that when the author refers to Abraham's inheritance as a city 'whose architect and builder is God' (11:10) and, at the same time, relates this city to a 'heavenly [country]' (11:16), he means for his readers to associate this city with the heavenly tabernacle and, therefore, to disassociate it from this creation, to disassociate it from *this* world.

Something similar should likely be inferred from the author's descrip-tion of the inheritance as a 'better country' in 11:16. Earlier in the letter the author associates this earth with Israel's priesthood and tabernacle, both of which anticipated the 'better' realities of Jesus' heavenly priesthood (7:11–28) and the heavenly tabernacle (8:5; 9:1–10, 24; etc.). 'If [Jesus] were on earth,' the author reasons, 'he would not be a priest, for there are already priests who offer the gifts prescribed by the law' (8:4). What this suggests, therefore, is that if the (anticipated) better priesthood and sacred space were heavenly and not earthly, then so also is the 'better country'.[42]

The distinction between the present world and the believer's hope is underscored elsewhere in the letter. In Hebrews 12:22–29 and 13:14 the author says that Abraham's inheritance (see 'city' and 'heavenly Jerusalem' in 12:22; cf. 11:10, 16), which he refers to as an unshakable kingdom (12:28), will remain (*meinē*) only after the present world – 'the earth . . . [and] heavens . . . that is, created things' – is 'remov[ed]' (vv. 26–27; cf. 1:10–12).[43] Similarly, in 13:14 he says, 'Here we do not have an enduring city [*menousan polin*], but we are looking for the city that is to come' (13:14; cf. 12:27–28; also 10:34).[44] One cannot have an enduring city (13:14) in a place that is itself not enduring (12:27; cf. 1:10–12).[45]

Similarly, in Hebrews 2:5 the author straightforwardly distinguishes the inheritance from this world, calling it 'the world to come [*mellousan*]' (cf. 13:14). This world in 2:5–18 is the heavenly place to which Jesus was exalted (2:9; cf. 1:6; also 1:3, 13; etc.) and from which he is presently

[42] Read in the light of 11:16 (and, moreover, the discussion to follow), vv. 8–9's description of Canaan as Abraham's 'inheritance' and as 'the promised land' should be understood e.g. like the real, if ultimately typological, efficacy of Israel's cult (on this, see Compton 2015: 121–124) or God's real, if also typological, presence in Israel's tabernacle. What is more, 11:16 may also suggest that v. 13's description of Abraham as a foreigner and stranger 'on earth [. . .]' (*epi tēs gēs*) and v. 38's note about this world not being 'worthy of [the ancients]' should take on added significance.

[43] Hebrews distinguishes between the shakable heavens and the unshakable heavens where the believer's inheritance lies. Cockerill e.g. describes the 'heavenly Jerusalem' of 12:22 as 'beyond creation and creation's divinely intended goal' (2012: 669–670, including nn. 37–38; see also Easter 2014: 80, including n. 7).

[44] See Attridge 1989: 399, including n. 128.

[45] Here we should note that some early Jewish texts also describe Abraham's inheritance as other-worldly but define this other world as a renewal of this creation (see e.g. *Jub.* 1.29; *4 Ezra* 6.16; 7.75; *L.A.B.* 3.10; 19.7, 12–13; *2 Bar.* 32.1–7; 57.2). Many of these texts also suggest that Abraham's inheritance will encompass the entirety of the renewed world (see e.g. *CD-A* 3.20; also 2.8–12; 4QpPs^a 4.10–12; *Jub.* 32.18–19; *L.A.B.* 3.10, in the light of 19.7, 12–13 and 23.11–13; *2 Bar.* 4.2–6; 15.1–8; 85.3–5) and can be accessed only in a resurrected body (see e.g. *Jub.* 15.27; *4 Ezra* 7.10–14; *L.A.B.* 3.10; 19.12–13; *2 Bar.* 49.2–3; 51.1; see Moffitt 2011: 81–118; Harris 2009: 104–164, 291–292; cf. also *EDEJ* 797–799.). What we have seen from Hebrews, however, appears to set its eschatology slightly apart (see Moffitt's similar admission, 2011: 117). This world, according to Hebrews, will instead one day 'wear out', 'be changed' and 'remov[ed]' (1:10–12; 12:26–27; see e.g. Bruce 1990: 364–365; Cockerill 2012: 668, n. 34; et al.).

leading 'Abraham's descendants' (2:16) to the glory and honour given them at creation but lost in the fall (2:5–10).[46]

This description of Abraham's inheritance, both in the author's story of Israel and elsewhere in his letter, suggests one final point about the author's structural emphases on the believer's anticipated resurrection and heavenly home: they are related. If the believer's heavenly inheritance comes (13:14; 'remain[s]', 12:27) only after the 'remov[al] of . . . created things' (12:27) and if these created things include (mortal) human bodies, as Hebrews elsewhere implies (2:7; 11:3; cf. 9:28), then human participation in the inheritance requires the type of bodily existence that can be described as unshakable (12:27–28), which is precisely the kind of existence those 'refusing to be released' in Hebrews 11:35b sought. They sought a 'better resurrection', one not to a revivified mortal life (11:35a) but to an enduring life (cf. 13:14; also 6:2). To put it simply, Hebrews's description of the heavenly inheritance suggests that entrance requires a resurrection body.

This reading corresponds to the way Hebrews talks about Jesus' own entrance into heaven.[47] It too was necessarily preceded by resurrection. In Hebrews 7:15–17 the author says that Jesus' resurrection was necessarily preliminary to his priestly appointment, which Hebrews closely associates with his entrance into heaven.[48] Appointment to the Levitical priesthood required a specific 'ancestry', while appointment to the Melchizedekian priesthood required a specific kind of life, something the author calls 'indestructible life' (7:16) and infers from the fact that Psalm 110:4 addresses a priest who remains 'for ever' (v. 17). In the light of his earlier insistence that Jesus' priestly appointment was necessarily preceded by death (5:7–10),[49] the author's reference to 'indestructible life' in 7:16 is

---

[46] Some insist that Heb. 4:8 also distinguishes between Canaan and Abraham's inheritance. Lincoln says e.g. 'Joshua (Greek *Iēsous*) did not give the people rest (4:8); his entry into the promised land can be compared to that of the high priest into the copy and shadow of the heavenly sanctuary (cf. 8:5)' (1983: 212; see also Martin 2015: 142–143, n. 44; Easter 2014: 81). What points against this, however, is the fact that the main emphasis in this part of Hebrews is not on the contrast between type (Canaan/this earth) and antitype (Israel's true place of rest) but on the fact that rest is for believers only. Unbelief, in other words, rather than the fact that Canaan was only a type, is the main reason emphasized for why Israel failed to enter God's rest (see e.g. 3:8, 10, 12–13, 15, 16, 18, 19; 4:2, 6, 11).

[47] Cf. Easter 2014: 95–97.

[48] In the inclusio of Heb. 1:5//1:13 the author describes Jesus' heavenly enthronement with the language of Pss 2:7 (also 2 Sam. 7:14//1 Chr. 17:13) and 110:1. In Heb. 5:5–6 he uses Ps. 2:7 and this time Ps. 110:4 to describe Jesus' priestly appointment.

[49] In Heb. 5:7–10 Jesus' appointment followed his perfection, which necessarily followed his death. On this see Compton 2015: 70–75.

likely a reference to Jesus' resurrection. Jesus' heavenly appointment, in other words, required the possession of a (better-)resurrected life (cf. 11:35b), the kind of indestructible life no longer susceptible to mortality.[50]

In fact, it is possible that the same rationale underlies what Hebrews says about the believer's perfection. Hebrews seems to imply that the believer's perfection, which gives access to God and the heavenly inheritance (11:39–40),[51] includes – leads to – the believer's resurrection. It does this by removing sin and all sin's effects (e.g. 'guilt', 10:2), including, according to Hebrews 2:5–18, both the 'power' and 'fear' of 'death' (vv. 14–15). Jesus 'bring[s] many sons and daughters to glory', he saves (see 'salvation', v. 10) and gives them access to and rule over 'the world to come' (v. 5), by 'mak[ing] atonement for [their] sins' and, thus, liberating them from death's lord (i.e. the devil) and menace.[52] If, as Hebrews elsewhere insists, humans still die (9:28), then Jesus' victory over death on behalf of believers likely refers to (and leads to) their post-mortem resurrection, which removes sin's final effect and fits humans for entrance to glory. It 'remov[es] what can be shaken' (12:27–28) and provides bodies appropriate for 'an enduring city' (13:14).[53]

Summary

If the author's summary functions to encourage persevering faith in the Christian confession by showing that such faith is possible, its structure serves this function by emphasizing and, therefore, explaining how such faith is possible. The 'great cloud' of ancients persevered in their faith precisely because they knew that their hope was beyond death – the emphasis at the centre of Lists 1 and 2 – and this world – the principal emphasis of the author's editorial comments. The ancients, in other words, persevered because they knew, as the audience itself must know, that the believer's hope rests on a bodily resurrection to a heavenly inheritance to come.

---

[50] See similarly e.g. Koester 2001: 355; also Moffitt 2011: 203.

[51] Perfection, which was not available during the ancients' era (11:39–40), completely removes sin (10:1–4; see also vv. 16–18), giving worshippers access to God's heavenly presence (9:6–10; cf. 9:11, 24), spiritually now (10:19–22; cf. 12:23) and bodily later (2:5–18; cf. 11:35b; also 6:2).

[52] The precise relationship between sin and death is not clearly stated in Heb. 2, but the fact that atonement rescues humans from death's 'power' and terror ('fear of death', v. 15) suggests that sin is, in some way, responsible for the devil's power, which is to say for the human predicament. This, of course, accords well with early Christian teaching elsewhere (see e.g. Rom. 6:23; Col. 2:13–15).

[53] Paul makes a similar argument in 1 Cor. 15:50–57.

Thematic emphases

The story's themes of faith's triumphs and sufferings, like the author's structure, serve a specific purpose. Both themes highlight the similarity between the ancients' and the audience's experiences. The ancients and the audience experienced social alienation and the threat of death. The story's themes, however, do more than this. The focus on faith's sufferings underscores the possibility of persevering in faith and, at the same time, the fact that such sufferings cannot touch the believer's hope. The focus on faith's triumphs underscores the reality of the believer's hope. The ancients' triumphs against obstacles similar to those troubling the audience are intended to foreshadow and, thus, guarantee the audience's own future and lasting triumph.

Faith's sufferings

In the light of the overall function of the author's summary – to show that persevering faith is possible – it is not hard to discern the specific function of the story's thematic emphasis on faith's sufferings. In nineteen examples of faith's sufferings (vv. 4, 8, 9–10, 20, 21, 22, 23, 24–26, 27, 35b, 36, 37a, 37b, 37c, 37d, 37e, 37f, 37g, 38b) the author insists that the ancients maintained their faith even in the face of social alienation and death, not least because they knew that such sufferings could not touch the object of their hope, which was in another world and another life. And his point is simple: if the ancients could do this, so too can the audience.

This focus on faith's suffering, in fact, appears to be the story's main thematic focus. Suffering is, after all, the subject of the first and last events in the extended Abraham story of List 1 (List 1B, vv. 8–22) and of the author's longest editorial comment, which nearly divides this Abraham narrative right in half (vv. 13–16). Suffering, moreover, concludes the story's climax, found in List 2's rapid-fire list of ancients (List 2C, vv. 35b–38).[54] And not only does List 2 end with ten final examples of suffering, but it also includes the author's final editorial note, also focusing on suffering (v. 38a). The author's story concludes, moreover, with the same emphasis, noting that even where faith triumphed, these triumphs were but temporary, since all of the ancients died and 'none . . . received what had been promised' (v. 39).

---

[54] Cockerill 2000: 232.

Faith's triumphs

The author's nineteen positive examples (see vv. 3, 5, 7, 11–12, 17–19, 28, 29, 30, 31, 33a, 33b, 33c, 33d, 34a, 34b, 34c, 34d, 34e, 35a) serve a different purpose. They give the audience a typology of triumph. The triumphs, to say it another way, point the audience forward to and give them assurance of the better triumphs awaiting them.[55] The triumphs foreshadow and, therefore, fortify the audience's hope, specifically hope in an enduring (i.e. resurrected) life. After all, almost every example of faith's triumphs (except v. 3) has to do with temporal triumph over death. Each is meant to point to the better triumph over death – the 'better resurrection' (v. 35b) – that God's people await.

Two observations point us in this direction. First, as noted above, the structural centres of both Lists 1 and 2 focus on resurrection. And each points to the typological role played by its respective example of triumph. Thus, in List 1's centre (vv. 17–19) the author describes Abraham's triumph – his 'receiv[ing] Isaac back from death' – as a *parabolē* (cf. the NIVUK's 'in a manner of speaking'). Abraham's triumph in Isaac was like a resurrection. But, more than this, the author's earlier use of the same word (9:9)[56] indicates that what Isaac experienced was not only like a resurrection, but also pointed to resurrection, just as Israel's tabernacle and priesthood pointed to (NIVUK, 'illustrat[ed]', 9:9) Jesus' better priesthood and the better access to God Jesus' priesthood brings.

A similar point is made at the centre of List 2, where the author contrasts the triumph of resurrection in verse 35a ('raised to life again') with the suffering in verse 35b, endured due to a hope in a 'better resurrection'. Throughout Hebrews 'better' is used to describe the realities of the Christian era to which the former (good) things pointed. In other words, the triumphs in both verses 17–19 and verse 35a are types (or parables) meant to point beyond themselves and to assure the audience of the coming better reality: the coming better, which is to say, lasting, resurrection.

Second, this same point is made in the author's contrast between Abel and Enoch, a paradigmatic contrast between the sufferings and triumphs of faith that opens the author's story and prepares the way for the ebb and flow of suffering and triumph of List 1 and the contrast between the

---

[55] See the similar function Cockerill assigns to the triumphs of vv. 33–35a (ibid. 223).
[56] Cf. BDAG, s.v., *'parabolē'*.

triumphs of List 2B and sufferings of List 2C (vv. 33–35a; 35b–38). Abel suffers in faith as an example for the audience. And Enoch triumphs, 'not experienc[ing] death' (v. 5). Enoch's experience, at first, seems rather more to illustrate the antitype, the reality, of triumph rather than its type, its anticipation, in apparent contrast with verses 17–19 and 35a. However, the author maintains that even Enoch failed to receive what had been promised (see vv. 13 and 39), a comment indicating that Enoch did not experience the reality for which he longed, namely, resurrection to a heavenly home. This conclusion is required by the fact that the author insists that none of the ancients received what had been promised because none was 'perfect[ed]' (v. 40). They all lived and died (or were translated) prior to the perfection and, thus, forgiveness (10:15–18) provided by Jesus' sacrifice (v. 14), a prerequisite for entrance into the heavenly inheritance. In fact, as we noted above, even though Hebrews's audience lives in the era of perfection and has unprecedented access to God (see e.g. 4:3; 10:19–22; 12:22), it too still awaits the consummation of the era and the resurrection to the heavenly home that consummation brings (see e.g. 9:28; cf. 1:14; 2:10; 4:11; 13:14; etc.).[57]

Therefore, the typology highlighted by the structure of Hebrews – both the chiastic centres of Lists 1 and 2 and the paradigmatic role of verses 4–5 – suggests that each triumph over death is meant to point to and assure the audience of the better triumph awaiting in the resurrection. Thus, Noah's (v. 7), Abraham's (and Sarah's; vv. 11–12), Israel's (vv. 28–30), Rahab's (v. 31) and others' rescue from or victory over death (or the threat of death; 33a, b, c, d, 34a, b, c, d, e) serves to fortify the audience's faith in the certainty of their resurrection hope.[58]

Summary

As we noted, all the negative examples of faith's sufferings, whether death or social alienation, serve to fortify the audience by showing that others – many others – persevered under similar circumstances and did so based on the firm conviction that their hope was neither in this life

---

[57] On this tension, see Lincoln 1983: 210–212.

[58] In fact, this typological understanding of the triumphs of the author's summary helps explain what the author means in v. 33c when he says some 'gained what was promised'. The author's competence, everywhere indicated, rules out a sloppy contradiction between vv. 13 and 39 and suggests instead that what was 'gained' was the temporal, typological experience of triumph, something that was meant to point, as we have seen, to the final, antitypical experience of triumph awaited by and assured for all of God's people.

nor in this world. All the positive examples of faith's triumphs – except verse 3 – relate to temporary rescue from or victory over death. Each serves to fortify the audience by showing that others – many others – experienced triumph in the face of death and, thereby, points to the real and indeed better triumph awaiting all of God's people. In sum, the story's themes emphasize both the possibility of persevering in faith even in the midst of suffering and the promise and reality of the 'joy set before' them.

Summary of content

If the summary functions to encourage persevering faith in the Christian confession by showing that such faith is possible, then the content of the summary serves this function and, at the same time, corroborates it by showing how such faith is possible. Persevering in faith is possible, even in the face of social alienation and death, because the believer's hope cannot be touched by either. The believer's hope is, as it has always been, in another world and in an enduring life. The summary's structure emphasizes the nature of the believer's hope, while the repeated themes of suffering and triumph underscore both the possibility of persevering in hope and the reality of hope's – faith's – object.

In short, the author wisely curates a list of faithful believers – a 'great cloud' – from Israel's past to show his audience that what God calls for is possible because it was done before in circumstances just like those the audience itself has experienced. Like the ancients, and indeed like Jesus, the audience too must fix their eyes on the 'joy set before [them]' (12:2), a joy that neither social alienation nor death can touch. They must fix their eyes on the heavenly home and the enduring life – the resurrected life – God will give them to enter and enjoy.

The contribution of Hebrews's summary

Having taken a close look at the author's summary, both its context and content, we are now in a position to take a step back and describe its biblical-theological contribution. There are at least two contributions that Hebrews's story makes to our understanding of how the earliest Christians put their Bibles together. The first relates to the function of Israel's story. The second relates to its plot. And both, as we shall see, are related to one another.

First, Hebrews's story tells us something about the function of Israel's story. It can be used pastorally. It can be used, in other words, morally to exhort, challenge and inspire behaviour. Its characters, including one or two unlikely ones (e.g. Samson!),[59] can be used, alongside Jesus (12:1–4), as models to emulate, examples to follow. This is, as we have already suggested, a fresh contribution. It suggests that Israel's story can be read not simply negatively (see e.g. Matthew's summaries or Acts's; cf. 1 Cor. 10:6 or esp. Heb. 3:7 – 4:13) but also positively.

Second, and, as we shall see, related, Hebrews's story tells us something about the plot of Israel's story. Israel's story, we saw, is only one part of a larger story, begun at creation and extending through the present era and to the 'world to come'. One implication of this – in fact, the author makes this quite clear – is that the present era, that of the audience and our own, is a continuation of Israel's, and therefore of creation's, story. Hebrews's story shows us that Israel's story *necessarily* continues into the present era (see e.g. 11:39–40). The continuity between the audience's story and Israel's is underscored, moreover, by the fact, implied by the author, that *all* believers are, like Abraham, 'strangers in a foreign country'. We 'together' (11:40) wait for 'the city that is to come'. Abraham's sojourn, his exile, if we can call it that, is different from the exile theme we noted elsewhere – for example, in Matthew's two summaries. In Hebrews's case Abraham's status and ours too does not owe, at least according to Hebrews 11,[60] to disobedience and, therefore, to God's retributive justice (i.e. his wrath) but rather simply to our place in the story. All believers wander in exile during their time on this earth, whether in Canaan, Babylon or elsewhere simply because our homeland, our inheritance, is yet to come.

At the same time that Hebrews highlights its audience's continuity with Israel's story, it highlights its discontinuity as well, though a better way to put this would be to talk not of discontinuity but rather of progress or fulfilment. What Israel's institutions – the 'characters' of Israel's plot – pointed to, whether a better covenant, sacrifice, priesthood or sacred space, has finally arrived in part with Jesus' first advent. The story, in other words, has *progressed*. Its promises have begun to be *fulfilled*. This motif of progress and fulfilment, therefore, suggests something fundamental

---

[59] Here we might also add 'non-canonical' ones (see e.g. 11:35b, 36a). This in fact provides warrant for the spiritual value of e.g. post-canonical Christian biography.

[60] There is a sense in which our wandering is indeed a form of exile, considering what Hebrews says elsewhere about what humans lost in the fall (see esp. Heb. 2:7; cf. 3:7 – 4:13).

about the role of Israel's story in the Bible's larger plot arc of creation-to-'the world to come' (i.e. what John and others call 'new creation'). Israel's story, as Hebrews makes clear, plays the role of foreshadowing and preparing for the audience's new-covenant era.[61] Israel's story is meant, as we have seen, to show how the human problem is to be solved and the human vocation and destiny fulfilled. And it does this in 'shadow[s]' cast by the new-covenant realities themselves (see 10:1). Israel's institutions, in other words, are related to but not identical with the realities themselves, in the same way that a tree's shadow is related to – cast by – the tree but is not the tree itself.

We saw this very clearly in the way Hebrews's story described one of Israel's central 'institutions', one of the central 'characters' in Israel's story: the land inheritance. Hebrews 11 tells us that this inheritance should be understood in the same way we understand Israel's cult and covenant, as shadows of a better reality. The author tells us that Israel's true, *real* inheritance is, unlike Canaan, part of another, heavenly world, which remains (or comes) only once this present world is removed. Here we must remember that the author says this – he uses Israel's story in this way – precisely due to his sense of his audience's need. The author recalls this element from Israel's story – the other-worldly nature of Israel's inheritance – to encourage his friends to persevere in their faith in the face of painful social alienation. To put it one more way, he draws his audience's attention to the true nature of their and the ancients' hope to remind them that their home is not in this world but in the world to come.

Closely related to this is the author's subtle connection between Israel's heavenly inheritance and resurrection hope. If the heavenly inheritance comes only after the removal of created things, then resurrection – of the kind described in 11:35 (a 'better' resurrection) – is needed to fit creatures – believers – for entrance. This connection between the inheritance and resurrection is, we noted, of a piece with the way the author earlier talks about Jesus' own resurrection, which necessarily preceded his entrance into the heavenly inheritance. And, moreover, it is coordinate with the way the author elsewhere talks about the believer's perfection, which is not only necessary for entrance into the heavenly inheritance but also includes resurrection. After all, as we noted, perfection speaks of the

---

[61] NB: It does this, as we see esp. elsewhere in Hebrews (see e.g. 7:11–28; 8:6–13), self-consciously (on this, see Caird 1959).

removing of sin *and all of sin's effects*, including mortality. This connection, this biblical-theological contribution, too is rooted in the author's pastoral agenda. How else can believers persevere in faith in the face of death if not by holding fast to the promise of enduring life after death, which fits one for entrance into the long-awaited and unshakable world to come?

Conclusion

In retelling Israel's story in Hebrews 11 the author commends Israel's faithfulness to his audience and reminds them and us too that God's people are able to persevere in faith, even in the face of profound suffering, precisely because our hope is not in this world nor in this life. The believer's hope, rather, has always been and remains heavenly and is accessed by and only by those with lives of the same quality as the inheritance itself – enduring.

7
Conclusion: a biblical-theological rule of faith

For the earliest Christians the story of Israel could never be separated from its culmination in Jesus Christ. As we observed in the introduction, SIS are not mere historical records but stories that actualize Israel's history for the present and future. In the case of the authors of the NT the story always finds its culmination in the person and work of Jesus, the promised Messiah. Time and again we have observed that the writers of the NT were unable to tell the story of Israel apart from its climax in the life, death and resurrection of Jesus. Following from this, the story continues in the work of Jesus and everyone who belongs to him by faith, Jew and Gentile alike. Consequently, according to the apostles, the story of Israel found in the OT continues to this very day and even into the eschatological future.

In this final chapter we will summarize our findings and consider the implications for our own practice of biblical theology. In so doing we will summarize our best understanding of an apostolic biblical theology and what we can learn from it. If the SIS in the NT are inspired examples of biblical theology, then they provide a kind of biblical-theological 'rule of faith' that should shape our own retellings of Israel's story. This is not to say that the NT will tell us everything we need to know about the OT. The OT itself should also be generative in our study of biblical theology, just as it was for the apostles. But it should be generative only *within* a biblical-theological rule of faith provided by the apostles.

Summary of the contributions

The diversity of genres in the NT is evident in our analysis of the SIS. In Matthew and Acts the stories are primarily advancing the narrative purposes of their authors. Therefore, we find the primary contributions of these retellings in narrative terms as they instruct us about the plot and characters found in Israel's story. They teach us about the nature of Israel's continuing story, the climax of its plot in the life of Jesus and the function of some of the story's characters. In the argumentative settings of Galatians and Romans we see specific aspects of the story elucidated as Paul teases out the implications of the coming of the Messiah for Jews and Gentiles. And in the highly structured, urgently pastoral argument of Hebrews we see the story of Israel folded into the overall structure of the book in a complex argument that culminates in Jesus, the pioneer and perfecter of faith (Heb. 12:2). While these stories differ in emphases and detail, they all share the fundamental premise that the story of Israel culminates in the Messiah; following this, the story of Israel continues with the life and mission of the church.

In Matthew we are introduced to the continuing story of Israel. Matthew's genealogy walks us from Abraham to David to the exile and finally to Christ. In this story we see the narrative tension of Israel's story is the unresolved exile. Near the end of the book the parable of the tenants indicates that the exile is a result of Israel's rejection of the Lord's messengers, which culminates in Israel's rejecting the cornerstone himself. Yet through this rejected cornerstone the experience of exile comes to an end for those who follow him, and the story reaches its climax. Yet this story is not yet complete, for Matthew invites us into this story as Jesus sends his followers out to proclaim him to the end of the earth.

The two SIS in Acts are similar to Matthew's in several ways, but they also add unique emphases that help us to grasp key features of Israel's story better. The emphasis on the covenantal substructure of Israel's story accounts for the content of Stephen's speech before the Sanhedrin and Paul's sermon in Pisidian Antioch. These two SIS also emphasize individual characters in the story, especially the rejected and vindicated servants of the Lord in Stephen's speech. Finally, these two stories, and Acts in general, emphasize the positive aspects of the life of David more than the summaries in Matthew. Still, Paul's sermon emphasizes that God's fulfilment of the covenant with David required a greater David, the Messiah, Jesus.

As we turn to Paul's letters, we observe that in Galatians 3 – 4 the apostle gives several different SIS, reminding us that the story of Israel can be summarized faithfully in different ways, even within the same chapter. The most important contribution to our understanding of Israel's story is Paul's elucidation of the law's role in Israel's story. He argues that it plays a secondary role to the Abrahamic covenant, a negative role by imprisoning the world in sin, a temporary role until the coming of Messiah and a preparatory role for the era of grace and faith. The law plays a tragic role in Israel's story. But it also teaches us that Abrahamic sonship and inheritance come about by God's own grace.

The grace of God in Israel's story is teased out even further in Romans 9 – 11, where Paul reflects deeply on the identity of 'Israel'. Here he argues that 'Israel' has always been a theological category, a people determined not by ethnic descent or moral effort but ultimately by God's own gracious call. And yet this does not mean that God has rejected the physical descendants of Jacob, for his plan is to show mercy to all, both Jews and Gentiles. Thus, we are again reminded that the story of Israel continues in a surprising way through the mission of the church and beyond. Romans 9 – 11 reminds us that we should also be nuanced in our understanding of 'God's people', avoiding a rigid ethnic understanding that roots our understanding of Israel in human descent or effort rather than in God's call, as well as avoiding replacement theology that ignores God's irrevocable calling and his purpose in hardening Israel and that acts as if mercy is only for Gentiles.

Finally, in his retelling of Israel's story in Hebrews 11, the author of Hebrews tells Israel's story to encourage his own audience's faith. He reminds it and us too that God's people are able to persevere in faith, even in the face of social alienation and death, precisely because our hope, the long-awaited inheritance, first promised to Abraham, is not in this world or in this life. Our hope, rather, has always been heavenly and is accessed only with an enduring, which is to say a resurrected, life.

Biblical-theological prescriptions

Our view of Scripture makes it impossible to read the NT without some measure of prescription. Until this point in the book we have largely avoided making prescriptive biblical-theological observations. Here, however, we will consider more directly how the stories of Israel in the NT should affect our own biblical-theological method and practice. In what follows, we will reflect on the implications of our investigation for our own biblical-theological practice, specifically focusing on three areas: plot, characters and method.

To be clear, we are not claiming that every summary will include all of these points nor that any one of these points is necessary to summarize Israel's story. For example, while exile is a major theme in Matthew, it is all but absent in Hebrews 11; conversely, while the land promises loom large in Hebrews, they are given little direct attention in Matthew. What we are claiming is that a faithful Christian SIS should not contradict the points outlined in these summaries; moreover, every faithful summary will in some way demonstrate that the story climaxes with Christ, continues with the church and concludes with the expectation that the story is heading towards its final fulfilment of God's promises in the 'city that is to come'.

Therefore, in this section, we will gather those aspects of Israel's story that we have observed throughout this study, considering where the summaries both converge and diverge, but primarily emphasizing their fundamental unity. This overview will help us identify the apostolic rule of faith within which our own retellings of Israel's story will flourish.

Plot

The earliest Christians shaped Israel's story to emphasize different key plot points. They chose different emphases, and thus told the story in different ways. Yet the similarities of their summaries show that it is the same story: it is Israel's story that climaxes in Christ and continues in the life and mission of the church. Not all of the details of the plot are equally pronounced (if pronounced at all); however, observing the unity and diversity in these emphases will help us read and retell the story of Israel more faithfully.

Climax: Christ

Though the earliest Christians highlight different aspects of the plot of Israel's story, they all agree that the climax of the story is the person and work of Jesus Christ. Matthew's genealogy indicates that the story of Israel has inevitably led to the birth of Jesus, the one who will resolve the tension in this story. Similarly, Stephen's speech in Acts 7 reveals that the story of Israel culminates in the rejected and vindicated servant, Jesus the Messiah. Paul famously tells us that the seed of Abraham to whom the promises were made is Christ (Gal. 3:16) and all who belong to Christ (Gal. 3:29).

Moreover, Christ is the 'culmination of the law so that there may be right-eousness for everyone who believes' (Rom. 10:4). And Hebrews tells us that Israel's story is exemplified in and fulfilled by Jesus' faithfulness, who gives all believers access to 'the city that is to come' (13:14).

In Galatians 3 – 4 the apostle Paul gives us an interesting window into his messianic reading of Israel's story. He says that 'Scripture foresaw that God would justify the Gentiles by faith, and announced the gospel in advance to Abraham: "All nations will be blessed through you"' (Gal. 3:8). The verb 'announced the gospel in advance' (*proeuēngelizomai*), which Paul applies to Genesis 12:3, nicely captures his understanding of the OT story as a 'fore-proclamation' of the gospel of Christ. This verb recognizes that there is a sense in which this gospel was not clearly proclaimed until Christ came. It was only *fore*-proclaimed. This means that Paul's telling of Israel's story is one that could be given only in the light of God's new revelation in Jesus Christ. His reading of the OT is distinctly *Christian* because of an awareness that God has sent his Son and Spirit and brought about the new-covenant era of faith.[1] He is reading the story 'backwards'. And yet there is also a sense in which he is reading the story 'forwards', because he genuinely views the OT as a fore-*proclamation* or prophetic witness to the gospel.[2] This is why he uses the word 'Scripture': to communicate that the OT is the divinely inspired Word of God and thus a prophetic witness to the gospel.

We submit, then, that in our own biblical theology we should read the story both backwards and forwards. The OT witness to Christ is seen more clearly through the lens of the NT and thus we should use the end of the story to enlighten the beginning. On the other hand, we should also read the story forwards. We should expect the OT, as the very Word of God, to bear prophetic witness to the person and work of Jesus Christ.

---

[1] The word 'Christian' is meant to communicate that Paul's hermeneutic is both 'Christological' and 'ecclesiological'. Hays has argued for a distinctly 'ecclesiological hermen-eutic' in Paul, observing that Paul rarely appeals to Scripture to prove that Jesus is the Messiah/Christ, but more often appeals to it in order to make a point about the church (1989: 34–39). His observation is insightful, but we should not exclude Paul's Christological hermeneutic as seen e.g. in Gal. 3:13 and 3:16.

[2] Watson sees a twofold hermeneutic of Paul the Christian who rereads Jewish Scripture: Paul 'remains accountable' to both the OT texts *and* to the new revelation of Jesus Christ (2016: 190–191). This is a recurring thesis of Watson's work (see e.g. Watson 2016: 16–17) and a helpful correction to Hays's overemphasis on 'reading backwards'. Cf. Longenecker: 'though in his own experience a true understanding of Christ preceded a proper understanding of Scrip-ture, in his exegetical endeavors he habitually began with Scripture and moved on to Christ' (1999: 104).

Tension: exile

If the climax of Israel's story is the person and work of Christ, then a central tension of the story, at least in most of the summaries we have addressed, is God's judgment on sinners that the work of Christ addresses. As we have observed, the most concrete expression of this tension is God's judgment in the exile. This tension appears in different ways in the genealogy and in the parable of the tenants in the Gospel of Matthew, yet in both the solution to the tension is the coming of the Messiah. Paul expresses this same reality in a different way in Galatians 3:13. 'Christ redeemed us from the curse of the law' implies that Christ delivers believers, Jews and Gentiles alike, from both the present and future experience of the covenant curse of the law.

To be clear, we are not claiming that the universal self-understanding of first-century Jews was that they continued in exile. The evidence for such a claim is limited and inconclusive.[3] Moreover, Israel's story can also be told without emphasizing the exile, as the author of Hebrews largely does. We noted earlier that God's judgment for sin is not presented as the cause of exile in Hebrews. Nonetheless, our claim is that at least some of the SIS in the NT emphasize the exile as the covenant curse imposed on Israel for the unfaithfulness of the people as led by unfaithful rulers. Moreover, the judgments of this curse were unresolved before the coming of the Messiah.

In the parable of the tenants, the unfaithful within Israel who finally reject the Messiah, the experience of exile is only intensified as they endure the continued absence of God's presence and later the destruction of the temple. Paul describes this same phenomenon: 'They stumbled over the stumbling stone' (Rom. 9:33; our tr.). Therefore, in our readings of Israel's story, we must recognize the central role of God's judgment, particularly in the exile, as the central tension that the work of Christ resolves.

Tension: land promises

Related to the tension of the exile, another key tension in Israel's story is the anticipation of the land inheritance. This tension is present to a degree in Stephen's speech, in that he alludes to the land promises to Abraham

---

[3] We find Douglas Moo's assessment of the notion of a continuing exile persuasive: 'As long as we understand how broadly the term is being used, "still in exile" is not necessarily an incorrect way to describe the plight from which Israel still awaits rescue' (2004: 205).

but does not specify how they will be fulfilled (Acts 7:4–8). More fundamentally, however, in Hebrews 11, the main narrative tension in the story is the as-yet-unfulfilled land promise. Hebrews tells us that God's people throughout Israel's history faithfully waited for the inheritance first promised to Abraham. According to Hebrews, therefore, the story of Israel is a story full of anticipation for the day when Jesus will finally lead his 'many sons and daughters' into their long-awaited inheritance. This tension remains in place until the 'shaking' of this world and the establishment of the new creation.

A continuing story

The story of Israel reaches its climax in and through Christ, who resolves the fundamental tensions in this story, but this does not mean the apostles believed the story had ended. Rather, it continues in the mission of the church. As noted above, the continued anticipation of the land promises in Hebrews 11 indicates that the story of Israel continues beyond the NT era, and we see this plot point in several other summaries in the NT.

Matthew's reading of the story of Israel helps us see that the judgments of the exile – particularly the removal of God's presence – have begun to come to an end with the coming of the Messiah. However, the parable of the tenants demonstrates that the experience of exile continues for everyone who rejects Jesus, for the vineyard, which represents the covenantal blessing of God's presence in the kingdom, is given to all who will produce its fruit, Jew and Gentile alike. Consequently, the church is the place where the covenant blessing of God's presence now dwells. We find a similar emphasis in the summaries in Acts. The ministries of Stephen, Paul and the church en masse continue the story of Israel.[4]

Paul also assumes the continuing nature of Israel's story in Romans 9 – 11. Regardless of how one interprets 'all Israel will be saved', it is clear that this SIS not only includes Israel's history, but also includes the present and future. Paul's expectation is that he is participating in Israel's story (Rom. 11:1) and that this story will continue until 'all Israel will be saved' (Rom. 11:26). Consequently, the church, consisting of Jew and Gentile together, is presently participating in Israel's story.

---

[4] As Michael Bird observes, 'The church, as the vanguard of the restored Israel and the renewed human race, was to project God's salvation into the world like a beacon of light beaming into the darkness. The Christians were not a replacement for national Israel, but the eschatological representatives of Israel in the messianic age' (2006: 131).

Similarly, the author of Hebrews uses Israel's story to encourage his own audience. He tells the story of Israel's unflagging hope in a future resurrection and heavenly inheritance in order to encourage his audience's own faith in these same realities. And right at the end of his story he goes a step further and explicitly weaves his own audience right into Israel's story, noting that neither Israel nor his audience will enter the long-awaited inheritance without the other. 'God had', he insists, 'planned' it this way, 'so that only together with us [i.e. the audience] would they [i.e. Israel] be made perfect' and thus be suited for entrance into heaven (Heb. 11:39–40).

All of these summaries explicitly or implicitly invite followers of Christ to share in God's covenant promises; we must therefore read the story of Israel with an eye towards this plot in which the church participates. As noted above, the earliest Christians summarize Israel's story in several ways and with several emphases, yet what is common to all of these stories is that the plot of Israel's story includes a narrative tension that is resolved with the coming of the Messiah; yet this story continues in the present through the church.

Characters

The fundamental elements of any story are plot and characters, and it is no different with the story of Israel. Just as we observed several important plot points in the summaries of the story in the NT, so also the characters of Israel's story ought to inform our own biblical theology. Admittedly, some of the summaries include more characters than others. One might compare Matthew's genealogy or Hebrews 11, which are bursting with characters from the story, with Galatians 3 – 4, which includes only a handful of characters in its three retellings of the story. In every case, however, the characters included in the summary can teach us more about how to retell the story ourselves.

Exemplars

The first note to make about the characters in Israel's story, especially in Hebrews's summary, is that characters from Israel's story can be used simply to exhort, challenge and inspire behaviour. Abel's and Abraham's faith, for example, are held out as examples for us to emulate. In fact, in Hebrews they are held out right alongside Jesus himself. What this tells us is that the earliest Christians read Israel's story not simply looking for anticipations of the new-covenant era (or the gospel); they also read the story for the moral lessons it can provide and the virtues these lessons can cultivate.

Types

Not only are the characters moral examples, but they also often prefigure the Christ and the church. The genealogy in Matthew obviously highlights Jesus' Davidic lineage. As we noted, it also portrays several Gentile women as saviour figures who not only prefigure the Messiah but also foreshadow the multinational character of the new-covenant messianic community. The parable of the tenants presents the messianic Son as the culmination of a series of prophetic messengers whom the Father sent to Israel, only to see them rejected. This final rejection then becomes the means by which the last chapter of Israel's history begins, as the rejected Messiah is installed as the reigning Davidic king.

We might even call the Gentile women and the rejected servants of the Lord in Israel's story types of Jesus. The Gentile women in the genealogy are prefiguring the ministry of Jesus and, perhaps to a lesser degree, his mother, Mary, as they intervene in surprising ways to preserve the line of promise and ensure the fulfilment of God's covenant promises. Jesus himself intervenes on behalf of his people to ensure God's covenant promises through his prophetic ministry and ultimately his sacrificial death.

In the parable of the tenants we are also introduced to a theme that becomes more explicit in Acts. The rejection of God's messengers throughout Israel's story foreshadows the rejection of the Son. But the rejection of the Son becomes the very means by which he is vindicated, as the rejected cornerstone becomes the foundation of the new-covenant temple. In both of these stories the historical characters prefigure Jesus the Messiah, for their place in the story is intended to point us towards him as the final fulfilment.

As we consider the role of the rejected and vindicated servants of the Lord in both Stephen's speech and Paul's sermon in Acts, we see a continuation of the typological significance of individual characters in the story of Israel. In Acts 7 Joseph and Moses are prominent as figures of the rejected and vindicated Messiah. However, at the end of his speech Stephen introduces a wrinkle in this pattern when he also includes himself as a figure of the rejected and vindicated Messiah. In a similar way Paul indicates that he and Barnabas are continuing the ministry of the suffering servant as they proclaim the good news to the nations. Therefore, as we read the story of Israel and observe key figures who prefigure the Messiah, we must also recognize that many prefigure the church in some way as well. This was, of course, true with all the characters in Hebrews's story. Each both prefigures Jesus' faithfulness and (the author certainly hoped) the audience's.[5]

We can observe similar ecclesial interpretations of the OT in Romans 9 – 11 as well. As noted above, Paul occasionally cites the OT as a promise now fulfilled in Christ (e.g. Rom. 9:33), but more often he appeals to patterns of Scripture that foreshadow God's present work in Christ and the church. Paul explains the present in the light of how God dealt with Pharaoh, Elijah and Israel's exile in the past. Moreover, his reasoning in Romans 11:5 presents perhaps the clearest example of typological reasoning in this section. Following this, Paul contends that the pattern of mercy to Gentiles and Jews continues into the future.

If we are following the patterns of the NT authors, an ecclesial reading ought to follow a Christological reading of Israel's story. Therefore, as we read and tell the story of Israel, we ought to look carefully for individual characters in the story who point forward (and, at times, back) to the coming of the Messiah and highlight the correspondence between the two. At times the correspondence between the characters in Israel's story and Christ and his church can be more or less pronounced; nonetheless, if we are reading the story of Israel the way the earliest Christians did, typology should be an important part of putting our Bibles together rightly.

The primary typological pattern in the summaries of Israel's stories are seen in the characters who prefigure Christ and the church; however, the land promises in Hebrews 11 also serve a typological function. God's promise to give Abraham a land in Palestine was anticipatory, looking forward to a greater inheritance to come (Heb. 11:8–10). We will return to this point in our discussion of method below.

Finally, typology is not the only contribution that the characters in Israel's story make: individual characters and key institutions play a more

---

[5] While this observation is superficially similar to what Hays has called an 'ecclesial' reading of the OT in these SIS, the church is a post-figuration of the Messiah; Hays argues that the OT prefigures the church but does not emphasize the messianic link between OT and NT covenant communities (see 1989: 34–39).

robust role in several of the NT SIS. In our investigation we have observed the important role that Abraham, David, Moses, the law and the main character of the story, God himself, play in the SIS.

Abraham

In virtually all of the summaries we have examined, the authors highlight Abraham in some way. The only exception to this is the highly symbolic summary in the parable of the tenants, but even this summary assumes the Abrahamic covenant, for the planting of the vineyard likely alludes to God's covenant with Abraham.

In Matthew and Acts the importance of Abraham is assumed, for he is the ancestor of God's people, the one with whom God made the covenant of circumcision (Acts 7:8). But the summaries in these books provide little additional explanation of the covenant with Abraham. In Galatians 3 – 4 Paul asserts that the two main characters in Israel's story are Abraham and his offspring. Moreover, as we will observe below, Abraham plays a central role in Paul's figural reading that spans Israel's past and present in Galatians 4. In Hebrews 11 Abraham is once more one of two main characters in Israel's story, this time along with Moses. Moreover, it is in the author's description of Abraham's exemplary faith that we are first explicitly introduced to the key motifs of his story; namely, the heavenly inheritance (vv. 8–10) and the resurrection hope (vv. 17–19).

In brief, therefore, Abraham plays a number of roles in the story of Israel. He is the founder of Israel, for he is the progenitor of the line that will culminate in Christ. More than this, he is the covenant head, for God's covenant promises were given particularly to him and later fulfilled in his seed, Christ. However, he also is the paradigm for Israel's faith, for Hebrews teaches us about the nature of his hope as a hope that lies beyond this world. Therefore, in our readings of Israel's story, we have warrant to highlight different aspects of Abraham's place in the story, but we would do well to emphasize his central place in the story.

David

While he plays a crucial role in NT biblical theology, David is mentioned only in passing in Matthew's genealogy, and his role in the story is largely negative (as seen in his sin with Bathsheba). Paul mentions him only once in Romans 9 – 11.[6] In Hebrews David is included among those characters the author does not 'have time to tell about' (Heb. 11:32).

However, this does not imply that David is incidental to the story. The parable of the tenants cites Psalm 118, which is closely tied to the Davidic covenant. In Galatians Paul reads the Abrahamic covenant in the light of the later Davidic promises; consequently, the Davidic covenant informs the rest of the story even in those places where 'David' is absent. The same is true in Hebrews, for the messianic enthronement that is central to the argument of Hebrews is built upon the Davidic covenant.[7]

In Acts David has a more central and largely positive place. Stephen notes that David 'enjoyed God's favour' (Acts 7:46), and Paul's sermon in Acts 13 has a particular focus on David. In several of the speeches in Acts the covenant with David is fundamental for understanding the person and work of the Messiah (Acts 2:25–35; 7:46; 13:32–37). In his Pisidian Antioch sermon Paul cites Psalm 89:20, where God describes David as 'a man after my own heart; he will do everything I want him to do' (Acts 13:22). Thus, David is also both covenant head and faithful example for God's people. Again, we have warrant to highlight different aspects of David's part in the story in our retellings of Israel's story while also recognizing the important role he plays, both positively and negatively.

Moses and the law

Like David, Moses is absent from several of the SIS we have surveyed; in Matthew's and Paul's summaries he is hardly mentioned at all.[8] However, this does not imply that he is irrelevant even in those summaries where he is not named, for Moses and the law covenant are closely linked, and the law is frequently assumed in Israel's story and explicitly discussed by Paul.

Moses' role is especially prominent in Acts 7 and Hebrews 11. In Acts 7 Stephen structures a large part of his speech around Moses, the exodus and the events that follow. This is unsurprising given the setting of his

---

[6] Paul's quotation of Ps. 69 in Rom. 9:9–10 indicates that he sees David's experience prefiguring that of Christ. However, this prefiguration is not a crucial part of his retelling of the story.

[7] See Compton 2015: 19–65.

[8] Matthew does not name Moses at all in his summaries; Paul does not mention him in his three retellings of Israel's story in Gal. 3 – 4 (though the 'mediator' in Gal. 3:19 likely refers to Moses). While he names Moses three times in Rom. 9 – 11, his role in these chapters is to receive or convey divine revelation (Rom. 9:15; 10:5, 19); he does not play a direct role as a character in the story of Israel.

speech as an answer to the charge that he was denigrating the law. Yet Moses is also included as a key example of one of the rejected and vindicated servants of the Lord in Israel's story. In Hebrews 11 the author presents Moses as one of the fundamental examples of Israel's faith. His hope was in an inheritance beyond what the law covenant itself could offer.

Moses and the law are closely linked, yet at times in Paul's letters the law is almost personified as a character itself. In Galatians 3 – 4 and Romans 9 – 11 the law plays a fundamentally negative role in Israel's story, for the law was a guardian until the coming of Christ (Gal. 3:24). It was unable to reach the gracious Abrahamic promises (Gal. 3:18) and the law was misused by Israel to try to attain righteousness (Rom. 9:32).[9]

Notably, in those places where Moses is highlighted the negative role of the law is muted. While Stephen emphasizes the failure of Israel's leaders to understand the purposes of the law, the law itself is not considered negatively. Rather, Moses is contrasted with those fathers of Israel who rejected him (Acts 7:39). As noted above, Hebrews 11 also highlights Moses, featuring him as a positive example without giving attention to the negative aspects of either the law or the failure of Israel's leaders.

Therefore, in our own biblical theology our discussions of Moses and the law should reflect this nuance. On the one hand, Moses is an example for the church and even prefigures the rejection and vindication of Christ. On the other hand, while it has God-ordained purposes and goals, the law covenant plays a negative role in Israel's story. If the exile is a fundamental tension in Israel's story, the law is the character most associated with that fundamental tension. Additionally, many of the SIS in the NT do not emphasize the law covenant to the degree that they focus on the covenants with Abraham and David or present Moses as a positive example in spite of the negative effect of the law. Therefore, our own retellings of the story can emphasize Moses and the law in varying degrees as our context demands. This understanding should guard us from conflating the Abrahamic promises and their fulfilment with the Jewish law, or, in Lutheran terms, from conflating the law and the gospel.

---

[9] The law plays a similar role in Acts 13:38, but its negative role is somewhat muted in Paul's sermon.

Main character: God

Abraham, Moses and David are central characters in Israel's story and the law is the negative foil in the story; however, there is an important sense in which the main character in Israel's story is God himself. As noted in our discussion of Acts 7, different characters emerge throughout the story but ultimately the main character of Stephen's speech is God, for he is present throughout the story and is actually directing the story. While God's power and promises are fundamental in all of the summaries in the NT, in Romans 9 – 11 God's sovereign hand is especially prominent, for he is the one who determines the identity of the true, spiritual Israel. Therefore, as we recount the story of Israel, we should emphasize that God is the author of this story and the whole scope of the story is under his sovereign control.

The NT retellings of Israel's story give us a clear warrant for including different characters and even different aspects of those characters' places in the story. However, a faithful retelling of Israel's story will recognize the links between the diverse actors in Israel's story and the culmination of Israel's story in Christ. These characters will often prefigure Christ and/or display faith in God's promises that are fulfilled in Christ. However, standing behind the story as its main character is God himself. Moreover, the conclusion of Romans 9 – 11 reminds us that the goal of Israel's story is the glory of God: 'For from him and through him and for him are all things. To him be the glory for ever! Amen' (Rom. 11:36).

Method

While the summaries of Israel's story in the NT include plotlines and central characters that guide us as we read and retell this story, the SIS also instruct us in our own biblical-theological methods. As we synthesize our findings, we can make four observations that ought to influence our own biblical-theological method.

Warranted allegories

Our first methodological observation is rooted in Paul's reading of Scripture in Galatians 4. We noted above that Israel's story is pregnant with patterns and prefigurations of Christ and the church that encourage not only typological readings but even warranted allegorical readings. We might call this 'allegory with a seatbelt'.[10]

---

[10] We are indebted to John Biegel for this phrase.

Paul's allegory of Abraham's two sons and their mothers is a well-known hermeneutical conundrum. Should Christians follow the apostle in this method?[11] While some might reject such an approach because of a modern commitment to historical-grammatical hermeneutics, Paul offers a warranted allegorical reading of the story of Ishmael and Isaac. Thus, we suggest that Christians should follow the apostle's allegorical method, but should carefully observe the scriptural roots of this method rather than embracing a kind of reader-response hermeneutics.

The apostle's allegory is warranted by at least four factors. First, his allegory is warranted by his view of the law as 'Scripture' that was written as a divine, prophetic witness to the gospel (4:30). Christian readers should not force the OT to speak of Christ but we should expect it to be a witness to the gospel. Second, the apostle's allegory is rooted in typology or the correspondence of OT figures to NT realities. The point of correspondence that Paul sees in the text is slavery–flesh and freedom–promise, points clearly seen in the OT text and in the NT reality. Third, Paul's allegory builds upon the typology already found within the OT; namely, Isaiah's use of Sarah's barrenness as a type of the future repopulation of Jerusalem in the new covenant. Paul builds on this typology to explain the freedom from the enslaving authority of the law in the era of the new covenant. Fourth, the apostle uses allegory to reinforce theological points he has already come to on other grounds; namely, the imprisoning role of the law and the Abrahamic sonship of Gentile believers. Thus, we suggest that Christian interpreters should pursue warranted allegory in the practice of biblical theology, expecting the OT narratives to be a prophetic witness of Christ, looking for points of correspondence both in the OT text and the NT fulfilment, seeking to build upon previous biblical typology, and reinforcing rather than introducing points of theology.

Covenantal substructure

A second point on method comes primarily from Acts. In Acts 7 Stephen is accused of blaspheming the temple and the law. In response he tells a story of Israel that demonstrates that his accusers had a faulty biblical theology.

---

[11] R. N. Longenecker famously answers 'no' and suggests that Gal. 4:21–31 'should probably be seen as an extreme form of Palestinian allegorical interpretation that was triggered by polemical debate and is largely *ad hominem* in nature' (1999: 112–113). Interpreters differ on how important this argument is to Paul: Burton regards it as an 'after-thought' (1921: 251), whereas others see it as the climax of his argument (Myers 2010: 295–308; Hahn 2009: 243–244).

His speech is structured around the major covenants in Israel's story and intended to show the purposes behind these covenants as the story climaxes with the coming of the Messiah. In a similar way Paul's sermon in Acts 13 is structured around Israel's major covenants. As noted above, these covenants explain the emphases and plot points in each of these summaries.

Thus, Acts highlights the covenantal substructure of Israel's story to demonstrate the consequences of putting our Bibles together wrongly. If we do not put it together rightly, we are going to put ourselves in danger of misunderstanding or ignoring the acts of God. That is to say, if we want to understand Israel's story correctly, we must understand how the covenants fit together. This is not to say we must always shape our retellings around the covenants, for Hebrews 11 does not do this in the way that Acts does; however, even Hebrews 11 assumes a basic old- and new-covenant structure that culminates in Christ.

This reading of Israel's history largely fits with Peter Gentry and Stephen Wellum's proposal for a 'progressive covenantalism'. While Gentry and Wellum divide Stephen's speech in Acts 7 into three coven-antal eras that we have observed above, they do not otherwise comment on the structure of either Acts 7 or Acts 13 in detail.[12] However, the coven-antal substructure of Stephen's speech and Paul's sermon affirms – or at least coincides with – Gentry and Wellum's observations about the nature and place of the covenants in the biblical story. In our reading of the OT we ought to recognize this same covenantal substructure as the backbone of the stories of Israel.

This covenantal substructure also provides a possible explanation for the surprising silence of the NT with respect to the covenants. Explicit references to the covenants are few and far between in the NT; however, the covenantal substructure of the story of Israel helps mitigate against the suggestion that the apostles were indifferent to a covenant theology.

New-covenant referents

Hebrews 11 generates our third methodological observation: we ought to read God's covenant promises in the story of Israel with their new-covenant

---

[12] For Acts 7, see Gentry and Wellum 2012: 96. They also repeat Gentry's interpretation of Acts 13:34 cited above (ibid. 418–421). While we are not as convinced that their position is exactly the via media between dispensationalism and covenant theology that they claim it is, their general argument for a progressive unfolding of God's redemptive plans as each covenant builds on and administers the previous one is well represented in Stephen's speech.

referents in view. We saw that Abraham's land inheritance is distinguished from Canaan and this world. The inheritance, Hebrews insists, has always been other-worldly, in a heavenly city built by God, which will come only after the removal of this world and all created things. This would rule out readings of Israel's story, therefore, that depend on fulfilment in this world. Much the same can be said for what Hebrews says about how one enters this heavenly inheritance. If the inheritance can be entered only by those with enduring bodies, then, as Paul says elsewhere, 'flesh and blood cannot inherit the kingdom of God' (1 Cor. 15:50). This would rule out readings of Israel's story, therefore, that depend on fulfilment in this life, which is to say, that suggest mortality and the heavenly inheritance (i.e. new creation) can be overlapping categories.

Fundamentally, Hebrews's SIS tells us that Israel's inheritance, like Israel's priesthood, sacrifices, sacred space and covenant, is typological. Each foreshadows and prepares for realities of the new-covenant era. The larger structure of Hebrews, in fact, corroborates this observation. It shows us that Israel's story, summarized in Hebrews 11 and fuelling the expositions of Hebrews 5 – 10, is part of a larger story, begun with Adam and seeking its resolution not in a single place, whether Canaan or elsewhere, but in a 'world to come', one to which Jesus, Israel's Messiah, is presently leading all of God's sons and daughters. In short, Hebrews teaches us that we are to read so much of Israel's story, from beginning to end, as a 'shadow of the good things that are coming – not the realities themselves' (Heb. 10:1).

Contextual retellings

Our final methodological point builds on the diversity of the SIS. This diversity instructs us about what we might label the situational applicability of Israel's story. Thus, the story of Israel should be told in such a way as to highlight Israel's contemporary significance.

Many within the church often instinctively apply the OT situationally. If we encounter a drift towards legalism, we will emphasize the inability of the commandments of the law to fulfil God's promises; when our congregations are doubting the veracity of God's promises, we emphasize the longsuffering hope of Israel's patriarchs. That is to say, we tend to emphasize those aspects of the story that have particular relevance to our own situations. We find warrant for this practice in the differences between the different tellings of the stories in the NT.

In Matthew Jesus continues the story of Israel as he repeats this story and propels it forwards. Similarly, Acts emphasizes the climax of the story as Jesus fulfils God's covenant promises and the church now embodies the continuing story of Israel. In Paul's letters the role of the law and the identify of Israel help us better understand the contours of the story. Finally, in Hebrews 11 the story of Israel is inevitably driving towards the heavenly inheritance for the true heirs of God's covenant promises. This diversity in the summaries largely reflects the various circumstances of the authors and audiences; yet, as we have observed, there is a fundamental unity to these retellings, and this unity is centred in Jesus Christ as the fulfilment of God's covenant promises and as the means by which these covenant promises continue to advance to the world.

Consequently, there is not only one correct way to tell Israel's story. Admittedly, there are certainly incorrect ways to summarize the story (e.g. a failure to emphasize the messianic climax of the story or to highlight the continuation of the story in the mission of the church), but the SIS in the NT remind us that our setting and context may require us to highlight different aspects of Israel's story without undermining parts of the story emphasized elsewhere. We too ought to make allowance for a diversity in our summaries and tell them in a way that fits our own circumstances.

Therefore, in our own biblical theology we have a warrant to retell the story of Israel with emphases that correspond to our circumstances, provided that our summaries are similarly centred on the person and work of Jesus Christ.

Israel's story and our stories

The SIS in the NT ought to reorient our priorities when reading the OT and retelling this story. These summaries instruct us about the climax of the story with Christ, the continuation of the story in the church and the conclusion of the story in the new creation. Although the apostles emphasized certain aspects of the story of Israel that fitted their context and argumentative situations well, all of the stories of Israel in the NT are faithful retellings of the story of Israel. While we cannot say that the writers of the NT were always operating with the story of Israel explicitly in view, the assumptions that these stories reveal are invariably connected to their other uses of Scripture and should therefore influence our overall understanding of the use of the OT in the NT.

Not only should these retellings influence our exegesis of the citations of the OT, but also for those who are seeking to live faithfully according to the Scriptures, understanding the story of Israel and our place in this story is of utmost importance. As Lesslie Newbigin reminds us:

> Authentic Christian thought and action begin not by attending to the aspirations of people, not by answering the questions they are asking in their terms, not by offering solutions to the problems as the world sees them. It must begin and continue by attending to what God has done in the story of Israel and supremely in the story of Jesus Christ. It must continue by indwelling that story so that it is our story, the way we understand the real story. And then, and this is the vital point, to attend with open hearts and minds to the real needs of people.[13]

Let us go and do likewise.

---

[13] Newbigin 1989: 151.

Bibliography

Aageson, J. W. (1986), 'Scripture and Structure in the Development of the Argument in Romans 9–11', *CBQ* 48: 265–289.

Attridge, H. W. (1989), *The Epistle to the Hebrews: A Commentary on the Epistle to the Hebrews*, Hermeneia, Philadelphia: Fortress.

Bacon, B. W. (1930), *Studies in Matthew*, New York: Holt.

Baker, M. (2005), 'Paul and the Salvation of Israel: Paul's Ministry, the Motif of Jealousy, and Israel's Yes', *CBQ* 67: 469–484.

Barclay, J. M. G. (1987), 'Mirror-Reading a Polemical Letter: Galatians as a Test Case', *JSNT* 10.31: 73–93.

—— (2015), *Paul and the Gift*, Grand Rapids: Eerdmans.

Barrett, C. K. (1982), 'The Allegory of Abraham, Sarah and Hagar in the Argument of Galatians', in C. K. Barrett (ed.), *Essays on Paul*, Philadelphia: Westminster, 197–219.

Bauckham, R. (1995), 'Tamar's Ancestry and Rahab's Marriage: Two Problems in the Matthean Genealogy', *NovT* 37: 313–329.

Beale, G. K. (2004), *The Temple and the Church's Mission: A Biblical Theology of the Dwelling Place of God*, NSBT 17, Leicester: Apollos; Downers Grove: InterVarsity Press.

—— (2011), *A New Testament Biblical Theology: The Unfolding of the Old Testament in the New*, Grand Rapids: Baker Academic.

—— (2012), *Handbook on the New Testament Use of the Old Testament: Exegesis and Interpretation*, Grand Rapids: Baker Academic.

Beale, G. K., and D. A. Carson (2007), *Commentary on the New Testament Use of the Old Testament*, Grand Rapids: Baker Academic.

Beale, G. K., and B. L. Gladd (2014), *Hidden but Now Revealed: A Biblical Theology of Mystery*, Downers Grove: IVP Academic.

Beers, H. (2015), *The Followers of Jesus as the 'Servant': Luke's Model from Isaiah for the Disciples in Luke–Acts*, LNTS 535, London: T&T Clark.

Bell, R. H. (1994), *Provoked to Jealousy: The Origin and Purpose of the Jealousy Motif in Romans 9–11*, Tübingen: Mohr Siebeck.

Bergen, R. D. (1996), *1, 2 Samuel*, NAC 7, Nashville: B&H.

Betz, H. D. (1979), *Galatians: A Commentary on Paul's Letter to the Churches in Galatia*, Hermeneia, Philadelphia: Fortress.

Bird, M. F. (2006), 'A Light to the Nations (Isaiah 42:6 and 49:6): Inter-Textuality and Mission Theology in the Early Church', *RTR* 65: 122–131.

Blomberg, C. L. (2007), 'Matthew', in G. K. Beale and D. A. Carson (eds.), *Commentary on the New Testament Use of the Old Testament*, Grand Rapids: Baker Academic, 1–110.

Bock, D. L. (2007), *Acts*, vol. 1, BECNT, Grand Rapids: Baker Academic.

—— (2010), *Acts*, vol. 2, BECNT, Grand Rapids: Baker Academic.

Boer, M. C. de (2004), 'Paul's Quotation of Isaiah 54.1 in Galatians 4.27', *NTS* 50: 370–389.

Brooke, G. J. (1995), '4Q500 1 and the Use of Scripture in the Parable of the Vineyard', *DSD* 2: 268–294.

Brown, R. E. (1977), *The Birth of the Messiah*, New York: Doubleday.

Bruce, F. F. (1969), *New Testament Development of Old Testament Themes*, Grand Rapids: Eerdmans.

—— (1990), *The Epistle to the Hebrews*, NICNT, Grand Rapids: Eerdmans.

Bruno, C. R. (2008), 'The Deliverer from Zion: The Source(s) and Function of Paul's Citation in Romans 11:26–27', *TynBul* 59: 119–134.

—— (2010), 'Jesus Is Our Jubilee . . . But How? The OT Background and Lukan Fulfillment of the Ethics of Jubilee', *JECS* 53: 81–101.

—— (2013), *God Is One: The Function of 'Eis ho Theos' as a Ground for Gentile Inclusion in Paul's Letters*, LNTS 497, London: T&T Clark.

Burton, E. D. W. (1921), *A Critical and Exegetical Commentary on the Epistle to the Galatians*, ICC, Edinburgh: T&T Clark.

Caird, G. B. (1959), 'The Exegetical Method of the Epistle to the Hebrews', *CJT* 5: 44–51.

Carson, D. A. (2010), 'Matthew', in *Matthew-Mark*, EBC, rev. edn Grand Rapids: Zondervan.

Chilton, B. D. (1990), 'The Isaiah Targum', in *The Aramaic Bible*, vol. 11, Collegeville: Liturgical Press.

Cockerill, G. L. (2000), 'The Better Resurrection (Heb 11:35): A Key to the Structure and Rhetorical Purpose of Hebrews 11', *TynBul* 51: 215–234.

—— (2012), *The Epistle to the Hebrews*, NICNT, Grand Rapids: Eerdmans.

Collins, C. J. (2003), 'Galatians 3:16: What Kind of Exegete Was Paul?', *TynBul* 54: 75–86.

Compton, J. M. (2015), *Psalm 110 and the Logic of Hebrews*, LNTS 537, New York: Bloomsbury.

Coppins, W. (2009), *The Interpretation of Freedom in the Letters of Paul*, WUNT 2.261, Tübingen: Mohr Siebeck.

Cosby, M. R. (1988), 'The Rhetorical Composition of Hebrews 11', *JBL* 107: 257–273.

Cosgrove, C. H. (1987), 'Justification in Paul: A Linguistic and Theological Reflection', *JBL* 106: 654–661.

Cranfield, C. E. B. (1975), *The Epistle to the Romans*, vol. 1, ICC, Edinburgh: T&T Clark.

—— (1979), *The Epistle to the Romans*, vol. 2, ICC, Edinburgh: T&T Clark.

Dahood, M. J. (1970), *Psalms III: 101–150*, AB 17A, Garden City: Doubleday.

Davies, W. D., and D. C. Allison (1988), *A Critical and Exegetical Commentary on the Gospel According to Matthew*, vol. 1, ICC, Edinburgh: T&T Clark.

—— (2004), *A Critical and Exegetical Commentary on the Gospel According to Matthew*, vol. 3, ICC, Edinburgh: T&T Clark.

Dempster, S. G. (2003), *Dominion and Dynasty: A Biblical Theology of the Hebrew Bible*, Leicester: Apollos; Downers Grove: InterVarsity Press.

Dever, M. E. (2004), *Nine Marks of a Healthy Church*, Wheaton: Crossway.

DiTommaso, L. (2010), 'Jerusalem, New', in J. J. Collins and D. C. Harlow (eds.), *The Eerdmans Dictionary of Early Judaism*, Grand Rapids: Eerdmans, 797–799.

Dodd, C. H. (1932), *The Epistle of Paul to the Romans*, London: Hodder and Stoughton.

—— (1953), *According to the Scriptures: The Sub-Structure of New Testament Theology*, London: Nisbet.

Donaldson, T. L. (1986), 'The Curse of the Law and the Inclusion of the Gentiles: Galatians 3:13–14', *NTS* 32: 94–112.

—— (1993), 'Riches for the Gentiles (Rom 11:12): Israel's Rejection and Paul's Gentile Mission', *JBL* 112: 81–98.

Dunn, J. D. G. (1988), *Romans 9–16*, WBC 38B, Dallas: Word.

—— (1993), *The Epistle to the Galatians*, Peabody: Hendrickson.

—— (1997), '4QMMT and Galatians', *NTS* 43: 147–153.

Dupont, J. (1985), 'La Structure Oratoire Du Discours d'Étienne (Actes 7)', *Bib* 66: 153–167.

Easter, M. C. (2014), *Faith and the Faithfulness of Jesus in Hebrews*, SNTSMS 160, New York: Cambridge University Press.

Eastman, S. G. (2010), 'Israel and the Mercy of God: A Re-Reading of Galatians 6:16 and Romans 9–11', *NTS* 56: 367–395.

Eisenbaum, P. M. (1997), 'Heroes and History in Hebrews 11', in C. A. Evans and J. A. Sanders (eds.), *Early Christian Interpretation of the Scriptures of Israel: Investigations and Proposals*, JSNTSup 148, Sheffield: Sheffield Academic Press, 380–396.

Ellis, E. E. (1977), 'How the New Testament Uses the Old', in I. H. Marshall (ed.), *New Testament Interpretation*, Grand Rapids: Eerdmans, 201–208.

Eloff, M. (2004), 'Exile, Restoration, and Matthew's Genealogy of Jesus Ὁ Χριστός', *Neot* 38: 75–87.

Filtvedt, O. J. (2016), 'God's Israel in Galatians 6:16: An Overview and Assessment of the Key Arguments', *CurBR* 15: 123–140.

Fitzmyer, J. A. (1993), *Romans*, AB 33, New York: Anchor Bible.

—— (2010), *The Acts of the Apostles: A New Translation with Introduction and Commentary*, New Haven: Yale University Press.

Gathercole, S. J. (2002), *Where Is Boasting? Early Jewish Soteriology and Paul's Response in Romans 1–5*, Grand Rapids: Eerdmans.

Gaventa, B. R. (2003), *The Acts of the Apostles*, ANTC, Nashville: Abingdon.

—— (2010), 'On the Calling-Into-Being of Israel: Romans 9:6–29', in F. Wilk and J. R. Wagner (eds.), *Between Gospel and Election: Explorations in the Interpretation of Romans 9–11*, Tübingen: Mohr Siebeck, 255–269.

Gentry, P. J. (2007), 'Rethinking the Sure Mercies of David in Isaiah 55:3', *WTJ* 69: 279–304.

Gentry, P. J., and S. Wellum (2012), *Kingdom Through Covenant: A Biblical-Theological Understanding of the Covenants*, Wheaton: Crossway.

Goldsworthy, G. (2008), 'Lecture 1: The Necessity and Viability of Biblical Theology', *SBJT* 12: 4–18.

Goodrich, J. K. (2016), 'The Word of God Has Not Failed: God's Faithfulness and Israel's Salvation in Tobit 14:3–7 and Romans 9–11', *TynBul* 67: 41–62.

Goswell, G. (2017), 'The Shape of Kingship in Deut 17: A Messianic Pentateuch?', *TJ* 38: 169–181.

Guthrie, G. H. (1998), *The Structure of Hebrews: A Text-Linguistic Analysis*, Grand Rapids: Baker.

—— (2007), 'Hebrews', in D. A. Carson and G. K. Beale (eds.), *Commentary on the New Testament Use of the Old Testament*, Grand Rapids: Baker, 919–995.

Haacker, K. (2010), 'Das Thema von Römer 9–11 als Problem der Auslegungsgeschichte', in F. Wilk and J. R. Wagner (eds.), *Between Gospel and Election: Explorations in the Interpretation of Romans 9–11*, Tübingen: Mohr Siebeck, 55–72.

Hafemann, S. J. (1988), 'The Salvation of Israel in Romans 11:25–32: A Response to Krister Stendahl', *ExAud* 4: 38–58.

Hagner, D. A. (1995), *Matthew 14–28*, WBC 33B, Dallas: Word.

Hahn, S. W. (2009), *Kinship by Covenant: A Canonical Approach to the Fulfillment of God's Saving Promises*, New Haven: Yale University Press.

Hakh, S. B. (2014), 'Women in the Genealogy of Matthew', *Exch* 114: 109–118.

Hamilton, J. M. (2010), *God's Glory in Salvation Through Judgment: A Biblical Theology*, Wheaton: Crossway.

Hansen, G. W. (1989), *Abraham in Galatians: Epistolary and Rhetorical Contexts*, JSNTSup 29, Sheffield: JSOT Press.

Harmon, M. S. (2010), *She Must and Shall Go Free: Paul's Isaianic Gospel in Galatians*, Berlin: de Gruyter.

Harriman, K. R. (2017), 'For David Said Concerning Him: Foundations of Hope in Psalm 16 and Acts 2', *JTI* 11: 239–257.

Harris, D. M. (2009), 'The Eternal Inheritance in Hebrews: The Appropriation of the Old Testament Inheritance Motif by the Author of Hebrews', PhD diss., Trinity Evangelical Divinity School.

Hartman, L. F. (1978), *The Book of Daniel*, AB 23, Garden City: Doubleday.

Hays, R. B. (1989), *Echoes of Scripture in the Letters of Paul*, New Haven: Yale University Press.

—— (2002), *The Faith of Jesus Christ: The Narrative Substructure of Galatians 3:1–4:11*, 2nd edn, Grand Rapids: Eerdmans.

—— (2016), *Echoes of Scripture in the Gospels*, repr. 2017, Waco: Baylor University Press.

Hester, J. D. (1992), 'Socio-Rhetorical Criticism and the Parable of the Tenants', *JSNT* 45: 27–56.

Hood, J. B. (2011), *The Messiah, His Brothers, and the Nations: Matthew 1:1–17*, LNTS 441, London: T&T Clark.

Hood, J. B., and M. Y. Emerson (2013), 'Summaries of Israel's Story: Reviewing a Compositional Category', *CurBR* 11: 328–348.

Hooker, M. D. (2002), 'Heirs of Abraham: The Gentile's Role in Israel's Story. A Response to Bruce W. Longenecker', in B. W. Longenecker (ed.), *Narrative Dynamics in Paul: A Critical Assessment*, Louisville: Westminster John Knox, 85–96.

Horne, E. H. (1998), 'The Parable of the Tenants as Indictment', *JSNT* 71: 111–116.

Horst, P. W. van der (2000), ' "Only Then Will All Israel Be Saved": A Short Note on the Meaning of καὶ οὕτως in Romans 11:26', *JBL* 119.3: 521–539.

Hunn, D. (2007), 'Ἐὰν μὴ in Galatians 2:16: A Look at Greek Literature', *NovT* 49: 281–290.

—— (2015), 'Galatians 3.10–12: Assumptions and Argumentation', *JSNT* 37: 253–266.

—— (2016), 'Galatians 3:6–9: Abraham's Fatherhood and Paul's Conclusions', *CBQ* 78: 500–514.

Hutchison, J. C. (2001), 'Women, Gentiles, and the Messianic Mission in Matthew's Genealogy', *BSac* 158: 152–164.

Iverson, K. R. (2012), 'Jews, Gentiles, and the Kingdom of God: The Parable of the Wicked Tenants in Narrative Perspective (Mark 12:1–12)', *BibInt* 20: 305–335.

Jerome (2010), *St. Jerome's Commentaries on Galatians, Titus, and Philemon*, tr. and ed. T. P. Scheck, Notre Dame: University of Notre Dame Press.

Jeska, J. (2001), *Die Geschichte Israels in der Sicht des Lukas: Apg 7,2b–53 und 13,17–25 im Kontext antik-jüdischer Summarien der Geschichte Israels*, Göttingen: Vandenhoeck & Ruprecht.

Jewett, R. (2007), *Romans: A Commentary*, Hermeneia, Minneapolis: Fortress.

Jobes, K. H. (1993), 'Jerusalem, Our Mother: Metalepsis and Inter-Textuality in Galatians 4:21–31', *WTJ* 55: 299–320.

Jones, J. M. (1994), 'Subverting the Textuality of Davidic Messianism: Matthew's Presentation of the Genealogy and the Davidic Title', *CBQ* 56: 256–272.

Joslin, B. C. (2007), 'Can Hebrews Be Structured? An Assessment of Eight Approaches', *CurBR* 6: 99–129.

Käsemann, E. (1980), *Commentary on Romans*, tr. and ed. G. W. Bromiley, Grand Rapids: Eerdmans.

Kee, H. C. (1993), 'Appropriating the History of God's People: A Survey of Interpretations of the History of Israel in the Pseudepigrapha, Apocrypha and the New Testament', in J. H. Charlesworth and C. A. Evans (eds.), *The Pseudepigrapha and Early Biblical Interpretation*, JSPSup 14, Sheffield: JSOT Press, 44–64.

Keener, C. S. (2013), *Acts: An Exegetical Commentary, vol. 2: 3:1–14:28*, Grand Rapids: Baker Academic.

Kennedy, G. A. (1984), *New Testament Interpretation Through Rhetorical Criticism*, Chapel Hill: University of North Carolina Press.

Khobnya, S. (2013), '"The Root" in Paul's Olive Tree Metaphor (Romans 11:16–24)', *TynBul* 64.2: 257–273.

Kidner, D. (1973), *Psalms 1–72*, TOTC, Leicester: Inter-Varsity Press; Downers Grove: InterVarsity Press.

—— (1994), 'Isaiah', in D. A. Carson, R. T. France, J. A. Motyer and G. J. Wenham (eds.), *New Bible Commentary: 21st Century Edition*, Leicester: Inter-Varsity Press; Downers Grove: InterVarsity Press, 629–670.

Kilgallen, J. J. (1975), *The Stephen Speech: A Literary and Redactional Study of Acts 7:2–53*, AnBib 67, Rome: Biblical Institute Press.

Kim, J. D. (2000), *God, Israel, and the Gentiles: Rhetoric and Situation in Romans 9–11*, SBLDS 176, Atlanta: SBL.

—— (2007), 'Explicit Quotations from Genesis Within the Context of Stephen's Speech in Acts', *Neot* 41: 341–360.

Kimball, C. A. (1994), *Jesus' Exposition of the Old Testament in Luke's Gospel*, JSNTSup 94, Sheffield: JSOT Press.

Kistemaker, S. (1990), 'The Speeches in Acts', *CTR* 5: 31–41.

Klink III, E. W., and D. R. Lockett (2012), *Understanding Biblical Theology: A Comparison of Theory and Practice*, Grand Rapids: Zondervan.

Koester, C. R. (2001), *Hebrews: A New Translation with Introduction and Commentary*, AB 36, New York: Doubleday.

—— (2014), *Revelation*, New Haven: Yale University Press.

Köstenberger, A. J., B. L. Merkle and R. L. Plummer (2016), *Going Deeper with New Testament Greek: An Intermediate Study of the Grammar and Syntax of the New Testament*, Nashville: B&H Academic.

Kugler, C. (2016), 'ΠΙΣΤΙΣ ΧΡΙΣΤΟΥ: The Current State of Play and the Key Arguments', *CurBR* 14: 244–255.

Lee, A. H. I. (2005), *From Messiah to Preexistent Son: Jesus' Self-Consciousness and Early Christian Exegesis of Messianic Psalms*, WUNT 2.192, Tübingen: Mohr Siebeck.

LéGasse, S. (1998), 'Les Généalogies de Jésus', *BLE* 99: 443–454.

Leithart, P. J. (2018), *The Gospel of Matthew Through New Eyes: Jesus as Israel*, Monroe: Athanasius.

Lincoln, A. T. (1983), 'Sabbath, Rest, and Eschatology in the New Testament', in D. A. Carson (ed.), *From Sabbath to Lord's Day: A Biblical, Historical, and Theological Investigation*, Grand Rapids: Zondervan, 197–220.

Loader, J. A. (2011), 'The Beautiful Infant and Israel's Salvation', *HvTSt* 67: 913–922.

Longenecker, B. W. (2002), 'Sharing in Their Spiritual Blessings? The Stories of Israel in Galatians and Romans', in B. W. Longenecker (ed.), *Narrative Dynamics in Paul: A Critical Assessment*, Louisville: Westminster John Knox, 58–84.

Longenecker, R. N. (1990), *Galatians*, WBC 41, Dallas: Word, 1990.

—— (1999), *Biblical Exegesis in the Apostolic Period*, 2nd edn, Grand Rapids: Eerdmans.

—— (2016), *The Epistle to the Romans: A Commentary on the Greek Text*, NIGTC, Grand Rapids: Eerdmans.

—— (2017), *Acts*, EBC, rev. edn, Grand Rapids: Zondervan.

Lucas, E. C. (2002), *Daniel*, AOTC 20, Leicester: Apollos; Downers Grove: InterVarsity Press.

Lyons, M. A. (2013), 'Paul and the Servant(s): Isaiah 49:6 in Acts 13:47', *ETL* 89: 345–359.

McFadden, K. W. (2015), 'Does Πίστις Mean Faith(Fulness) in Paul?', *TynBul* 66: 251–270.

McFarland, O. (2012), 'Whose Abraham, Which Promise? Genesis 15:6 in Philo's De Virtutibus and Romans 4', *JSNT* 35: 107–129.

McLean, B. H. (1996), *The Cursed Christ: Mediterranean Expulsion Rituals and Pauline Soteriology*, JSNTSup 126, Sheffield: Sheffield Academic Press.

Marsden, G. M. (2003), *Jonathan Edwards: A Life*, New Haven: Yale
University Press.

Marshall, I. H. (1978), *The Gospel of Luke: A Commentary on the Greek
Text*, NIGTC, Grand Rapids: Eerdmans.

—— (1993), 'Acts and the Former Treatise', in B. W. Winter and A. D.
Clarke (eds.), vol. 1, *The Book of Acts in Its First-Century Setting*, ed.
B. W. Winter, Grand Rapids: Eerdmans, 163–182.

Martin, O. R. (2015), *Bound for the Promised Land: The Land Promise
in God's Redemptive Plan*, NSBT 34, Nottingham: Apollos; Downers
Grove: InterVarsity Press.

Martyn, J. L. (1997), *Galatians*, AB, New York: Doubleday.

Maston, J. S. (2012), 'The Nature of Salvation History in Galatians',
JSPL 2: 89–103.

Mathews, K. A. (2005), *Genesis 11:27–50:26*, NAC, Nashville: B&H.

Matlock, R. B. (2007), 'The Rhetoric of Πίστις in Paul: Galatians 2:16,
3:22, Romans 3:22, and Philippians 3:9', *JSNT* 30: 173–203.

—— (2009), 'Helping Paul's Argument Work? The Curse of Galatians
3.10–14', in T. Michael and P. Oakes (eds.), *The Torah in the New
Testament*, LNTS 401, New York: T&T Clark, 154–179.

Matthews, S. (2010), *Perfect Martyr: The Stoning of Stephen and the
Construction of Christian Identity*, Oxford: Oxford University
Press.

Merkle, B. L. (2000), 'Romans 11 and the Future of Ethnic Israel',
JETS 43: 709–721.

Mittelstadt, M. W. (2004), *The Spirit and Suffering in Luke-Acts:
Implications for a Pentecostal Pneumatology*, JPTS 26, London:
T&T Clark.

Moffitt, D. M. (2011), *Atonement and the Logic of Resurrection in the
Epistle to the Hebrews*, NovTSup 141, Boston: Brill.

Moo, D. J. (1996), *The Epistle to the Romans*, NICNT, Grand Rapids:
Eerdmans.

—— (2002), 'The Theology of Romans 9–11: A Response to E. Elizabeth
Johnson', in D. M. Hay and E. E. Johnson (eds.), *Pauline Theology*,
vol. 3, *Romans*, Atlanta: Society of Biblical Literature, 240–258.

—— (2004), 'Israel and the Law in Romans 5–11: Interaction with the
New Perspective', in D. A. Carson (ed.), *Justification and Variegated
Nomism. The Paradoxes of Paul Vol. 2*, WUNT 181.2, Tübingen:
Mohr Siebeck; Grand Rapids: Baker, 185–216.

—— (2013), *Galatians*, BECNT, Grand Rapids: Baker.

—— (2018), *The Letter to the Romans*, 2nd edn, NICNT, Grand Rapids: Eerdmans.

Morgan-Wynne, J. E. (2014), *Paul's Pisidian Antioch Speech (Acts 13)*, Eugene: Pickwick.

Morris, L. (1992), *The Gospel According to Matthew*, PNTC, Grand Rapids: Eerdmans.

Motyer, J. A. (1993), *The Prophecy of Isaiah: An Introduction and Commentary*, Leicester: Inter-Varsity Press; Downers Grove: InterVarsity Press.

Moyise, S. (2010), *Paul and Scripture*, London: SPCK.

Munck, J. (1967), *Christ and Israel: An Interpretation of Romans 9–11*, Philadelphia: Fortress.

Myers, A. D. (2010), 'For It Has Been Written: Paul's Use of Isa 54:1 in Gal 4:27 in Light of Gal 3:1–5:1', *PRSt* 37: 295–308.

Nauck, W. (1960), 'Zum Aufbau Des Hebräerbriefes', in W. Eltester (ed.), *Judentum, Urchristentum, Kirche: Festschrift für Joachim Jeremias*, BZNW 26, Berlin: Töpelmann, 199–206.

Newbigin, L. (1989), *The Gospel in a Pluralist Society*, Grand Rapids: Eerdmans.

Nolland, J. (1996), 'Genealogical Annotation in Genesis as Background for the Matthean Genealogy of Jesus', *TynBul* 47: 115–122.

—— (2005), *The Gospel of Matthew*, NIGTC, Grand Rapids: Eerdmans.

Nowell, I. (2008), 'Jesus's Great-Grandmothers: Matthew's Four and More', *CBQ* 70: 1–15.

Ó Fearghail, F. (1988), *The Introduction to Luke-Acts: A Study of the Role of Lk 1, 1–4, 44 in the Composition of Luke's Two-volume Work*, AnBib 126, Rome: Editrice Pontificio Istituto Biblico.

Ortlund, D. C. (2012), *Zeal Without Knowledge: The Concept of Zeal in Romans 10, Galatians 1, and Philippians 3*, LNTS 472, New York: T&T Clark.

Osborne, G. R. (2010), *Matthew*, ZECNT, Grand Rapids: Zondervan.

Parsons, M. C. (2008), *Acts*, PCNT, Grand Rapids: Baker Academic.

Pelikan, J. (2005), *Acts*, BTCB, Grand Rapids: Brazos.

Penner, T. C. (2003), *In Praise of Christian Origins: Stephen and the Hellenists in Lukan Apologetic Historiography*, London: T&T Clark.

Pennington, J. T. (2012), *Reading the Gospels Wisely: A Narrative and Theological Introduction*, Grand Rapids: Baker Academic.

—— (2017), *The Sermon on the Mount and Human Flourishing: A Theological Commentary*, Grand Rapids: Baker Academic.

Pervo, R. I. (2008), *The Mystery of Acts: Unraveling Its Story*, Santa Rosa: Polebridge.

Peterson, D. G. (2009), *The Acts of the Apostles*, PNTC, Grand Rapids: Eerdmans; Nottingham: Apollos.

Piotrowski, N. G. (2015), 'After the Deportation: Observations in Matthew's Apocalyptic Genealogy', *BBR* 25: 189–204.

Piper, J. S. (1993), *The Justification of God: An Exegetical and Theological Study of Romans 9:1–23*, Grand Rapids: Baker.

Reasoner, M. (2010), 'Romans 9–11 Moves from Margin to Center, from Rejection to Salvation: Four Grids for Recent English-Language Exegesis', in F. Schleritt, J. R. Wagner and F. Wilk, *Between Gospel and Election*, Tübingen: Mohr Siebeck, 73–89.

Reicke, B. I. (1951), 'The Law and This World According to Paul: Some Thoughts Concerning Galatians 4:1–11', *JBL* 70: 274–276.

Rhee, V. (1998), 'Chiasm and the Concept of Faith in Hebrews 11', *BSac* 155 (619): 327–345.

Ridderbos, H. N. (1975), *Paul: An Outline of His Theology*, Grand Rapids: Eerdmans.

Sanders, E. P. (1983), *Paul, the Law, and the Jewish People*, Philadelphia: Fortress.

—— (2015), *Paul the Apostle's Life, Letters, and Thought*, Minneapolis: Fortress.

Sandys-Wunsch, J., and L. Eldredge (1980), 'J. P. Galber and the Distinction between Biblical and Dogmatic Theology: Translation, Commentary, and Discussion of His Originality', *SJT* 33: 133–158.

Schnabel, E. J. (2004), *Early Christian Mission: Paul and the Early Church*, Downers Grove: InterVarsity Press; Leicester: Apollos.

—— (2012), *Acts*, ZECNT, Grand Rapids: Zondervan.

Schreiner, T. R. (1991), 'Works of the Law in Paul', *NovT* 33: 217–244.

—— (2001), *Paul, Apostle of God's Glory in Christ: A Pauline Theology*, Downers Grove: InterVarsity Press; Leicester: Apollos.

—— (2010), *Galatians*, ZECNT, Grand Rapids: Zondervan.

—— (2018), *Romans*, 2nd edn, BECNT, Grand Rapids: Baker.

Seifrid, M. A. (2007), 'Romans', in G. K. Beale and D. A. Carson (eds.), *Commentary on the New Testament Use of the Old Testament*, Grand Rapids: Baker, 607–694.

Shepherd, M. B. (2013), *The Textual World of the Bible*, New York: Peter Lang.

Silva, M. (2007), 'Galatians', in G. K. Beale and D. A. Carson (eds.), *Commentary on the New Testament Use of the Old Testament*, Grand Rapids: Baker, 785–812.

Smith, D. L. (2012), *The Rhetoric of Interruption: Speech-Making, Turn-Taking, and Rule-Breaking in Luke-Acts and Ancient Greek Narrative*, BZNW 193, Berlin: de Gruyter.

Snodgrass, K. R. (1998), 'Recent Research on the Parable of the Wicked Tenants: An Assessment', *BBR* 8: 187–216.

—— (2011), *The Parable of the Wicked Tenants: An Inquiry into Parable Interpretation*, WUNT 27, Tübingen: Mohr Siebeck.

Stanley, C. D. (1992), *Paul and the Language of Scripture: Citation Technique in the Pauline Epistles and Contemporary Literature*, SNTSMS 69, Cambridge: Cambridge University Press.

Stanton, G. N. (1995), *The Interpretation of Matthew*, Edinburgh: T&T Clark.

Stauffer, E. (1955), *New Testament Theology*, London: SCM.

Stendahl, K. (1960), 'Quis et Unde? An Analysis of Matthew 1–2', in W. Eltester (ed.), *Judentum, Urchristentum, Kirche: Festschrift für J. Jeremias*, Berlin: Töpelmann, 94–105.

Stenschke, C. W. (2010), 'Römer als Teil des Römerbriefs', in F. Schleritt, J. R. Wagner and F. Wilk, *Between Gospel and Election*, Tübingen: Mohr Siebeck, 197–225.

Stettler, H. (2015), 'Did Paul Invent Justification by Faith?', *TynBul* 66: 161–196.

Steyn, G. J. (2015), 'Observations on the Text Form of the Minor Prophets in Romans 9–11', *JSNT* 38: 49–67.

Streett, D. R. (2015), 'Cursed by God? Galatians 3:13, Social Status, and Atonement Theory in the Context of Early Jewish Readings of Deuteronomy 21:23', *JSPL* 5: 189–210.

Taylor, J. W. (2012), 'The Eschatological Interdependence of Jews and Gentiles in Galatians', *TynBul* 63: 291–316.

Thielman, F. (1994), 'Unexpected Mercy: Echoes of a Biblical Motif in Romans 9–11', *SJT* 47: 169–181.

Thompson, A. J. (2011), *The Acts of the Risen Lord: Luke's Account of God's Unfolding Plan*, NSBT, Nottingham: Apollos; Downers Grove: InterVarsity Press.

Waetjen, H. C. (1976), 'The Genealogy as the Key to the Gospel According to Matthew', *JBL* 95: 207–211.

Wagner, J. R. (2002), *Heralds of the Good News: Isaiah and Paul 'in Concert' in the Letter to the Romans*, Leiden: Brill.

Wall, R. W. (2000), 'The Function of LXX Habakkuk 1:5 in the Book of Acts', *BBR* 10: 247–258.

Walton, J. H. (2006), *Ancient Near Eastern Thought and the Old Testament: Introducing the Conceptual World of the Hebrew Bible*, Grand Rapids: Baker Academic.

Watson, F. (2016), *Paul and the Hermeneutics of Faith*, 2nd edn, New York: T&T Clark.

Weren, W. J. C. (1998), 'The Use of Isaiah 5,1–7 in the Parable of the Tenants (Mark 12,1–12; Matthew 21,33–46)', *Bib* 79.1: 1–26.

Whitenton, M. R. (2012), 'Rewriting Abraham and Joseph: Stephen's Speech (Acts 7:2–16) and Jewish Exegetical Traditions', *NovT* 54: 149–167.

Wilken, R. L. (2003), *The Spirit of Early Christian Thought: Seeking the Face of God*, New Haven: Yale University Press.

Williamson, H. G. M. (1978), 'The Sure Mercies of David: Subjective or Objective Genitive?', *JSS* 23: 31–49.

Willitts, J. (2005), 'Isa 54,1 and Gal 4,24b–27: Reading Genesis in Light of Isaiah', *ZNW* 96: 188–210.

Wilson, T. A. (2007), *The Curse of the Law and the Crisis in Galatia: Reassessing the Purpose of Galatians*, WUNT 2.225, Tübingen: Mohr Siebeck.

Wolter, M. (2013), 'Die Unfruchtbare Frau und Ihre Kinder: Zur Rezeptionsgeschichte von Jes 54 (1)', in P. G. Klumbies and D. S. DuToit (eds.), *Paulus – Werk und Wirkung: Festschrift für Andreas Lindemann zum 70. Geburtstag*, Tübingen: Mohr Siebeck, 103–127.

—— (2015), *Paul: An Outline of His Theology*, Waco: Baylor University Press.

—— (2018), 'Ein Exegetischer und Theologischer Blick auf Röm 11:25–32', *NTS* 64: 123–142.

Wright, N. T. (1991), *The Climax of the Covenant: Christ and the Law in Pauline Theology*, Minneapolis: Fortress.

—— (1992), *The New Testament and the People of God*, vol. 1, *Christian Origins and the Question of God*, Minneapolis: Fortress.

—— (1996), *Jesus and the Victory of God*, vol. 2, *Christian Origins and the Question of God*, Minneapolis: Fortress.

—— (2013), *Paul and the Faithfulness of God*, vol. 4, *Christian Origins and the Question of God*, Minneapolis: Fortress.

Index of authors

Index of authors

Gentry, P. J., 22, 73–74, 99, 198
Gladd, B. L., 120
Goldsworthy, G., 3
Goodrich, J. K., 118
Goswell, G., 26
Guthrie, G. H., 149, 152

Haacker, K., 118, 146
Hafemann, S. J., 117, 135, 140
Hagner, D. A., 34
Hahn, S. W., 197
Hakh, S. B., 14
Hamilton, J. M., 3
Hansen, G. W., 87, 90, 105
Harmon, M. S., 97
Harriman, K. R., 54
Harris, D. M., 171, 173
Hartman, L. F., 39
Hays, R. B., 2, 14, 17–18, 28, 39,
    44–45, 87, 90, 102, 108, 131, 144,
    187, 192
Hester, J. D., 32
Hoekema, A. A., 141
Hood, J. B., 3–8, 11, 14, 18–19, 21,
    24–25, 44, 115
Hooker, M. D., 83
Horne, E. H., 34
Horst, P. W. van der, 142
Hunn, D. 87, 91, 94
Hutchison, J. C., 21

Iverson, K. R., 33–34, 41

Jeska, J., 5, 8, 51, 55, 62, 66, 80
Jewett, R., 122
Jobes, K. H., 108–109
Jones, J. M., 28, 109
Joslin, B. C., 152

Käsmann, E., 121, 129
Kee, H. C., 54, 68, 80
Keener, C. S., 52, 56–59, 66
Kennedy, G. A., 68

Khobnya, S., 140
Kidner, D., 33, 37–38
Kilgallen, J. J., 55
Kim, J. D., 59, 117–118
Kimball, C. A., 50
Kistemaker, S., 53
Klink III, E. W., 3
Koester, C. R., 6, 163, 175
Köstenberger, A. J., 24
Kugler, C., 87

Lee, A. H. I., 30
LéGasse, S., 14
Leithart, P. J., 13
Lincoln, A. T., 178
Loader, J. A., 60
Lockett, D. R., 3
Longenecker, B. W., 83, 117
Longenecker, R. N., 2, 57, 85, 92,
    102, 104, 116, 121, 135, 187, 197
Lucas, E. C., 38
Lyons, M. A., 77

McFadden, K. W., 102
McFarland, O., 91
McLean, B. H., 95
Marsden, G. M., 1
Marshall, I. H., 50, 52
Martin, O. R., 174
Martyn, J. L., 83–84, 88, 95, 98,
    105–107, 110
Maston, J. S., 83
Mathews, K. A., 92
Matlock, R. B., 87, 93–94
Matthews, S., 55, 92
Merkle, B. L., 141–142
Mittelstadt, M. W., 56
Moffitt, D. M., 173, 175
Moo, D. J., 86–87, 93, 96, 98,
    100–103, 106–108, 119, 121–123,
    127, 135, 140, 146, 188
Morgan-Wynne, J. E., 51, 68–70,
    72–74

Index of Scripture references

Index of Scripture references

Titles in this series:

An index of Scripture references for all the volumes may be found at http://www.thegospelcoalition.org/resources/nsbt.